MOON SPOTLIGHT

YOSEMITE & MAMMOTH LAKES CAMPING & HIKING

TOM STIENSTRA • ANN MARIE BROWN

Some of nature's most perfect artwork and the most profound natural phenomena imaginable have been created in Yosemite and the adjoining eastern Sierra near Mammoth Lakes.

Yosemite Valley is the world's greatest showpiece. It is also among the most highly visited and well-known destinations on earth. Many of the campgrounds listed in this section are within close driving proximity of Yosemite National Park. When it comes to cabin rentals in this region, the variety is extraordinary.

Anything in Yosemite, or in its sphere of influence, is going to be in high demand almost year-round, and the same is true near Mammoth Lakes.

Many family recreation opportunities exist at lake-based settings, including at Lake Alpine, Pinecrest Lake on the western slopes of the Sierra, and June Lake, Silver Lake, Lake Mary, Twin Lakes, Convict Lake, and Rock Creek Lake on the eastern Sierra.

Of course, most visits to this region start with a tour of Yosemite Valley. It is framed on one side by El Capitan, the Goliath of Yosemite, and the three-spired Cathedral Rocks on the other. As you enter the valley, Bridalveil Falls comes to view, a perfect free fall over the south canyon rim, then across a meadow. To your left you'll see the two-tiered Yosemite Falls, and finally, Half Dome, the single most awesome piece of rock in the world.

The irony is that this is all most people ever see of the region, even though it represents but a fraction of the fantastic land of wonder, adventure, and unparalleled natural beauty. Though 24,000 people jam into five square miles of Yosemite Valley each summer day, the park is actually 90 percent wilderness. Other landmark areas you can reach by car include the Wawona Grove of Giant Sequoias, Tenaya Lake, Tuolumne Meadows, and Hetch Hetchy.

But that's still only scratching the surface. For those who hike, another world will open up: Yosemite has 318 lakes, dozens of pristine streams, the Grand Canyon of the Tuolumne River, Matterhorn Peak, Benson Lake (with the largest white-sand beach in the Sierra), and dozens of spectacular waterfalls.

If you explore beyond the park boundaries, the adventures just keep getting better. Over Tioga Pass, outside the park and just off Highway 120, are Tioga Lake, Ellery Lake, and Saddlebag Lake (10,087 feet), the latter of which is the highest lake in California accessible by car. To the east is Mono Lake and its weird tufa spires, which create a stark moonscape.

The nearby June Lake Loop and Mammoth Lakes area is a launch point to another orbit. Both have small lakes with on-site cabin rentals, excellent fishing, great hiking and mountain biking for all levels, and phenomenal skiing and winter sports. In addition, just east of Mammoth Lakes airport is a series of hot springs, including a famous spot on Hot Creek, something of a legend in these parts.

More hiking and fishing opportunities abound at Devils Postpile National Monument, where you can hike to Rainbow Falls. At nearby Agnew Meadows, you'll find a trail that hugs the pristine San Joaquin River up to Thousand Island Lake and leads to the beautiful view from Banner and Ritter Peaks in the Ansel Adams Wilderness. Horseback riding is also popular in this area, with pack trips available from Reds Meadow.

In case you didn't already know, many of California's best lakes for a chance to catch giant rainbow and brown trout are in this region. They include Bridgeport Reservoir, Twin Lakes, June Lake, Convict Lake, and Crowley Lake in the eastern Sierra.

This region has it all: beauty, variety, and a chance at the hike or fish of a lifetime. There is nothing else like it.

How to Use This Book

ABOUT THE CAMPGROUND PROFILES

The campgrounds are listed in a consistent, easy-to-read format to help you choose the ideal camping spot. Here is a sample profile:

Site name and number →

1 SOMEWHERE USA

Icons noting activities and facilities at or nearby the campground

Scenic rating: 10

Rating of scenic beauty on a scale of 1-10 with 10 the highest rating

General location of the site in relation to the nearest major town or landmark →

south of Somewhere USA Lake

BEST

Symbol indicating that the site is listed among the author's top picks

Each campground in this book begins with a brief overview of its setting. The description typically covers ambience, information about the attractions, and activities popular at the campground.

Campsites, facilities: This section notes the number of campsites for tents and RVs and indicates whether hookups are available. Facilities such as restrooms, picnic areas, recreation areas, laundry, and dump stations will be addressed, as well as the availability of piped water, showers, playgrounds, stores, and other amenities. The campground's pet policy and wheelchair accessibility is also mentioned here.

Reservations, fees: This section notes whether reservations are accepted, and provides rates for tent sites and RV sites. If there are additional fees for parking or pets, or discounted weekly or seasonal rates, they will also be noted here.

Directions: This section provides mile-by-mile driving directions to the site from the nearest major town or highway.

Contact: This section provides an address, phone number, and website, if available, for each site.

ABOUT THE ICONS

The camping icons are designed to provide at-a-glance information on activities, facilities, and services available on-site or within walking distance of each campground.

- Hiking trails
- Biking trails
- Swimming
- Fishing
- Boating
- Canoeing and/or kayaking
- Winter sports
- Hot Springs
- Pets permitted
- Playground
- Wheelchair accessible
- RV sites
- Tent sites

ABOUT THE SCENIC RATING

Each campground profile employs a scenic rating on a scale of 1 to 10, with 1 being the least scenic and 10 being the most scenic. A scenic rating measures only the overall beauty of the campground and environs; it does not take into account noise level, facilities, maintenance, recreation options, or campground management. The setting of a campground with a lower scenic rating may simply not be as picturesque that of as a higher rated campground, however other factors that can influence a trip, such as noise or recreation access, can still affect or enhance your camping trip. Consider both the scenic rating and the profile description before deciding which campground is perfect for you.

ABOUT THE TRAIL PROFILES

Each hike in this book is listed in a consistent, easy-to-read format to help you choose the ideal hike. From a general overview of the setting to detailed driving directions, the profile will provide all the information you need. Here is a sample profile:

Map number and hike number

Round-trip mileage (unless otherwise noted) and the approximate amount of time needed to complete the hike (actual times can vary widely, especially on longer hikes)

Difficulty and quality ratings

General location of the trail, named by its proximity to the nearest major town or landmark

Symbol indicating that the hike is listed among the author's top picks

1 SOMEWHERE USA HIKE

9.0 mi/5.0 hrs 3 8

at the mouth of the Somewhere River

BEST

Each hike in this book begins with a brief overview of its setting. The description typically covers what kind of terrain to expect, what might be seen, and any conditions that may make the hike difficult to navigate. Side trips, such as to waterfalls or panoramic vistas, in addition to ways to combine the trail with others nearby for a longer outing, are also noted here. In many cases, mile-by-mile trail directions are included.

User Groups: This section notes the types of users that are permitted on the trail, including hikers, mountain bikers, horseback riders, and dogs. Wheelchair access is also noted here.

Permits: This section notes whether a permit is required for hiking, or, if the hike spans more than one day, whether one is required for camping. Any fees, such as for parking, day use, or entrance, are also noted here.

Maps: This section provides information on how to obtain detailed trail maps of the hike and its environs. Whenever applicable, names of U.S. Geologic Survey (USGS) topographic maps and national forest maps are also included.

Directions: This section provides mile-by-mile driving directions to the trail head from the nearest major town.

Contact: This section provides an address and phone number for each hike. The contact is usually the agency maintaining the trail but may also be a trail club or other organization.

ABOUT THE ICONS

The hiking icons are designed to provide at-a-glance information on the difficulty and quality of each hike.

The **difficulty rating** (rated **1-5** with **1** being the lowest and **5** the highest) is based on the steepness of the trail and how difficult it is to traverse

The **quality rating** (rated **1-10** with **1** being the lowest and **10** the highest) is based largely on scenic beauty, but also takes into account how crowded the trail is and whether noise of nearby civilization is audible

ABOUT THE DIFFICULTY RATINGS

Trails rated 1 are very easy and suitable for hikers of all abilities, including young children.

Trails rated 2 are easy-to-moderate and suitable for most hikers, including families with active children 6 and older.

Trails rated 3 are moderately challenging and suitable for reasonably fit adults and older children who are very active.

Trails rated 4 are very challenging and suitable for physically fit hikers who are seeking a workout.

Trails rated 5 are extremely challenging and suitable only for experienced hikers who are in top physical condition.

MAP SYMBOLS

Expressway	Interstate Freeway	Airfield
Primary Road	U.S. Highway	Airport
Secondary Road	State Highway	City/Town
Unpaved Road	County Highway	Mountain
Ferry	Lake	Park
National Border	Dry Lake	Pass
State Border	Seasonal Lake	State Capital

ABOUT THE MAPS

This book is divided into chapters based on major regions in the state; an overview map of these regions precedes the table of contents. Each chapter begins with a map of the region, which is further broken down into detail maps. Sites are noted on the detail maps by number.

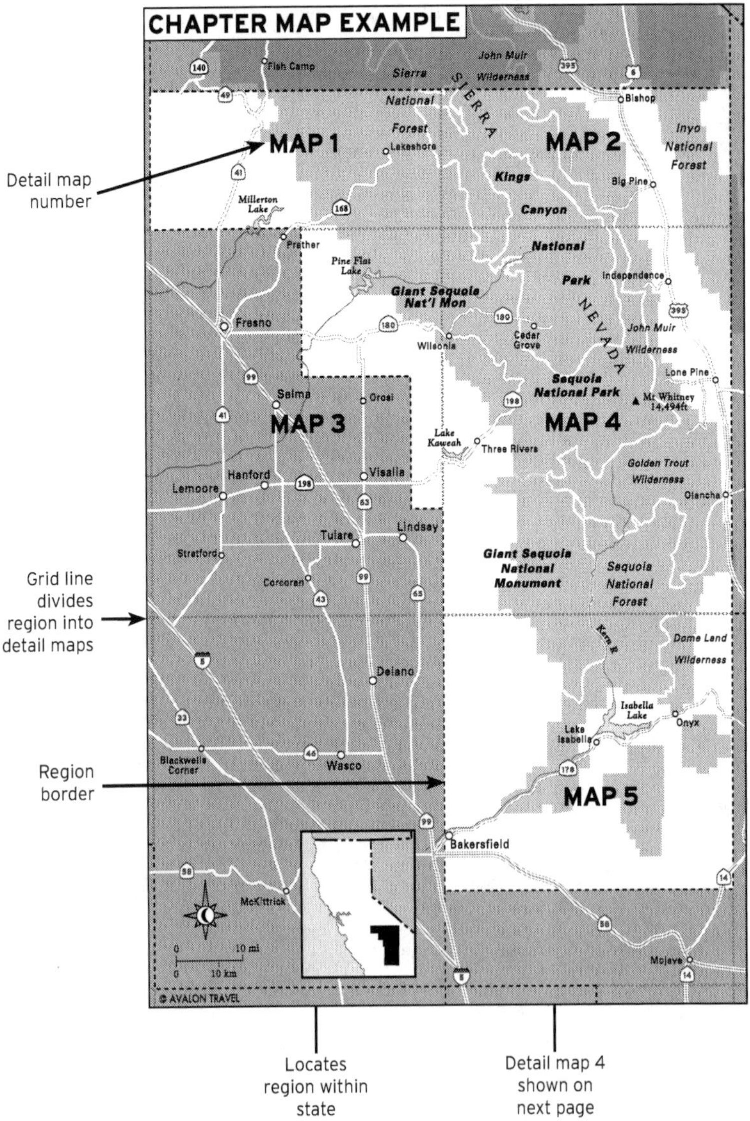

Locates detail map within region

Map number → **Map 4**

Sites shown on detail map → **Sites 105-117**

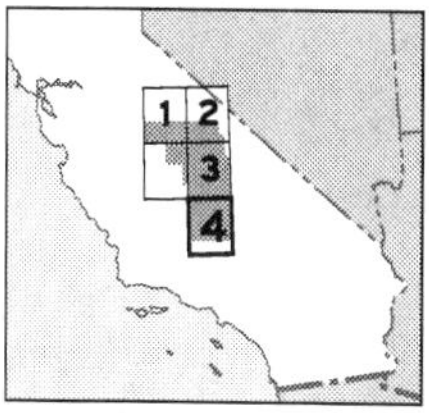

Site number →

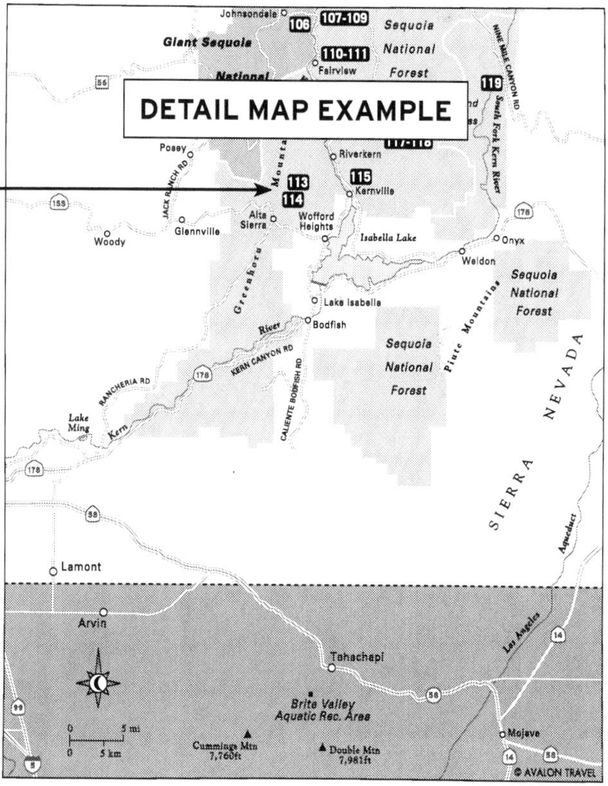

YOSEMITE & MAMMOTH LAKES CAMPING

COURTESY OF THE NATIONAL PARK SERVICE

BEST CAMPGROUNDS

Scenic Destinations
Bridalveil Creek and Equestrian and Group Camp, **page 24**

Hikes with Views
Tuolumne Meadows, **page 17**
Yosemite Creek, **page 19**

Family Destinations
Convict Lake, **page 54**

Fishing
Lower Twin Lake, **page 35**
Agnew Meadows and Equestrian Camp, **page 44**

White-Water Rafting
Merced Recreation Area, **page 25**

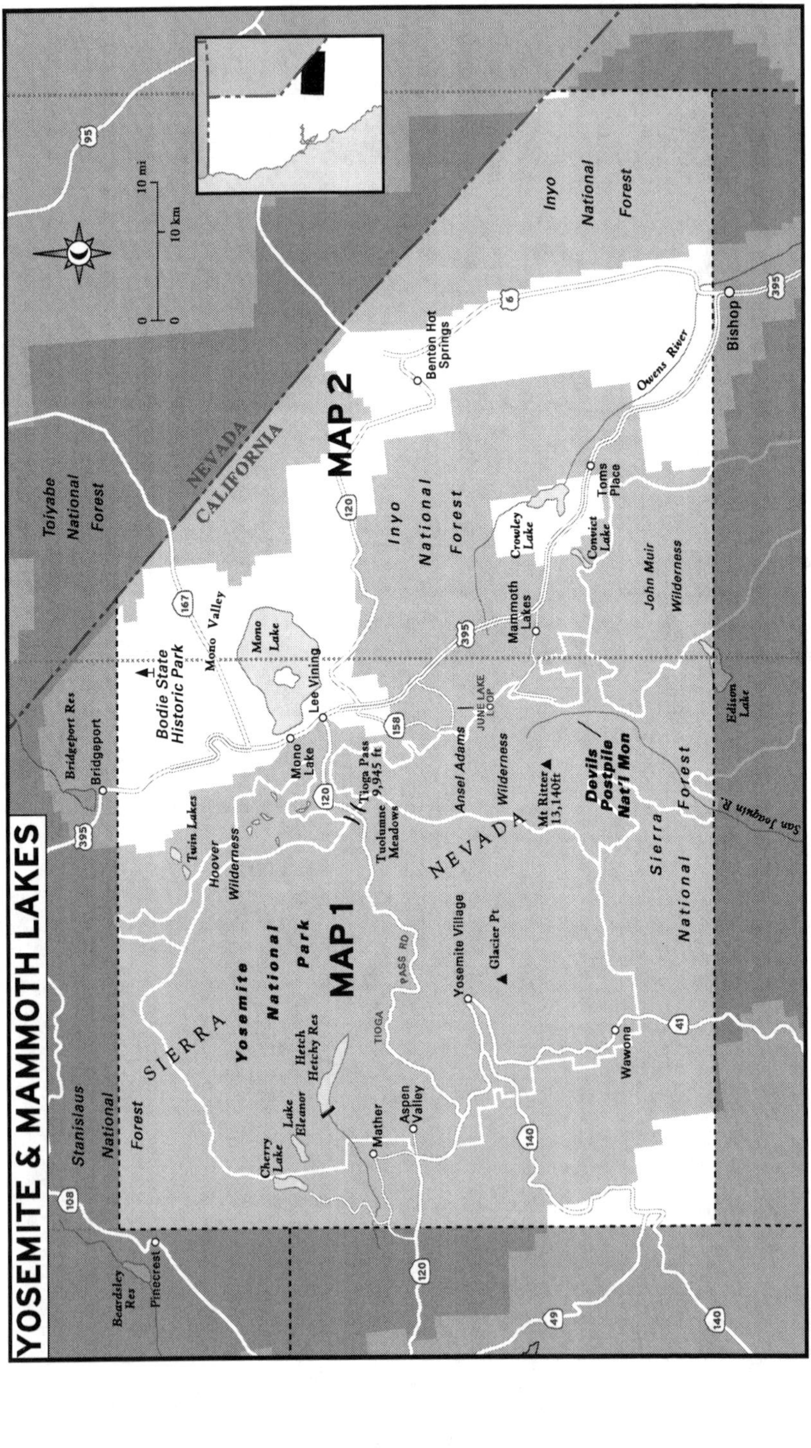
YOSEMITE & MAMMOTH LAKES
MAP 1
MAP 2
0
10 mi
10 km
Toiyabe National Forest
NEVADA
CALIFORNIA
Bridgeport Res
Bridgeport
Bodie State Historic Park
Mono Valley
Mono Lake
Lee Vining
Twin Lakes
Hoover Wilderness
Tioga Pass 9,945 ft
Tuolumne Meadows
JUNE LAKE LOOP
Ansel Adams Wilderness
Mt Ritter 13,140ft
Devils Postpile Nat'l Mon
Mammoth Lakes
Crowley Lake
Convict Lake
Toms Place
Inyo National Forest
John Muir Wilderness
Benton Hot Springs
Owens River
Bishop
Edison Lake
San Joaquin R.
SIERRA NEVADA
Sierra National Forest
Yosemite National Park
TIOGA PASS RD
Yosemite Village
Glacier Pt
Wawona
Hetch Hetchy Res
Lake Eleanor
Cherry Lake
Mather
Aspen Valley
Stanislaus National Forest
Pinecrest
Beardsley Res
95
6
395
167
120
158
108
140
41
49

Map 1

Campgrounds 1-71

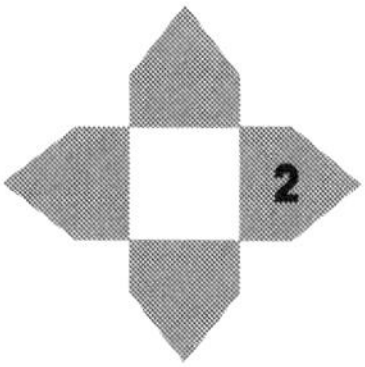

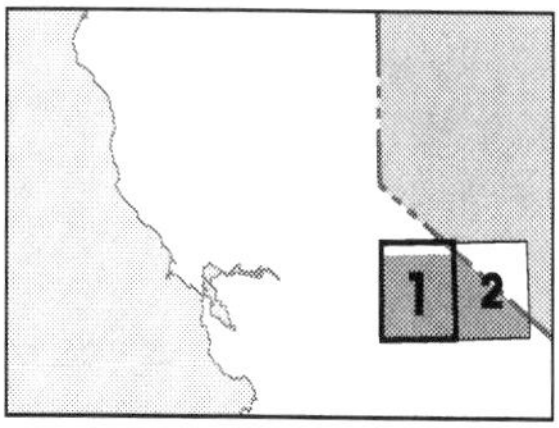

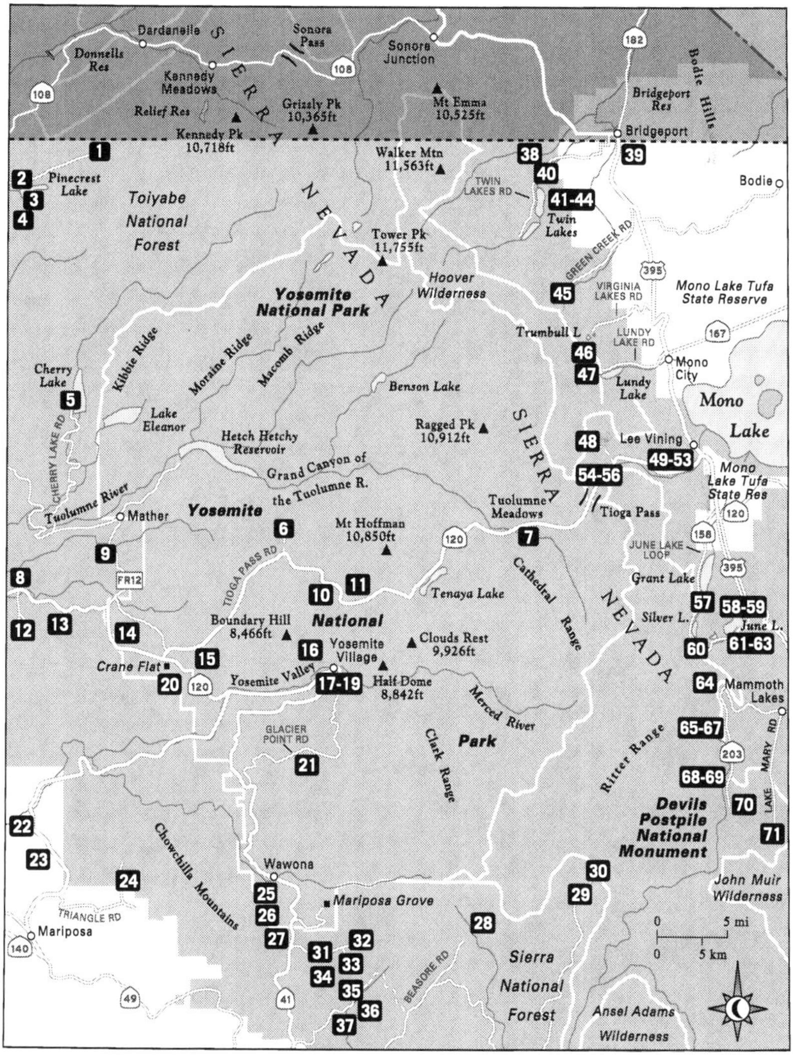

CAMPING

Map 2

Campgrounds 72-101

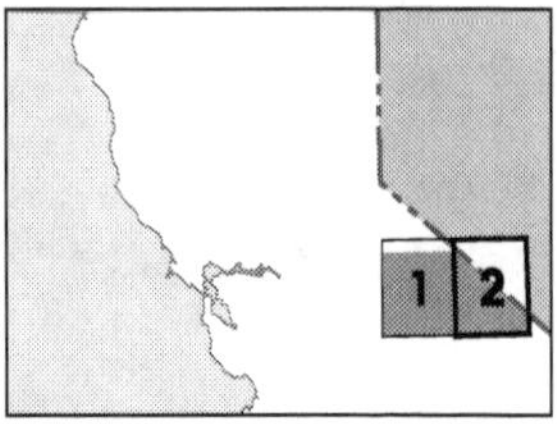

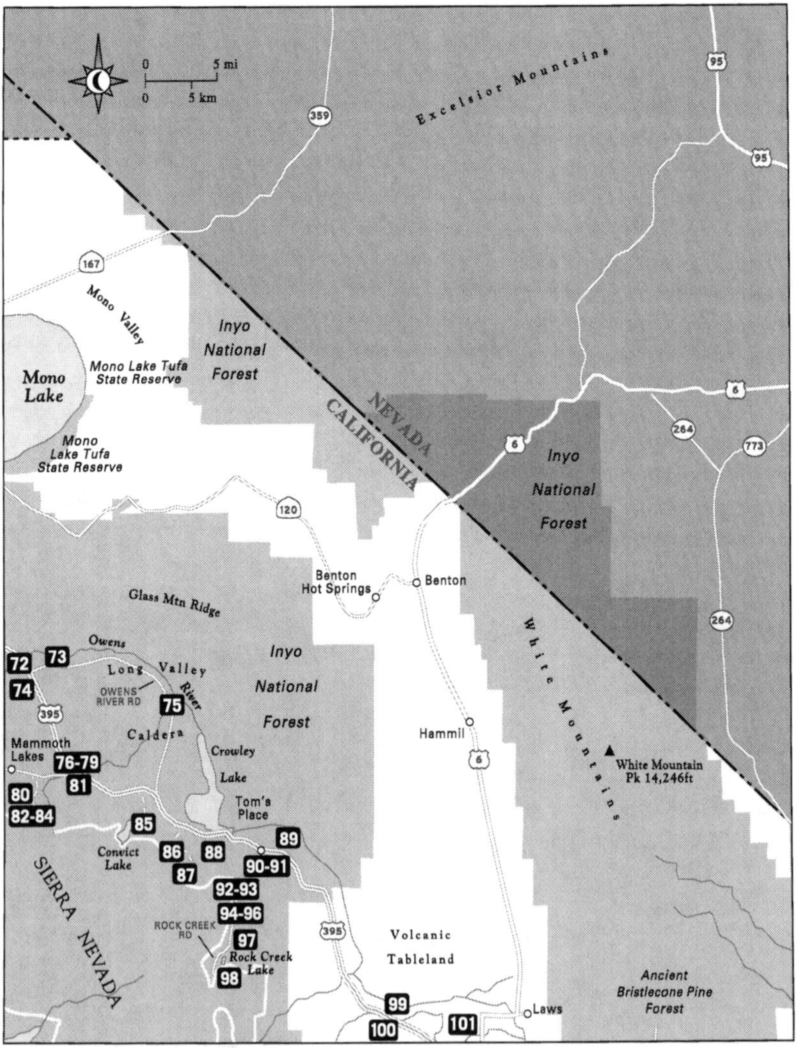

1 HERRING RESERVOIR

Scenic rating: 8

at Herring Lake in Stanislaus National Forest

This is a pretty little spot, a rustic campground set near Herring Creek as it enters Herring Lake, set at an elevation of 7,350 feet. There is no boat ramp, but hand-launched boats, such as kayaks, canoes, rafts, prams, and float tubes, are ideal. The lake is shallow, with fair fishing for brook trout and rainbow trout. No horses are permitted.

Campsites, facilities: There are 42 sites for tents or RVs up to 22 feet (no hookups). Fire rings are provided. Vault toilets are available. No drinking water is available. Garbage must be packed out. Leashed pets are permitted.

Reservations, fees: Reservations are not accepted. There is no camping fee. Open May through October, weather permitting.

Directions: From Sonora, drive east on Highway 108 for about 25 miles to Strawberry. Continue past Strawberry for two miles to Herring Creek Road/Forest Road 4N12. Turn right and drive seven miles to Hamill Canyon Road/Forest Road 4N12. Bear right and drive 0.25 mile to Herring Creek Reservoir. Continue another 0.25 mile (cross the bridge) and turn right and drive to the campground. The road is rough and not recommended for RVs or low-clearance vehicles.

Contact: Stanislaus National Forest, Summit Ranger District, 209/965-3434, fax 209/965-3372.

2 PINECREST

Scenic rating: 7

near Pinecrest Lake in Stanislaus National Forest

This monster-sized Forest Service camp is set near Pinecrest Lake. A launch ramp is available, and a 20-mph speed limit is enforced on the lake. A trail circles the lake and also branches off to nearby Catfish Lake. In early summer, there is good fishing for stocked rainbow trout. The elevation is 5,600 feet. Winter camping is allowed near the Pinecrest Day-Use Area. (For details about Pinecrest Lake, see the *Meadowview* listing in this chapter.)

Campsites, facilities: There are 200 sites for tents or RVs up to 22 feet (no hookups). Picnic tables and fire grills are provided. Drinking water and flush toilets are available. Garbage must be packed out. A grocery store, coin laundry, coin showers, boat ramp, and propane gas are nearby at Pinecrest Lake Resort. Some facilities are wheelchair-accessible. Leashed pets are permitted.

Reservations, fees: Reservations are required mid-May–mid-September at 877/444-6777 or www.recreation.gov ($10 reservation fee). Sites are $19 per night. Open May through October, weather permitting.

Directions: From Sonora, drive east on Highway 108 for about 30 miles to the signed turn for Pinecrest Lake on the right. Turn right and drive to the access road (0.7 mile past the turnoff signed "Pinecrest") for the campground. Turn right and drive a short distance to the campground.

Contact: Stanislaus National Forest, Summit Ranger District, 209/965-3434, fax 209/965-3372.

3 PIONEER TRAIL GROUP CAMP

Scenic rating: 8

near Pinecrest Lake in Stanislaus National Forest

If you're going to Pinecrest Lake with a Scout troop, this is the spot, since it is set up specifically for groups. You get beautiful creek and lake views, with the camp set at an elevation of 5,700 feet. (For recreation information, see the *Meadowview* listing in this chapter.)

Campsites, facilities: There are three group areas for tents or RVs up to 22 feet (no hookups) that can accommodate 50–100 people each. Picnic tables and fire grills are provided. Drinking water and vault toilets are available. Garbage must be packed out. A grocery store, coin laundry, boat ramp, coin showers, and propane gas are nearby. Some facilities are wheelchair-accessible. Leashed pets are permitted.

Reservations, fees: Reservations are accepted at 877/444-6777 or www.recreation.gov ($10 reservation fee). Sites are $60–75 per night. Open May through October, weather permitting.

Directions: From Sonora, drive east on Highway 108 for about 30 miles to the signed road for Pinecrest Lake. Turn right at the sign and drive 0.5 mile to the signed road for Pinecrest/Dodge Ridge Road. Turn right and drive about a mile to the campground entrance on the left.

Contact: Stanislaus National Forest, Summit Ranger District, 209/965-3434, fax 209/965-3372.

4 MEADOWVIEW

Scenic rating: 7

near Pinecrest Lake in Stanislaus National Forest

No secret here, folks. This camp is one mile from Pinecrest Lake, a popular weekend vacation area (and there's a trail that connects the camp with the town). Pinecrest Lake is set at 5,621 feet elevation, covers 300 acres and 2.5 miles of shoreline, has a sandy swimming beach, and has a 20-mph speed limit for boaters. The lake is the centerpiece of a fully developed family vacation area; boat rentals at the small marina are a big bonus. The lake is stocked with rainbow trout and also has a small resident population of brown trout. The easy hike around the lake is a popular walk. If you want something more ambitious, there is a cutoff on the north side of the lake that is routed one mile up to little Catfish Lake, which in reality is a set of shallow ponds surrounded by old-growth forest. The Dodge Ridge Ski Area is nearby, with many privately owned cabins in the area.

Campsites, facilities: There are 100 sites for tents or RVs up to 22 feet (no hookups). Picnic tables and fire grills are provided. Drinking water and flush toilets are available. A grocery store, coin laundry, boat ramp, boat rentals, coin showers, and propane gas are nearby. Garbage must be packed out. Some facilities are wheelchair-accessible. Leashed pets are permitted.

Reservations, fees: Reservations are not accepted. Sites are $14 per night. Open May through September, weather permitting.

Directions: From Sonora, drive east on Highway 108 for about 30 miles to the signed road for Pinecrest Lake. Turn right at the sign and drive 0.5 mile to Pinecrest/Dodge Ridge Road. Turn right and drive about 200 yards to the campground entrance on the right side of the road.

Contact: Stanislaus National Forest, Summit Ranger District, 209/965-3434, fax 209/965-3372.

5 CHERRY VALLEY AND BOAT-IN

Scenic rating: 8

on Cherry Lake in Stanislaus National Forest

Cherry Lake is a mountain lake surrounded by national forest at 4,700 feet elevation, just outside the western boundary of Yosemite National Park. It is much larger than most people anticipate and provides much better trout fishing than anything in Yosemite. The camp is on the southwest shore of the lake, a very pretty spot, about a mile ride to the boat launch on the west side of the Cherry Valley Dam. A bonus is that dispersed boat-in camping is allowed on the lake's east side. All water sports are allowed, yet because it takes a considerable drive to reach the lake, you won't find nearly the waterskiing traffic as at other regional lakes. Water levels can fluctuate here. The lake is bordered to the east by Kibbie Ridge; just on the other side are Yosemite Park and Lake Eleanor. Insider's tip: During periods of campfire restrictions, which is often most of the summer in this national forest, this campground is the only one in the area where campfires are permitted. A fire permit is required from the Forest Service.

Campsites, facilities: There are 45 sites for tents or RVs up to 22 feet (no hookups). Primitive boat-in camping is permitted on the lake's east side. Picnic tables and fire grills are provided. Drinking water and vault toilets are available. A boat ramp is nearby. Leashed pets are permitted.

Reservations, fees: Reservations are not accepted. Sites are $17 per night, $34 per night for double sites. There is no camping fee for boat-in sites. A 14-day limit is enforced. Open April through October, weather permitting.

Directions: From Groveland, drive east on Highway 120 for about 15 miles to Forest Road 1N07/Cherry Lake Road. Turn left and drive 20 miles to Cottonwood Road/Forest Road 1N04. Turn left and drive one mile to the campground entrance road. Turn right and drive one mile to the campground.

Contact: Stanislaus National Forest, Groveland Ranger District, 209/962-7825, fax 209/962-7412.

6 WHITE WOLF

Scenic rating: 8

in Yosemite National Park

This is one of Yosemite National Park's prime mountain camps for people who like to hike, either for great day hikes in the immediate area and beyond, or for overnight backpacking trips. The day hike to Lukens Lake is an easy two-mile trip, the payoff being this pretty little alpine lake set amid a meadow, pines, and granite. Just about everybody who camps at White Wolf makes the trip. Backpackers (wilderness permit required) can make the overnight trip into the Ten Lakes Basin, set below Grand Mountain and Colby Mountain. Bears are common at this camp, and campers are required to secure food in the bearproof lockers. The elevation is 8,000 feet.

Campsites, facilities: There are 74 sites for tents or RVs up to 27 feet (no hookups). Tent cabins are also available. Picnic tables, food lockers, and fire grills are provided. Drinking water and flush toilets are available. Evening ranger programs are occasionally offered. A small store with a walk-up window and limited items is nearby. Leashed pets are permitted in the campground, but not on trails.

Reservations, fees: Reservations are not accepted. Sites are $14 per night, plus $20 park entrance fee per vehicle. Open July to early September, weather permitting.

Directions: From Merced, drive east on Highway 140 to the Arch Rock entrance station. Continue east to the Big Oak Flat Road junction (0.5 mile before entering Yosemite Valley). Turn left and drive 14 miles to Tioga Road. Turn right and drive 15 miles to White Wolf Road on the left. Turn left and drive a mile to the campground entrance road on the right.

Contact: Yosemite National Park, 209/372-0200, for an automated menu of recorded information, www.nps.gov/yose.

7 TUOLUMNE MEADOWS

Scenic rating: 8

in Yosemite National Park

BEST

This is Yosemite's biggest camp, and for the variety of nearby adventures, it might also be the best. It is set in the high country, at 8,600 feet, and can be used as a base camp for fishing, hiking, and horseback riding, or as a start-up point for a backpacking trip (wilderness permits required). This is one of the top trailheads in North America. There are two outstanding and easy day hikes from here, one heading north on the Pacific Crest Trail for the near-level walk to Tuolumne Falls and Glen Aulin, the other heading south up Lyell Fork (toward Donohue Pass), with good fishing for small brook trout. With a backpack (wilderness permit required), either route can be extended for as long as desired into remote and beautiful country. The campground is huge, and neighbors are guaranteed, but it is well wooded and feels somewhat secluded even with all the RVs and tents. There are lots of food-raiding bears in the area, so use of the food lockers is required.

Campsites, facilities: There are 304 sites for tents or RVs up to 35 feet (no hookups), four horse camps, and seven group sites that can accommodate 30 people each. There are also an additional 25 hike-in sites available for backpackers (no parking is available for backpacker campsites, often reserved for those hiking the Pacific Crest Trail, for which a wilderness permit is required). Picnic tables, fire grills, and food lockers are provided. Drinking water, flush toilets, and dump station are available. Showers and groceries are nearby. Leashed pets are permitted, except in group sites, horse camps, and backpacker sites.

Reservations, fees: Reservations are accepted at 877/444-6777 or www.recreation.gov ($10 reservation fee); half of the sites are available through reservations, the other half are first come, first served. Sites are $20 per night for individual sites, $5 per night per person for walk-in (backpack) sites, $25 per night for horse camp, and $40 per night for group sites, plus a $20 per vehicle park entrance fee. Open July through late-September, weather permitting.

Directions: From Merced, drive east on Highway 140 to the Arch Rock entrance station. Continue east to the Big Oak Flat Road junction (0.5 mile before entering Yosemite Valley). Turn left and drive 14 miles to Tioga Road. Turn right and drive 46 miles to the campground on the right side of the road.

From just south of Lee Vining at the junction of U.S. 395 and Highway 120, turn west and drive to the Tioga Pass entrance station for Yosemite National Park. Continue for about eight miles to the campground entrance on the left.

Contact: Yosemite National Park, 209/372-0200, for an automated menu of recorded information, www.nps.gov/yose.

8 SWEETWATER

Scenic rating: 4

near the South Fork of the Tuolumne River in Stanislaus National Forest

This camp is set at 3,000 feet elevation, near the South Fork Tuolumne River, one of several camps along Highway 120 that provide a safety valve for campers who can't find space in Yosemite National Park to the east. Nearby, on the North Fork of the Tuolumne River, is a popular swimming area known as Rainbow Pools, with a waterfall and series of pools created by the river. Whitewater rafting and kayaking are also available a few miles from this camp; a Forest Service permit is required.

Campsites, facilities: There are 12 sites for tents or RVs up to 22 feet (no hookups). Picnic tables and fire grills are provided. Drinking water and vault toilets are available. Leashed pets are permitted.

Reservations, fees: Reservations are not accepted. Sites are $15 per night. A 14-day limit is enforced. Open April through October, weather permitting.

Directions: From Groveland, drive east on Highway 120 for about 15 miles (five miles past the Groveland District Office) to the campground on the left side of the road.

Contact: Stanislaus National Forest, Groveland Ranger District, 209/962-7825, fax 209/962-7412.

9 DIMOND "O"

Scenic rating: 7

in Stanislaus National Forest

Dimond "O" is set at 4,400 feet elevation on the eastern side of Stanislaus National Forest—just two miles from the western border of Yosemite National Park.

Campsites, facilities: There are 36 sites for tents or RVs up to 22 feet (no hookups). Picnic tables and fire grills are provided. Drinking water and vault toilets are available. Some facilities are wheelchair-accessible. Leashed pets are permitted.

Reservations, fees: Reservations are accepted at 877/444-6777 or www.recreation.gov ($10 reservation fee). Sites are $19 per night, double sites are $38 per night. Open April through October, weather permitting.

Directions: From Groveland, drive east on Highway 120 for 25 miles to Evergreen Road/Forest Road 12. Turn left on Evergreen Road and drive six miles to the campground.

Contact: Stanislaus National Forest, Groveland Ranger District, 209/962-7825, fax 209/962-7412.

10 YOSEMITE CREEK

Scenic rating: 9

on Yosemite Creek in Yosemite National Park

BEST

This is the most remote drive-to camp in Yosemite National Park, a great alternative to camping in the valley or at Tuolumne Meadows, and the rough, curvy access road keeps many visitors away. It is set along Yosemite Creek at 7,659 feet elevation, with poor trout fishing but a trailhead for a spectacular hike. If you arrange a shuttle ride, you can make a great one-way trip down to the north side of the Yosemite Canyon rim, skirting past the top of Yosemite Falls (a side trip to Yosemite Point is a must!), then tackling the unbelievable descent into the valley, emerging at Camp 4 Walk-In. Note: The narrow entrance road is a remnant of "Old Tioga Road."

Campsites, facilities: There are 40 sites with no hookups for tents or small RVs. Picnic tables, food lockers (mandatory use), and fire grills are provided. Vault toilets are available. No drinking water is available. Leashed pets are permitted.

Reservations, fees: Reservations are not accepted. Sites are $10 per night, plus $20 park entrance fee per vehicle. A 14-day stay limit is enforced. Open July through early September, weather permitting.

Directions: From Merced, drive east on Highway 140 to the Arch Rock entrance station. Continue east to the Big Oak Flat Road junction (0.5 mile before entering Yosemite Valley). Turn left and drive 14 miles to Tioga Road. Turn right and drive about 30 miles (just beyond the White Wolf turnoff on the left) to Yosemite Creek Campground Road on the right. Turn right (RVs over 24 feet and trailers are not recommended) and drive five miles to the campground at the end of the road.

Contact: Yosemite National Park, 209/372-0200, for an automated menu of recorded information, www.nps.gov/yose.

11 PORCUPINE FLAT

Scenic rating: 6

near Yosemite Creek in Yosemite National Park

Porcupine Flat, set at 8,100 feet elevation, is southwest of Mount Hoffman, one of the prominent nearby peaks along Tioga Road in Yosemite National Park. The trailhead for a hike to May Lake, set just below Mount Hoffman, is about five miles away on a signed turnoff on the north side of the road. There are several little peaks above the lake where hikers can gain great views, including one of the back side of Half Dome.

Campsites, facilities: There are 52 sites for tents or RVs up to 24 feet (no hookups). There is limited RV space. Picnic tables, fire rings, and food lockers (mandatory use) are provided. Pit toilets are available. No drinking water is available. No pets are allowed.

Reservations, fees: Reservations are not accepted. Sites are $10 per night, plus $20 park entrance fee per vehicle. Open July through mid-October, weather permitting.

Directions: From Merced, drive east on Highway 140 to the Arch Rock entrance station. Continue east to the Big Oak Flat Road junction (0.5 mile before entering Yosemite Valley). Turn left and drive 14 miles to Tioga Road. Turn right and drive about 25 miles to the campground on the left side of the road (16 miles west from Tuolumne Meadows).

Contact: Yosemite National Park, 209/372-0200, for an automated menu of recorded information, www.nps.gov/yose.

12 MOORE CREEK GROUP CAMP

Scenic rating: 6

in Stanislaus National Forest

This group camp is set at 3,100 feet elevation, just past where the Sierra alpine zone takes over from foothill oak woodlands. It is near the access route (Highway 120) to the Crane Flat entrance station of Yosemite National Park.

Campsites, facilities: There is one group site for tents or RVs up to 30 feet (no hookups) that can accommodate up to 40 people. Picnic tables and fire grills are provided. No drinking water is available. No toilet is available and campers are required to bring a portable toilet with them. Garbage must be packed out. Leashed pets are permitted.

Reservations, fees: Reservations are required at Groveland Ranger District at 209/962-7825. There is no camping fee. Open year-round.

Directions: From Groveland, drive east on Highway 120 for about 12 miles to Buck Meadows Road. Turn right and drive 1.5 miles (the road becomes Forest Road 2S05) to the campground on the right.

Contact: Stanislaus National Forest, Groveland Ranger District, 209/962-7825, fax 209/962-7412.

13 YOSEMITE LAKES

Scenic rating: 6

on Tuolumne River at Groveland

This is a 400-acre park set at 3,600 feet elevation along the South Fork Tuolumne River in the Sierra foothills near Groveland. Its proximity to Yosemite National Park, just five miles from the west entrance station, makes it ideal for many. The park is an affiliate of Thousand Trails, whose facilities usually are open only to members, but in this case, it is open to the general public on a limited basis. It is a family-oriented park with a large variety of recreation options and seasonal organized activities. Fishing and swimming are popular, and the river is stocked with trout. A plus is 24-hour security.

Campsites, facilities: There are 20 sites with full hookups (30 amps) for RVs of any length and 25 sites for tents available to the public (more sites available to Thousand Trails members only), and cabins, yurts, and a hostel. Picnic tables and fire rings are provided. Restrooms, drinking water, showers, flush toilets, fish-cleaning station, and coin laundry are available. A store, gas station, propane, and firewood are available. Kayak rentals, pedalboats, inner tubes, and bicycles are available for rent. Some facilities are wheelchair accessible. Leashed pets are permitted.

Reservations, fees: Reservations are accepted at 800/533-1001. Sites are $37–39.50 per night for RVs, $29.50–32 per night for tents. Credit cards accepted. Open year-round, weather permitting.

Directions: Drive east on Highway 120 to Groveland. From Groveland, continue east for 18 miles to the entrance road (signed) for Yosemite Lakes on the right. Turn right and drive a short distance to the park.

Contact: Yosemite Lakes, 209/962-0121, www.stayatyosemite.com.

14 HODGDON MEADOW

Scenic rating: 7

in Yosemite National Park

Hodgdon Meadow is on the outskirts of Yosemite, just inside the park's borders at the Big Oak Flat (Highway 120) entrance station, at 4,900 feet in elevation. It is near a small feeder creek to the South Fork Tuolumne River. It is about a 20-minute drive on Highway 120 to a major junction, where a left turn takes you on Tioga Road and to Yosemite's high country, including Tuolumne Meadows, and where staying on Big Flat Road routes you toward Yosemite Valley (25 miles from the camp). Because of the presence of bears, use of food lockers is required.

Campsites, facilities: There are 105 sites for tents or RVs up to 24 feet (no hookups) and four group sites for 13–30 people each. Picnic tables, fire rings, and food lockers are provided. Drinking water and flush toilets are available. Leashed pets are permitted in the campground, but not in group camps or on trails.

Reservations, fees: Reservations are accepted at 877/444-6777 or www.recreation.gov, and are required April through mid-October ($10 reservation fee). Sites are $20 per night May through October, $14 remainder of year, group campsite $40 per night, plus $20 park entrance fee per vehicle. Open year-round, except for group sites.

Directions: From Groveland, drive east on Highway 120 to the Big Oak Flat entrance station for Yosemite National Park. Just after passing the entrance station, turn left and drive a short distance to the campground on the right.

Contact: Yosemite National Park, 209/372-0200, for an automated menu of recorded information, www.nps.gov/yose.

15 TAMARACK FLAT

Scenic rating: 7

on Tamarack Creek in Yosemite National Park

The road to this campground looks something like the surface of the moon. Then you arrive and find one of the few primitive drive-to camps in Yosemite National Park, at 6,300 feet elevation. From the trailhead at camp, you can link up with El Capitan Trail and then hike across Ribbon Meadow on up to the north valley rim at El Capitan, at 7,569 feet elevation. This is the largest single piece of granite in the world, and standing atop it for both the sensation and the divine view is a breathtaking experience. From camp, Yosemite Valley is 23 miles away. Note that the use of food lockers is now required.

Campsites, facilities: There are 52 sites for tents or RVs up to 24 feet (no hookups). Note that the access road is difficult. Picnic tables, food lockers, and fire grills are provided. Vault toilets are available. No drinking water is available. No pets are allowed.

Reservations, fees: Reservations are not accepted. Sites are $10 per night, plus $20 park entrance fee per vehicle. Open June through September.

Directions: From Merced, drive east on Highway 140 to the Arch Rock entrance station.

Continue east to the Big Oak Flat Road junction (0.5 mile before entering Yosemite Valley). Turn left and drive 14 miles to Tioga Road. Turn right on Tioga Road and drive three miles to the campground entrance on the right side of the road. Turn right and drive 2.5 miles to the campground at the end of the road. Trailers and RVs are not advised.

Contact: Yosemite National Park, 209/372-0200, for an automated menu of recorded information, www.nps.gov/yose.

16 CAMP 4

Scenic rating: 8

in Yosemite Valley in Yosemite National Park

The concept at Camp 4 was to provide a climber's bivouac near the base of El Capitan, and so it is. It has also worked as a walk-in alternative to drive-in camps that sometimes resemble combat zones. The sites here are jammed together, and six people will be placed in your site, whether you know them or not. Regardless, the camp is in a great location, within walking distance of Yosemite Falls. It has a view of Leidig Meadow and the southern valley rim, with Sentinel Rock directly across the valley. A trail is routed from camp to Lower Yosemite Fall. In addition, the trailhead for Yosemite Falls Trail is a short distance away, a terrible, butt-kicking climb up Columbia Rock to the rim adjacent to the top of the falls, but providing one of the most incredible views in all the world. Insider's note: After originally being named Camp 4, the park once renamed this campground as "Sunnyside Walk-In." The name was switched back to the original, because climbers never stopped calling it Camp 4.

Campsites, facilities: There are 35 walk-in tent sites. Six people are placed in each campsite, regardless of the number of people in each party. Picnic tables, fire pits, and food lockers (mandatory use) are provided. Drinking water and flush toilets are available. A parking area, showers, groceries, and a coin laundry are nearby. No pets are allowed.

Reservations, fees: Reservations are not accepted. Sites are $5 per person per night, plus $20 park entrance fee per vehicle. There is a seven-day limit during the summer. Open year-round.

Directions: From Merced, drive east on Highway 140 to the Arch Rock entrance station. Continue east to the Big Oak Flat Road junction (0.5 mile before entering Yosemite Valley). Continue into Yosemite Valley, and drive past the chapel to a stop sign. Turn left, cross Sentinel Bridge, and drive one mile to another stop sign. Continue 1.5 miles and look for the large sign marking the parking area for Camp 4 Walk-In on the right (near the base of El Capitan).

Contact: Yosemite National Park, 209/372-0200, for an automated menu of recorded information, www.nps.gov/yose.

17 LOWER PINES

Scenic rating: 9

in Yosemite Valley in Yosemite National Park

Lower Pines sits right along the Merced River, quite pretty, in the center of Yosemite Valley. Of course, the tents and RVs are jammed in quite close together. Within walking distance is the trail to Mirror Lake (a zoo on parade), as well as the trailhead at Happy Isles for the hike up to Vernal Fall and Nevada Fall. The park's shuttle bus picks up riders near the camp entrance.

Campsites, facilities: There are 60 sites for tents or RVs up to 40 feet, one double site for tents or RVs up to 40 feet, and two group camps. No hookups. Fire rings, picnic tables, and food lockers (mandatory use) are provided. Drinking water and flush toilets are available. A grocery store, coin laundry, propane gas, recycling center, dump station and horse and bike rentals are nearby. Leashed pets are permitted.

Reservations, fees: Reservations are required at 877/444-6777 or www.recreation.gov ($10 reservation fee). Sites are $20 per night, $30 per night for double or group sites, plus $20 park entrance fee per vehicle. There is a seven-day limit during the summer. Open late March through October, weather permitting.

Directions: From Merced, drive east on Highway 140 to the Arch Rock entrance station. Continue east to the Big Oak Flat Road junction (0.5 mile before entering Yosemite Valley). Continue into Yosemite Valley, drive past Curry Village (on the right) to the campground entrance on the left side of the road (just before Clarks Bridge).

Contact: Yosemite National Park, 209/372-0200, for an automated menu of recorded information, www.nps.gov/yose.

18 UPPER PINES

Scenic rating: 9

in Yosemite Valley in Yosemite National Park

Of the campgrounds in Yosemite Valley, Upper Pines is the closest trailhead to paradise, providing you can get a campsite at the far south end of the camp. From here it is a short walk to Happy Isles trailhead and with it the chance to hike to Vernal Fall on Mist Trail (steep), or beyond to Nevada Fall (very steep) at the foot of Liberty Cap. But crowded this camp is, and you'd better expect it. People come from all over the world to camp here. Sometimes it appears as if they are from other worlds as well. The elevation is 4,000 feet.

Campsites, facilities: There are 238 sites for tents or RVs up to 35 feet (no hookups). Fire rings, picnic tables, and food lockers (mandatory use) are provided. Drinking water, flush toilets, and dump station are available. A grocery store, coin laundry, propane gas, recycling center, and horse and bike rentals are nearby. Three sites provide wheelchair access. Leashed pets are permitted in the campgrounds, but not on trails.

Reservations, fees: Reservations are required at 877/444-6777 or www.recreation.gov ($10 reservation fee). Sites are $20 per night, plus $20 park entrance fee per vehicle. There is a seven-day limit during the summer. Open year-round.

Directions: From Merced, drive east on Highway 140 to the Arch Rock entrance station. Continue east to the Big Oak Flat Road junction (0.5 mile before entering Yosemite Valley). Continue into Yosemite Valley, drive past Curry Village (on the right) to the campground entrance on the right side of the road (just before Clarks Bridge).

Contact: Yosemite National Park, 209/372-0200, for an automated menu of recorded information, www.nps.gov/yose.

19 NORTH PINES

Scenic rating: 9

in Yosemite Valley in Yosemite National Park

North Pines is set along the Merced River. A trail out of camp heads east and links with the paved road/trail to Mirror Lake, a virtual parade of people. If you continue hiking past Mirror Lake you will get astounding views of Half Dome and then leave the masses behind as you enter Tenaya Canyon. The elevation is 4,000 feet.

Campsites, facilities: There are 81 sites for tents or RVs up to 40 feet (no hookups). Picnic tables, fire grills, and food lockers (mandatory use) are provided. Drinking water and flush toilets are available. A grocery store, coin laundry, recycling center, propane gas, and horse and bike rentals are nearby. Leashed pets are allowed.

Reservations, fees: Reservations are required at 877/444-6777 or www.recreation.gov ($10 reservation fee). Sites are $20 per night, plus

$20 park entrance fee per vehicle. Open April through September, weather permitting.

Directions: From Merced, drive east on Highway 140 to the Arch Rock entrance station. Continue east to the Big Oak Flat Road junction (0.5 mile before entering Yosemite Valley). Continue into Yosemite Valley, drive past Curry Village (on the right), continue past Upper and Lower Pines Campgrounds, and drive over Clarks Bridge to a junction at the horse stables. Turn left at the horse stables and drive a short distance to the campground on the right.

Contact: Yosemite National Park, 209/372-0200, for an automated menu of recorded information, www.nps.gov/yose.

20 CRANE FLAT

Scenic rating: 6

near Tuolumne Grove of Big Trees in Yosemite National Park

Crane Flat is within a five-minute drive of the Tuolumne Grove of Big Trees and to the Merced Grove to the nearby west. This is the feature attraction in this part of Yosemite National Park, set near the western border in close proximity to the Big Oak Flat Entrance Station (Highway 120). The elevation is 6,200 feet. Yosemite Valley is about a 25-minute drive away.

Campsites, facilities: There are 166 sites for tents or RVs up to 35 feet (no hookups). Picnic tables, fire rings, and food lockers are provided. Drinking water and flush toilets are available. Groceries, propane gas, and a gas station are nearby. Leashed pets are allowed in the campground.

Reservations, fees: Reservations are required at 877/444-6777 or www.recreation.gov ($10 reservation fee). Sites are $20 per night, plus $20 park entrance fee per vehicle. Open July through September, weather permitting.

Directions: From Groveland, drive east on Highway 120 to the Big Oak Flat entrance station for Yosemite National Park. After passing through the entrance station, drive about 10 miles to the campground entrance road on the right. Turn right and drive 0.5 mile to the campground.

Contact: Yosemite National Park, 209/372-0200, for an automated menu of recorded information, www.nps.gov/yose.

21 BRIDALVEIL CREEK AND EQUESTRIAN AND GROUP CAMP

Scenic rating: 10

near Glacier Point in Yosemite National Park

BEST

There may be no better view in the world than the one from Glacier Point, looking down into Yosemite Valley, where Half Dome stands like nature's perfect sculpture. Then there are the perfect views of Yosemite Fall, Nevada Fall, Vernal Fall, and several hundred square miles of Yosemite's wilderness backcountry. This is the closest camp to Glacier Point's drive-to vantage point, but it is also the closest camp to the best day hikes in the entire park. Along Glacier Point Road are trailheads to Sentinel Dome (incredible view of Yosemite Fall) and Taft Point (breathtaking drop, incredible view of El Capitan), and McGurk Meadow (one of the most pristine spots on Earth). At 7,200 feet, the camp is more than 3,000 feet higher than Yosemite Valley. A good day hike out of camp leads you to Ostrander Lake, just below Horse Ridge.

Campsites, facilities: There are 110 sites for tents or RVs up to 35 feet (no hookups), three equestrian sites, and two group sites for 13–30 people each. Picnic tables, fire rings, and food lockers (mandatory use) are provided. Drinking water and flush toilets are available. Leashed pets are permitted, except in group sites.

Reservations, fees: Reservations are not accepted for individual sites, but they are required for equestrian sites and group sites at 800/444-6777 or www.recreation.gov ($10 reservation fee). Sites are $14 per night, $25 per night for equestrian site, $40 per night for group site, plus $20 park entrance fee per vehicle. A 14-day stay limit is enforced. Open July through early September, weather permitting.

Directions: From Merced, drive east on Highway 140 to the Arch Rock entrance station. Continue east (past Big Oak Flat Road junction) to the junction with Wawona Road/Highway 41 (just before Yosemite Valley). Turn right on Highway 41/Wawona Road and drive about 10 miles to Glacier Point Road. Turn left on Glacier Point Road and drive about five miles (a few miles past Badger Pass Ski Area) to Peregoy Meadow and the campground access road on the right. Turn right and drive a short distance to the campground.

Contact: Yosemite National Park, 209/372-0200, for an automated menu of recorded information, www.nps.gov/yose.

22 MERCED RECREATION AREA

Scenic rating: 8

on the Merced River east of Briceburg

BEST

What a spot: The campsites are along one of the prettiest sections of the Merced River, where you can enjoy great hiking, swimming, rafting, kayaking, and fishing, all on the same day. There are three campgrounds here: McCabe Flat, Willow Placer, and Railroad Flat. The access road out of camp leads downstream to the Yosemite Railroad Grade, which has been converted into a great trail. One of the best wildflower blooms anywhere in the Sierra foothills is found near here at Red Hills (just outside Chinese Camp), usually best in April. If you don't mind the cold water, swimming in the Merced River's pools can provide relief from summer heat. Evening fly-fishing is good in many of the same spots through July. But the true attraction on the Merced River is rafting and kayaking. An extraordinarily long stretch of river, 29 miles, can be run from the put-in at Red Bud Day-Use Area to the take-out at Bagby. A number of whitewater guide companies work this stretch of river.

Campsites, facilities: There are 21 walk-in tent sites and nine sites for tents or RVs up to 18 feet (no hookups). Picnic tables and fire grills are provided. Vault and pit toilets are available. No drinking water is available at the campsites (drinking water is available across from the Briceburg Bridge). Supplies are available in Mariposa. Some facilities are wheelchair-accessible. Leashed pets are permitted.

Reservations, fees: Reservations are not accepted. Sites are $10 per night. There is a 14-day limit. Open April through October, weather permitting.

Directions: From Merced, turn east on Highway 140 and drive 40 miles to Mariposa. Continue another 15 miles to Briceburg and the Briceburg Visitor Center on the left. Turn left at a road that is signed "BLM Camping Areas" (the road remains paved for about 150 yards). Drive over the Briceburg suspension bridge and turn left, traveling downstream on the road, parallel to the river. Drive 2.5 miles to McCabe Flat, 3.8 miles to Willow Placer, and 4.8 miles to Railroad Flat.

Contact: Bureau of Land Management, Folsom Field Office, 916/985-4474, fax 916/985-3259.

23 YOSEMITE-MARIPOSA KOA

Scenic rating: 7

near Mariposa

A little duck pond, swimming pool, and proximity to Yosemite National Park make this one a winner. A shuttle bus service (fee) to the national park is a great bonus. The RV sites are lined up along the entrance road. A 10 P.M. "quiet time" helps ensure a good night's sleep. It's a one-hour drive to Yosemite Valley, and your best bet is to get there early to enjoy the spectacular beauty before the park is packed with people.

Campsites, facilities: There are 49 sites with full or partial hookups (30 and 50 amps) for RVs up to 40 feet, 26 tent sites, 12 cabins, and three lodges. Picnic tables and barbecues are provided; no wood fires. Restrooms with showers, dump station, Wi-Fi, telephone/modem access, coin laundry, convenience store, propane gas, seasonal swimming pool, train caboose with arcade, and playground are available. Some facilities are wheelchair accessible. Leashed pets are permitted in RV and tent sites only, with certain restrictions.

Reservations, fees: Reservations are accepted at 800/562-9391. Sites are $35–60 per night, $6 per person per night for more than two people, $5 per night for each additional vehicle, $2 per pet per night. Call for cabin and lodge prices. Some credit cards accepted. Open March through October.

Directions: From Merced, drive east on Highway 140 to Mariposa. Continue on Highway 140 for seven miles to Midpines and the campground entrance on the left at 6323 Highway 140.

Contact: Yosemite-Mariposa KOA, 209/966-2201, www.yosemitekoa.com.

24 JERSEYDALE

Scenic rating: 5

in Sierra National Forest

This little camp gets overlooked by many visitors shut out of nearby Yosemite National Park simply because they don't realize it exists. Jerseydale is set southwest of the national park in Sierra National Forest, with two good side trips nearby. If you continue north on Jerseydale Road to its end (about six miles), you will come to a Forest Service road/trailhead that provides access east along a portion of the South Fork of the Merced River, where there is often good fishing, swimming, and rafting. In addition, a dirt road from the camp is routed east for many miles into the Chowchilla Mountains.

Campsites, facilities: There are 10 sites for tents or RVs up to 24 feet (no hookups). Picnic tables and fire grills are provided. Vault toilets are available. No drinking water. A few hitching posts are available and horses are permitted at these camps. Leashed pets are permitted.

Reservations, fees: Reservations are not accepted. There is no fee for camping. Open May through November.

Directions: From Mariposa, drive northeast on Highway 140 for about five miles to Triangle Road (if you reach Midpines, you have gone 1.5 miles too far). Turn right on Triangle Road and drive about six miles to Darrah and Jerseydale Road. Turn left and drive three miles to the campground on the left side of the road (adjacent to the Jerseydale Ranger Station).

Contact: Sierra National Forest, Bass Lake Ranger District, 559/877-2218, fax 559/877-3108.

25 WAWONA

Scenic rating: 9

on the South Fork of the Merced River in Yosemite National Park

Wawona is an attractive alternative to the packed camps in Yosemite Valley, providing you don't mind the relatively long drives to the best destinations. The camp is pretty, set along the South Fork of the Merced River, with the sites more spacious than at most other drive-to camps in the park. The nearest attraction is the Mariposa Grove of Giant Sequoias, but get your visit in by 9 A.M., because after that it turns into a zoo, complete with shuttle train. The best nearby hike is a strenuous 10-mile round-trip to Chilnualna Falls, the prettiest sight in the southern region of the park; the trailhead is at the east end of Chilnualna Road in North Wawona. It's a 45-minute drive to either Glacier Point or Yosemite Valley.

Campsites, facilities: There are 93 sites for tents or RVs up to 35 feet (no hookups), one group tent site for 13–30 people each, and two horse camps. Picnic tables, fire grills, and food lockers (mandatory use) are provided. Drinking water and flush toilets are available. There are some stock-handling facilities for camping with pack animals; call for further information. A grocery store, dump station, propane gas, gas station, post office, restaurant, and seasonal horseback-riding facilities are nearby. Leashed pets are permitted, but not in group sites, horse camps, or on trails.

Reservations, fees: From May through September, reservations are required at 877/444-6777 or www.recreation.gov ($10 reservation fee). No reservations are needed from October to April. Sites are $20 per night, $14 per night in off-season; horse camps are $25 per night, group tent site is $40 per night; plus $20 park entrance fee per vehicle. A seven-day camping limit is enforced during the summer. Open year-round, and horse camp open April through October.

Directions: From Oakhurst, drive north on Highway 41 to the Wawona entrance of Yosemite National Park. Continue north on Highway 41 past Wawona (golf course on the left) and drive one mile to the campground entrance on the left.

Contact: Yosemite National Park, 209/372-0200, for an automated menu of recorded information, www.nps.gov/yose.

26 SUMMIT CAMP

Scenic rating: 5

in Sierra National Forest

The prime attraction of tiny Summit Camp is its proximity to the Wawona entrance of Yosemite National Park. It sits along a twisty Forest Service road, perched in the Chowchilla Mountains at 5,800 feet, about three miles from Big Creek. It's a little-known alternative when the park campgrounds at Wawona are packed.

Campsites, facilities: There are six primitive sites for tents or RVs up to 16 feet (no hookups). Picnic tables and fire grills are provided. Vault toilets are available. No drinking water is available. Garbage must be packed out. Leashed pets are permitted.

Reservations, fees: Reservations are not accepted. There is no fee for camping. A 14-day limit is enforced. Open June through October, weather permitting.

Directions: From Oakhurst, drive north on Highway 41 toward the town of Fish Camp and to the gravel Forest Road 5S09X a mile before Fish Camp on the left. Turn left and drive six twisty miles to the campground on the left side of the road. High-clearance vehicles are required. Trailers are not advised.

Contact: Sierra National Forest, Bass Lake Ranger District, 559/877-2218, fax 559/877-3108.

27 SUMMERDALE

Scenic rating: 7

on the South Fork of the Merced River in Sierra National Forest

You can't get much closer to Yosemite National Park. This camp is within a mile of the Wawona entrance to Yosemite, about a five-minute drive to the Mariposa Grove. If you don't mind its proximity to the highway, this is a pretty spot in its own right, set along Big Creek, a feeder stream to the South Fork Merced River. Some good swimming holes are in this area. The elevation is 5,000 feet.

Campsites, facilities: There are 79 sites for tents or RVs up to 24 feet (no hookups). Picnic tables and fire grills are provided. Vault toilets are available. No drinking water is available. A grocery store is nearby (within one mile). Some facilities are wheelchair-accessible. Leashed pets are permitted.

Reservations, fees: Reservations are accepted at 877/444-6777 or www.recreation.gov ($10 reservation fee). Sites are $19 per night, $5 per night for each additional vehicle. Open May through October, weather permitting.

Directions: From Oakhurst, drive north on Highway 41 to Fish Camp and continue for one mile to the campground entrance on the left side of the road.

Contact: Sierra National Forest, Bass Lake Ranger District, 559/877-2218, fax 559/877-3108.

28 UPPER CHIQUITO

Scenic rating: 7

on Chiquito Creek in Sierra National Forest

Upper Chiquito is set at 6,800 feet elevation on a major access road to Sierra National Forest and the western region of the Ansel Adams Wilderness, about 15 miles to the east. The camp is set on Upper Chiquito Creek. About a mile down the road (southwest) is a Forest Service spur road (turn north) that provides access to a trail that is routed up Chiquito Creek for three miles to gorgeous Chiquita Lake (another route with a longer drive and shorter hike is available out of Fresno Dome).

Campsites, facilities: There are 20 sites for tents or RVs up to 20 feet (no hookups). Picnic tables and fire rings are provided. Vault toilets are available. No drinking water is available. Garbage service is located at the entrance to the campground. Leashed pets are permitted.

Reservations, fees: Reservations are not accepted. There is no fee for camping. Open June through September, weather permitting.

Directions: From Fresno, drive north on Highway 41 for 50 miles to Yosemite Forks and County Road 222. Turn right on County Road 222 (keeping to the right at each of two Y intersections) and drive six miles to Pines Village and Beasore Road. Turn left onto Beasore Road and drive 16 miles to the campground.

Contact: Sierra National Forest, Bass Lake Ranger District, 559/877-2218, fax 559/877-3108.

29 CLOVER MEADOW

Scenic rating: 8

in Sierra National Forest

This is one of two excellent jump-off camps in the area for backpackers; the other is Granite Creek. The camp is set at 7,000 feet elevation, adjacent to the Clover Meadow Ranger Station, where backcountry information is available. While a trail is available from camp heading east into the Ansel Adams Wilderness, most hikers drive about three miles farther northeast on Minarets Road to a trailhead for a five-mile hike to Cora Lakes.

Campsites, facilities: There are seven sites for tents or RVs up to 20 feet (no hookups). Picnic tables and fire rings are provided. Drinking water and vault toilets are available. Garbage must be packed out. Leashed pets are permitted.

Reservations, fees: Reservations are not accepted. There is no fee for camping. Open June through September, weather permitting.

Directions: From Fresno, drive north on Highway 41 for about 25 miles to North Fork Road/County Road 200. Turn right and drive northeast for 17.5 miles to Auberry Road/County Road 222. Turn left (north) and drive one mile to the town of North Fork and Mammoth Pool Road. Turn right and drive 1.5 miles to County Road 225 (still Mammoth Pool Road). Turn right and drive (the road eventually becomes Minarets Road) to the junction with Forest

Road 4S81. Bear left (north) on Forest Road 4S81 and drive to the campground entrance road. Bear left (signed "Clover Meadow") and drive to the campground, adjacent to the Clover Meadow Ranger Station. The total distance from North Fork to the entrance road is about 63 miles; it's 20 miles north of the well-signed Mammoth Pool Reservoir on Minarets Road.

Contact: Sierra National Forest, Bass Lake Ranger District, 559/877-2218, fax 559/877-3108.

30 GRANITE CREEK AND EQUESTRIAN CAMP

Scenic rating: 6

in Sierra National Forest

This camp is a good jump-off point for backpackers since a trail from camp leads north for five miles to Cora Lakes in the Ansel Adams Wilderness, with the option of continuing to more remote wilderness. Note that nearby Clover Meadow camp (see listing in this chapter) may be more desirable because it has both drinking water to tank up your canteens and a ranger station to obtain the latest trail information. In addition, the upper half of this campground is available for equestrians. The elevation is 6,900 feet.

Campsites, facilities: There are 20 sites for tents or RVs up to 20 feet (no hookups). Picnic tables and fire rings are provided. Vault toilets and a horse corral are available. No drinking water is available. Garbage must be packed out. Leashed pets are permitted.

Reservations, fees: Reservations are not accepted. There is no fee for camping. Open June through September, weather permitting.

Directions: From Fresno, drive north on Highway 41 for about 25 miles to North Fork Road/County Road 200. Turn right and drive northeast for 17.5 miles to Auberry Road/County Road 222. Turn left (north) and drive one mile to the town of North Fork and Mammoth Pool Road. Turn right and drive 1.5 miles to County Road 225 (still Mammoth Pool Road). Turn right and drive (the road eventually becomes Minarets Road) to the junction with Forest Road 4S81. Bear left (north) on Forest Road 4S81 and drive to the campground entrance road. Turn left (signed for Granite Creek) and drive 3.5 miles to the campground. (The total distance from North Fork to the entrance road is about 66.5 miles; it's 23.5 miles north of Mammoth Pool Reservoir on the well-signed Minarets Road.)

Contact: Sierra National Forest, Bass Lake Ranger District, 559/877-2218, fax 559/877-3108.

31 BIG SANDY

Scenic rating: 7

on Big Creek in Sierra National Forest

It's only six miles from the highway and just eight miles from the southern entrance to Yosemite National Park. Add that up: Right, when Wawona is full in southern Yosemite, this camp provides a much-needed option. It's a pretty camp set on Big Creek in the Sierra National Forest, one of two camps in the immediate area. The elevation is 5,800 feet. If you head into Yosemite for the tour of giant sequoias in Wawona, get there early, by 7:30 or 8:30 A.M., when the grove is still quiet and cool, and you will have the old, mammoth trees practically to yourself.

Campsites, facilities: There are 18 sites for tents or RVs up to 20 feet (no hookups). Picnic tables and fire grills are provided. Vault toilets are available. No drinking water is available. Leashed pets are permitted.

Reservations, fees: Reservations are not accepted. Sites are $16 per night, $5 per night for each additional vehicle. Open May through September, weather permitting.

Directions: From Oakhurst drive north on Highway 41 for 15 miles to Forest Road 6S07 (one mile before reaching Marriotts). Turn right on Forest Road 6S07 and drive about six miles (a slow, rough road) to the camp.

Contact: Sierra National Forest, Bass Lake Ranger District, 559/877-2218, fax 559/877-3108.

32 FRESNO DOME

Scenic rating: 7

on Big Creek in Sierra National Forest

This camp is named after nearby Fresno Dome to the east, at 7,540 feet elevation the dominating feature in the surrounding landscape. The trailhead for a mile hike to its top is two miles curving down the road to the east. This camp is set at 6,400 feet on Big Creek in Sierra National Forest, a good option to nearby Yosemite National Park.

Campsites, facilities: There are 15 sites for tents or RVs up to 20 feet (no hookups). Picnic tables and fire grills are provided. Vault toilets are available. No drinking water is available. Garbage service is located near the entrance to the campground. Leashed pets are permitted.

Reservations, fees: Reservations are not accepted. Sites are $14 per night, $5 per night for each additional vehicle. A 14-day limit is enforced. Open June through mid-October, weather permitting.

Directions: From Oakhurst, drive north on Highway 41 approximately five miles to Sky Ranch Road/Forest Road 6S10. Turn right and drive 12 miles to the campground on the left.

Contact: Sierra National Forest, Bass Lake Ranger District, 559/877-2218, fax 559/877-3108.

33 KELTY MEADOW AND EQUESTRIAN CAMP

Scenic rating: 6

on Willow Creek in Sierra National Forest

This primitive campground is often used by campers with horses. It is at Kelty Meadow by Willow Creek. Side-trip options feature nearby Fresno Dome, the Nelder Grove of giant sequoias and, of course, the southern entrance to nearby Yosemite National Park. The elevation is 5,800 feet.

Campsites, facilities: There are 11 sites for tents or RVs up to 20 feet. Fire grills and picnic tables are provided. Vault toilets and hitching posts are available. No drinking water is available. Garbage service is located near the entrance to the campground. Leashed pets are permitted.

Reservations, fees: Reservations are required for equestrian sites at 877/444-6777 or www.recreation.gov ($10 reservation fee). Sites are $16 per night, $5 per night for each additional vehicle. Open June through September, weather permitting.

Directions: From Oakhurst on Highway 41, drive five miles north to Sky Ranch Road/Forest Road 6S10. Turn left (northeast) and drive approximately 10 miles to the campground.

Contact: Sierra National Forest, Bass Lake Ranger District, 559/877-2218, fax 559/877-3108.

34 NELDER GROVE

Scenic rating: 7

in Sierra National Forest

Nelder Grove is a primitive spot, also pretty, yet it is a camp that is often overlooked. It is set amid the Nelder Grove of giant sequoias, the majestic mountain redwoods. There are two interpretive trails, each about a two-mile walk. Since the southern entrance to Yosemite National Park is just 10 miles away, Nelder Grove is overshadowed by Yosemite's Wawona Grove. The elevation is 5,300 feet. A good option.

Campsites, facilities: There are seven sites for tents or RVs up to 20 feet (no hookups). Picnic tables and fire grills are provided. Vault toilets are available. No drinking water is available. Garbage must be packed out. Leashed pets are permitted.

Reservations, fees: Reservations are not accepted. There is no fee for camping. Open May through September, weather permitting.

Directions: From Fresno, drive north on Highway 41 for 46 miles to the town of Oakhurst. Continue north on Highway 41 for five miles to Sky Ranch Road/Forest Road 6S10. Turn right (northeast) and drive about eight miles to Forest Road 6S47Y. Turn left and drive a short distance to the campground.

Contact: Sierra National Forest, Bass Lake Ranger District, 559/877-2218, fax 559/877-3108.

35 SOQUEL

Scenic rating: 7

on the North Fork of Willow Creek in Sierra National Forest

Soquel is at 5,400 feet elevation on the North Fork of Willow Creek, an alternative to nearby Grey's Mountain in Sierra National Forest. When the camps are filled at Bass Lake, these two camps provide overflow areas as well as more primitive settings for those who are looking for more of a wilderness experience.

Campsites, facilities: There are 11 sites for tents or RVs up to 20 feet (no hookups). Picnic tables and fire grills are provided. Vault toilets are available. No drinking water is available. Leashed pets are permitted.

Reservations, fees: Reservations are accepted at 877/444-6777 or www.recreation.gov ($10 reservation fee). Sites are $16 per night, $5 per night for each additional vehicle. Open June through October, weather permitting.

Directions: From Fresno, drive north on Highway 41 for 46 miles to the town of Oakhurst. Continue north on Highway 41 for five miles to Sky Ranch Road/Forest Road 6S10. Turn right (east) and drive approximately five miles to Forest Road 6S40. Turn right and drive about three-quarters of a mile to the campground.

Contact: Sierra National Forest, Bass Lake Ranger District, 559/877-2218, fax 559/877-3108.

36 TEXAS FLAT GROUP CAMP

Scenic rating: 5

on the North Fork of Willow Creek in Sierra National Forest

If you are on your honeymoon, this definitely ain't the place to be. Unless you like the smell of horses, that is. It's a pretty enough spot, set along the North Fork of Willow Creek, but the camp is primitive and designed for groups with horses. This camp is 15 miles from the south entrance of Yosemite National Park and 15 miles north of Bass Lake. The elevation is 5,400 feet.

Campsites, facilities: There are four group sites for tents or RVs up to 20 feet (no hookups) that can accommodate 25–100 people each. Fire grills and picnic tables are provided. Vault toilets and a corral are available. No drinking water is available. Leashed pets are permitted.

Reservations, fees: Reservations are accepted at 877/444-6777 or www.recreation.gov ($10 reservation fee). Sites are $60.50–90.20 per night. A 14-day limit is enforced. Open June through November.

Directions: From Fresno, drive about 52 miles north on Highway 41 to Sky Ranch Road/

County Road 632. Turn right (east) on Sky Ranch Road/Forest Road 6S10 and drive approximately five miles to Forest Road 6S40. Turn right and drive about three-quarters of a mile to Forest Road 6S08. Turn left and drive 2.5 miles to Forest Road 6S38 and the campground.

Contact: Sierra National Forest, Bass Lake Ranger District, 559/877-2218, fax 559/877-3108.

37 GREY'S MOUNTAIN

Scenic rating: 7

on Willow Creek in Sierra National Forest

This is a small, primitive campground to keep in mind when all the campgrounds are filled at nearby Bass Lake. It is one of a series of campgrounds on Willow Creek. The elevation is 5,400 feet, set just below Sivels Mountain to the east at 5,813 feet.

Campsites, facilities: There are 26 sites for tents or RVs up to 20 feet (no hookups). Picnic tables and fire grills are provided. Vault toilets are available. No drinking water is available. Leashed pets are permitted.

Reservations, fees: Reservations are not accepted. Sites are $16 per night, $5 per night for each additional vehicle. Open May through November, weather permitting.

Directions: From Oakhurst, drive north on Highway 41 for approximately five miles to Sky Ranch Road/Forest Road 6S10. Turn right and drive five miles to Forest Road 6S40. Turn right and drive 0.75 mile to Forest Road 6S08 and the camp.

Contact: Sierra National Forest, Bass Lake Ranger District, 559/877-2218, fax 559/877-3108.

38 BUCKEYE

Scenic rating: 8

near Buckeye Creek in Humboldt-Toiyabe National Forest

Here's a little secret: A two-mile hike out of camp heads to the undeveloped Buckeye Hot Springs. That is what inspires campers to bypass the fishing at nearby Robinson Creek (three miles away) and Twin Lakes (six miles away). The camp feels remote and primitive, set at 7,000 feet elevation on the eastern slope of the Sierra near Buckeye Creek. Another secret is that rainbow trout are planted at the little bridge that crosses Buckeye Creek near the campground. A trail that starts near camp is routed through Buckeye Canyon and into the Hoover Wilderness.

Campsites, facilities: There are 65 paved sites for tents or RVs up to 35 feet (no hookups). Picnic tables and fire grills are provided. Drinking water and vault and flush toilets are available. Some facilities are wheelchair-accessible. Leashed pets are permitted.

Reservations, fees: Reservations are not accepted. Sites are $15 per night, $5 per night for each additional vehicle. Open May through October, weather permitting.

Directions: On U.S. 395, drive to Bridgeport and the junction with Twin Lakes Road. Turn west and drive seven miles to Buckeye Road. Turn right (north) on Buckeye Road (dirt, often impassable when wet) and drive 3.5 miles to the campground.

Contact: Humboldt-Toiyabe National Forest, Bridgeport Ranger District, 760/932-7070, fax 760/932-5899; American Land and Leisure, 760/932-9888.

39 WILLOW SPRINGS RV PARK

Scenic rating: 6

near Bridgeport

Willow Springs RV Park is set at 6,800 feet elevation along U.S. 395, which runs along the eastern Sierra from Carson City south to Bishop and beyond to Lone Pine. The park is one mile from the turnoff to Bodie ghost town. A nice touch to the place is a central campfire that has been in place for more than 50 years. The country is stark here on the edge of the high Nevada desert, but there are many side trips that give the area life. The most popular destinations are to the nearby south: Mono Lake, with its tufa towers and incredible populations of breeding gulls and waterfowl, and the Bodie ghost town. For trout fishing, there's Bridgeport Reservoir to the north (good trolling) and downstream to the East Walker River (fly-fishing), both excellent destinations, as well as Twin Lakes to the west (huge brown trout).

Campsites, facilities: There are 25 sites with full hookups (30 amps) for RVs of any length. No tents. A motel is also available. Picnic tables are provided. Restrooms with showers, coin laundry, and nightly campfires are available. A restaurant is within walking distance. Leashed pets are permitted.

Reservations, fees: Reservations are accepted. Sites are $30 per night, $5 per person per night for more than two people. Open May through October.

Directions: From Bridgeport on U.S. 395, drive five miles south to the park, which is on the east side of the highway.

Contact: Willow Springs RV Park, 760/932-7725.

40 HONEYMOON FLAT

Scenic rating: 8

on Robinson Creek in Humboldt-Toiyabe National Forest

The camp is set beside Robinson Creek at 7,000 feet elevation, in the transition zone between the Sierra Nevada range to the west and the high desert to the east. It is easy to reach on the access road to Twin Lakes, only three miles farther. The lake is famous for occasional huge brown trout. However, the fishing at Robinson Creek is also often quite good, thanks to large numbers of trout planted each year.

Campsites, facilities: There are 35 sites with no hookups for tents or RVs up to 35 feet. Picnic tables and fire grills are provided. Drinking water, food lockers, and vault toilets are available. Some facilities are wheelchair-accessible. Leashed pets are permitted.

Reservations, fees: Reservations are accepted at 877/444-6777 or www.recreation.gov ($10 reservation fee). Sites are $13.39–15 per night, $5 per night for each additional vehicle. Open mid-April through October.

Directions: On U.S. 395, drive to Bridgeport and the junction with Twin Lakes Road. Turn west and drive eight miles to the campground.

Contact: Humboldt-Toiyabe National Forest, Bridgeport Ranger District, 760/932-7070, fax 760/932-5899; American Land and Leisure, 760/932-9888.

41 PAHA

Scenic rating: 8

near Twin Lakes in Humboldt-Toiyabe National Forest

This is one in a series of camps near Robinson Creek and within close range of Twin Lakes. The elevation at the camp is 7,000 feet. (See the *Lower Twin Lake* and *Honeymoon Flat* listings in this chapter for more information.)

Campsites, facilities: There are 22 sites for tents or RVs up to 35 feet (no hookups). Picnic tables and fire grills are provided. Drinking water, flush toilets, and food lockers are available. Two boat launches, a store, coin showers, and a coin laundry are available nearby at Twin Lakes Resort. Leashed pets are permitted.

Reservations, fees: Reservations are accepted at 877/444-6777 or www.recreation.gov ($10 reservation fee). Sites are $15.18–30.36 per night, $5 per night for each additional vehicle. Open May through October, weather permitting.

Directions: On U.S. 395, drive to Bridgeport and the junction with Twin Lakes Road. Turn west and drive 10 miles to the campground.

Contact: Humboldt-Toiyabe National Forest, Bridgeport Ranger District, 760/932-7070, fax 760/932-5899; American Land and Leisure, 760/932-9888.

42 ROBINSON CREEK

Scenic rating: 9

near Twin Lakes in Humboldt-Toiyabe National Forest

This campground, one of a series in the area, is set at 7,000 feet elevation on Robinson Creek, not far from Twin Lakes. The campground is divided into two areas. (For recreation options, see the *Lower Twin Lake* and *Honeymoon Flat* listings in this chapter.)

Campsites, facilities: There are 54 paved sites for tents or RVs up to 35 feet (no hookups). Picnic tables, food lockers, and fire grills are provided. Drinking water and flush and vault toilets are available. Some facilities are wheelchair-accessible. An amphitheater is nearby. Boat launches, a store, coin laundry, and coin showers are nearby at Twin Lakes Resort. Leashed pets are permitted.

Reservations, fees: Reservations are accepted at 877/444-6777 or www.recreation.gov ($10 reservation fee). Sites are $15.18–30.36 per night, $5 per night for each additional vehicle. Open mid-April through October, weather permitting.

Directions: On U.S. 395, drive to Bridgeport and the junction with Twin Lakes Road. Turn west and drive 10 miles to the campground.

Contact: Humboldt-Toiyabe National Forest, Bridgeport Ranger District, 760/932-7070, fax 760/932-5899; American Land and Leisure, 760/932-9888.

43 CRAGS CAMPGROUND

Scenic rating: 8

on Robinson Creek in Humboldt-Toiyabe National Forest

Crags Campground is set at 7,100 feet elevation in the Sierra, one of a series of campgrounds along Robinson Creek near Lower Twin Lake. While this camp does not offer direct access to Lower Twin, home of giant brown trout, it is very close. (See the *Lower Twin Lake* and *Honeymoon Flat* listings in this chapter.)

Campsites, facilities: There are 52 sites for tents or RVs up to 45 feet (no hookups). Picnic tables, food lockers, and fire grills are provided. Drinking water and flush toilets are available. Some facilities are wheelchair-accessible. A boat launch (at Lower Twin Lake), store, coin laundry, and coin showers are within a half mile. Leashed pets are permitted.

Reservations, fees: Reservations are accepted at 877/444-6777 or www.recreation.gov ($10 reservation fee). Sites are $15.18–30.36 per night, $5 per night for each additional vehicle. A group site is $95 per night. Open mid-May through mid-November, weather permitting.

Directions: On U.S. 395, drive to Bridgeport and the junction with Twin Lakes Road. Turn west and drive 11 miles to South Twin Road (just before reaching Lower Twin

Lake). Turn left and drive over the bridge at Robinson Creek to another road on the left. Turn left and drive a short distance to the campground.

Contact: Humboldt-Toiyabe National Forest, Bridgeport Ranger District, 760/932-7070, fax 760/932-5899; American Land and Leisure, 760/932-9888.

44 LOWER TWIN LAKE

Scenic rating: 9

in Humboldt-Toiyabe National Forest

BEST

The Twin Lakes are actually two lakes, set high in the eastern Sierra at 7,000 feet elevation. Each lake is unique. Lower Twin, known as the fishing lake, with a 5-mph speed limit, has a full resort, marina, boat ramp, and some of the biggest brown trout in the West. The state-record brown—26.5 pounds—was caught here in 1985. Of course, most of the trout are your typical 10- to 12-inch planted rainbow trout, but nobody seems to mind, with the chance of a true monster-sized fish always in the back of the minds of anglers. Upper Twin Lake, with a resort and marina, is a primary destination for boaters, personal watercraft, water-skiers, swimmers, and sailboarders. These lakes are very popular in summer. An option for campers is an excellent trailhead for hiking near Mono Village at the head of Upper Twin Lake. Here you will find Barney Lake Trail, which is routed up the headwaters of Robinson Creek, steeply at times, to Barney Lake, an excellent day hike.

Campsites, facilities: There are 15 paved sites for tents or RVs up to 35 feet (no hookups). Picnic tables and fire grills are provided. Drinking water, flush toilets, and food lockers are available. A boat launch, store, coin showers, and a coin laundry are available nearby. Leashed pets are permitted.

Reservations, fees: Reservations are accepted at 877/444-6777 or www.recreation.gov ($10 reservation fee). Sites are $15.18–17 per night, $5 per night for each additional vehicle. Open early May through mid-October, weather permitting.

Directions: On U.S. 395, drive to Bridgeport and the junction with Twin Lakes Road. Turn west and drive 11 miles to South Twin Road (just before reaching Lower Twin Lake). Turn left and drive over the bridge at Robinson Creek and to the campground entrance road on the right.

Contact: Humboldt-Toiyabe National Forest, Bridgeport Ranger District, 760/932-7070, fax 760/932-5899; American Land and Leisure, 760/932-9888.

45 GREEN CREEK

Scenic rating: 7

in Humboldt-Toiyabe National Forest

This camp is ideal for backpackers or campers who like to fish for trout in streams. That is because it is set at 7,500 feet, with a trailhead that leads into the Hoover Wilderness and to several high mountain lakes, including Green Lake, West Lake, and East Lake; the ambitious can hike beyond in remote northeastern Yosemite National Park. The camp is set along Green Creek, a fair trout stream with small rainbow trout.

Campsites, facilities: There are 11 sites for tents or RVs up to 35 feet and two group sites for tents or RVs of any length that can accommodate 25–30 people each. No hookups. Picnic tables and fire grills are provided. Drinking water and vault toilets are available. Leashed pets are permitted.

Reservations, fees: Reservations are not accepted for individual sites but are required for group sites at 877/444-6777 or www.recreation.gov ($10 reservation fee). Sites are $15.18 per night, $5 per night for each additional vehicle, and $46.43–58.04 per night for a group site. Open mid-May through early October, weather permitting.

Directions: From Bridgeport, drive south on U.S. 395 for four miles to Green Lakes Road (dirt). Turn right and drive seven miles to the campground.

Contact: Humboldt-Toiyabe National Forest, Bridgeport Ranger District, 760/932-7070, fax 760/932-5899; American Land and Leisure, 760/932-9888.

46 TRUMBULL LAKE

Scenic rating: 8

in Humboldt-Toiyabe National Forest

This is a high-mountain camp (9,500 feet) at the gateway to a beautiful Sierra basin. Little Trumbull Lake is the first lake on the north side of Virginia Lakes Road, with Virginia Lakes set nearby, along with the Hoover Wilderness and access to many other small lakes by trail. A trail is available that is routed just north of Blue Lake, and then it leads west to Frog Lake, Summit Lake, and beyond into a remote area of Yosemite National Park. If you don't want to rough it, cabins, boat rentals, and a restaurant are available at Virginia Lakes Resort. No gas motors, swimming, and water/body contact is permitted at Virginia Lakes.

Campsites, facilities: There are 45 sites for tents or RVs up to 35 feet (no hookups). Picnic tables and fire grills are provided. Drinking water and pit toilets are available. A store is nearby at the resort. Some facilities are wheelchair-accessible. Leashed pets are permitted.

Reservations, fees: Reservations are accepted at 877/444-6777 or www.recreation.gov ($10 reservation fee). Sites are $13.39–45 per night, $5 per night for each additional vehicle. Open June through September, weather permitting.

Directions: From Bridgeport, drive south on U.S. 395 for 13.5 miles to Virginia Lakes Road. Turn right on Virginia Lakes Road and drive 6.5 miles to the campground entrance road.

Contact: Humboldt-Toiyabe National Forest, Bridgeport Ranger District, 760/932-7070, fax 760/932-5899; American Land and Leisure, 760/932-9888.

47 LUNDY CANYON CAMPGROUND

Scenic rating: 7

near Lundy Lake

This camp is set high in the eastern Sierra at 7,400 feet elevation along pretty Lundy Creek, the mountain stream that feeds Lundy Lake and then runs downhill, eventually joining other creeks on its trip to nearby Mono Lake. Nearby Lundy Lake (at 7,800 feet elevation) is a long, narrow lake with good fishing for rainbow trout and brown trout. The water is clear and cold, even through the summer. There is a trailhead just west of the lake that is routed steeply up into the Hoover Wilderness to several small pretty lakes, passing two waterfalls about two miles in. A must-do side trip is visiting Mono Lake and its spectacular tufa towers, best done at the Mono Lake Tufa State Reserve along the southern shore of the lake.

Campsites, facilities: There are 50 sites for tents or RVs up to 24 feet (no hookups). Picnic tables and fire rings are provided. Pit toilets are available. No drinking water is available. You can buy supplies in Lee Vining, 8.5 miles away. Leashed pets are permitted.

Reservations, fees: Reservations are not accepted. Sites are $12 per night, with a limit of two vehicles and six people per site. Monthly rates available. Open May through mid-November.

Directions: From Lee Vining, drive north on U.S. 395 for seven miles to Lundy Lake Road. Turn left and drive a short distance to the campground.

Contact: Mono County Public Works, 760/932-5440, fax 760/932-5441.

48 SADDLEBAG LAKE

Scenic rating: 10

in Inyo National Forest

This camp is set in spectacular high country above tree line, the highest drive-to camp and lake in California, at 10,087 feet elevation. The camp is about a quarter mile from the lake, within walking range of the little store, boat rentals, and a one-minute drive for launching a boat at the ramp. The scenery is stark; everything is granite, ice, or water, with only a few lodgepole pines managing precarious toeholds, sprinkled across the landscape on the access road. An excellent trailhead is available for hiking, with the best hike routed out past little Hummingbird Lake to Lundy Pass. A hikers shuttle boat, which will ferry you across the lake, is a nice plus. Note that with the elevation and the high mountain pass, it can be windy and cold here, and some people find it difficult to catch their breath on simple hikes. In addition, RV users should note that level sites are extremely hard to come by.

Campsites, facilities: There are 20 sites for tents or RVs up to 30 feet (no hookups), and one group tent site for up to 25 people. Drinking water, fire grills, and picnic tables are provided. Flush toilets, boat rentals, and a primitive boat launch are available. A grocery store is nearby. Some facilities are wheelchair-accessible. Leashed pets are permitted.

Reservations, fees: Reservations are not accepted for individual sites, but are required for the group site at 877/444-6777 or www.recreation.gov ($10 reservation fee). Sites are $17 per night, $45 per night for the group site for up to 15 people, $60 per night for the group site for 16 people or more. Open late June through early September, weather permitting.

Directions: On U.S. 395, drive 0.5 mile south of Lee Vining and the junction with Highway 120. Turn west and drive about 11 miles to Saddlebag Lake Road. Turn right and drive 2.5 miles to the campground on the right.

From Merced, drive east on Highway 140 to the Arch Rock entrance station. Continue east to the Big Oak Flat Road junction (0.5 mile before entering Yosemite Valley). Turn left and drive 14 miles to Tioga Road. Turn right and drive about 65 miles (past Tuolumne Meadows) and through the Tioga Pass entrance station. Continue two miles to Saddlebag Lake Road. Turn left and drive 2.5 miles (rough road) to the campground on the right.

Contact: Inyo National Forest, Mono Basin Scenic Area Ranger Station and Visitor Center, 760/647-3044, fax 760/647-3046.

49 LOWER LEE VINING CAMP

Scenic rating: 7

near Lee Vining

This former Mono County camp and its neighboring camps—Cattleguard, Moraine, Aspen, Big Bend, and Boulder—can be a godsend for vacationers who show up at Yosemite National Park and make the discovery that there are no sites left, a terrible experience for some late-night arrivals. But these Forest Service campgrounds provide a great safety valve, even if they are extremely primitive, on the edge of timber. Lee Vining Creek is the highlight, flowing right past the campgrounds along Highway 120, bound for Mono Lake to the nearby east. It is stocked regularly during the fishing season. A must-do side trip is venturing to the south shore of Mono Lake to walk amid the bizarre yet beautiful tufa towers. There is good rock-climbing and hiking in the area. Although sunshine is the norm, be prepared for all kinds of weather: It can snow every month of the year here. Short but lively thunderstorms are common in early summer. Other nearby trips are available to Mammoth Lakes, June Lake, and Bodie State Park.

Campsites, facilities: There are 54 sites for

tents or RVs up to 40 feet (no hookups). Picnic tables, food lockers, and fire rings are provided. Portable toilets are available. No drinking water is available. You can buy supplies in Lee Vining (about two miles away). Leashed pets are permitted.
Reservations, fees: Reservations are not accepted. Sites are $14 per night. Open May through October, weather permitting.
Directions: On U.S. 395, drive to just south of Lee Vining and the junction with Highway 120. Turn west on Highway 120 and drive about 2.5 miles. Turn left into the campground entrance.
Contact: Inyo National Forest, Mono Basin Scenic Area Ranger Station and Visitor Center, 760/647-3044, fax 760/647-3046.

50 CATTLEGUARD CAMP

Scenic rating: 7

near Lee Vining

This camp is an alternative to Yosemite National Park. Though primitive, it has several advantages: It is quiet, gets more sun than the three neighboring camps (Lower Lee Vining, Moraine, and Boulder), and provides the best views of Dana Plateau. (For more information, see the *Lower Lee Vining Camp* listing in this chapter.)
Campsites, facilities: There are 15 sites for tents or RVs up to 40 feet (no hookups). Picnic tables, food lockers, and fire rings are provided. Pit toilets are available. No drinking water is available. You can buy supplies in Lee Vining (about two miles away). Leashed pets are permitted.
Reservations, fees: Reservations are not accepted. Sites are $14 per night. A 14-day limit is enforced. Open May through October, weather permitting.
Directions: On U.S. 395, drive to just south of Lee Vining and the junction with Highway 120. Turn west on Highway 120 and drive about three miles. Turn left into the campground entrance.
Contact: Inyo National Forest, Mono Basin Scenic Area Ranger Station and Visitor Center, 760/647-3044, fax 760/647-3046.

51 MORAINE CAMP

Scenic rating: 7

near Lee Vining

This camp provides an alternative to Yosemite National Park. (For more information, see the *Lower Lee Vining Camp* listing in this chapter.)
Campsites, facilities: There are 20 sites for tents or RVs up to 40 feet (no hookups). Picnic tables and fire rings are provided. Pit toilets are available. There is no drinking water. You can buy supplies in Lee Vining (about two miles away). Leashed pets are permitted.
Reservations, fees: Reservations are not accepted. Sites are $14 per night. Open May through October, weather permitting.
Directions: On U.S. 395, drive to just south of Lee Vining and the junction with Highway 120. Turn west on Highway 120 and drive 3.5 miles to Poole Power Plant Road. Exit left onto Poole Power Plant Road and drive 0.25 mile to the campground entrance at the end of the road.
Contact: Inyo National Forest, Mono Basin Scenic Area Ranger Station and Visitor Center, 760/647-3044, fax 760/647-3046.

52 BIG BEND

Scenic rating: 8

on Lee Vining Creek in Inyo National Forest

This camp is set in sparse but beautiful country along Lee Vining Creek at 7,800 feet elevation. Ancient pine trees are on site.

It is an excellent bet for an overflow camp if Tuolumne Meadows in nearby Yosemite is packed. The view from the camp to the north features Mono Dome (10,614 feet) and Lee Vining Peak (11,691 feet).

Campsites, facilities: There are 17 sites for tents or RVs up to 30 feet (no hookups). Picnic tables, food lockers, and fire grills are provided. Drinking water and vault toilets are available. Some facilities are wheelchair-accessible. Leashed pets are permitted.

Reservations, fees: Reservations are not accepted. Sites are $17 per night. A 14-day limit is enforced. Open late April through mid-October, weather permitting.

Directions: On U.S. 395, drive to just south of Lee Vining and the junction with Highway 120. Turn west on Highway 120 and drive about 3.5 miles to Poole Power Plant Road and the signed campground access road on the right. Turn right and drive a short distance to the camp.

Contact: Inyo National Forest, Mono Basin Scenic Area Ranger Station and Visitor Center, 760/647-3044, fax 760/647-3046.

53 ASPEN

Scenic rating: 8

on Lee Vining Creek

This high-country, primitive camp is set along Lee Vining Creek at 7,500 feet elevation, on the eastern slopes of the Sierra just east of Yosemite National Park. Take the side trip to moonlike Mono Lake, best seen at the south shore's Tufa State Reserve.

Campsites, facilities: There are 56 sites for tents or RVs up to 40 feet (no hookups). Picnic tables and fire rings are provided. Portable toilets are available. Drinking water is available. You can buy supplies in Lee Vining. Leashed pets are permitted.

Reservations, fees: Reservations are not accepted. Sites are $14 per night. A 14-day limit is enforced. Open May through October, weather permitting.

Directions: On U.S. 395, drive to just south of Lee Vining and the junction with Highway 120. Turn west on Highway 120 and drive about 3.5 miles. Exit onto Poole Power Plant Road. Turn left and drive about four miles west to the campground on the left.

Contact: Inyo National Forest, Mono Basin Scenic Area Ranger Station and Visitor Center, 760/647-3044, fax 760/647-3046.

54 JUNCTION

Scenic rating: 7

near Ellery and Tioga Lakes in Inyo National Forest

Which way do you go? From Junction, any way you choose, you can't miss. Two miles to the north is Saddlebag Lake, the highest drive-to lake (10,087 feet) in California. Directly across the road is Ellery Lake, and a mile to the south is Tioga Lake, two beautiful, pristine waters with trout fishing. To the east is Mono Lake, and to the west is Yosemite National Park. From camp, it is a one-mile hike to Bennetville, a historic camp. Take your pick. Camp elevation is 9,600 feet.

Campsites, facilities: There are 13 sites for tents or RVs up to 30 feet (no hookups). Picnic tables, food lockers, and fire grills are provided. Pit toilets are available. No drinking water is available. Some facilities are wheelchair-accessible. Leashed pets are permitted.

Reservations, fees: Reservations are not accepted. Sites are $12 per night. Open early June through mid-October, weather permitting.

Directions: On U.S. 395, drive to just south of Lee Vining and the junction with Highway 120. Turn west on Highway 120 and drive about 10 miles to Saddlebag Road and the campground on the right side of the road.

From Merced, drive east on Highway 140 to the Arch Rock entrance station. Continue east to the Big Oak Flat Road junction (0.5 mile before entering Yosemite Valley). Turn left and drive 14 miles to Tioga Road. Turn right and drive about 65 miles (past Tuolumne Meadows) and through the Tioga Pass entrance station. Continue two miles to Saddlebag Lake Road and the campground on the left side of the road.

Contact: Inyo National Forest, Mono Basin Scenic Area Ranger Station and Visitor Center, 760/647-3044, fax 760/647-3046.

55 TIOGA LAKE

Scenic rating: 9

in Inyo National Forest

Tioga Lake is a dramatic sight, with gemlike blue waters encircled by Sierra granite at 9,700 feet elevation. Together with adjacent Ellery Lake, it makes a pair of gorgeous waters with near-lake camping, trout fishing (stocked with rainbow trout), and access to Yosemite National Park and Saddlebag Lake. Conditions here are much like those at neighboring Ellery. The only downers: It can get windy here (no foolin'!) and the camps fill quickly from the overflow crowds at Tuolumne Meadows. (See the *Ellery Lake* listing for more information.)

Campsites, facilities: There are 13 sites for tents or RVs up to 30 feet (no hookups). Picnic tables, food lockers, and fire grills are provided. Drinking water and pit toilets are available. Some facilities are wheelchair-accessible. Leashed pets are permitted.

Reservations, fees: Reservations are not accepted. Sites are $17 per night. Open early June through mid-October, weather permitting.

Directions: On U.S. 395, drive to just south of Lee Vining and the junction with Highway 120. Turn west on Highway 120 and drive about 11 miles (just past Ellery Lake) to the campground on the left side of the road.

From Merced, drive east on Highway 140 to the Arch Rock entrance station. Continue east to the Big Oak Flat Road junction (0.5 mile before entering Yosemite Valley). Turn left and drive 14 miles to Tioga Road. Turn right and drive about 65 miles (past Tuolumne Meadows) and through the Tioga Pass entrance station. Continue one mile to the campground entrance road on the right side of the road.

Contact: Inyo National Forest, Mono Basin Scenic Area Ranger Station and Visitor Center, 760/647-3044, fax 760/647-3046.

56 ELLERY LAKE

Scenic rating: 9

in Inyo National Forest

Ellery Lake offers all the spectacular beauty of Yosemite but is two miles outside park borders. That means it is stocked with trout by the Department of Fish and Game (no lakes in Yosemite are planted, hence the lousy fishing). Just like neighboring Tioga Lake, here are deep-blue waters set in rock in the 9,500-foot-elevation range, one of the most pristine highway-access lake settings anywhere. Although there is no boat ramp, boats with small motors are allowed and can be hand-launched. Nearby Saddlebag Lake, the highest drive-to lake in California, is a common side trip. Whenever Tuolumne Meadows fills in Yosemite, this camp fills shortly thereafter. Camp elevation is 9,500 feet.

Campsites, facilities: There are 21 sites for tents or RVs up to 30 feet (no hookups). Picnic tables and fire grills are provided. Drinking water, food lockers, and pit toilets are available. A grocery store is nearby. Some facilities are wheelchair-accessible. Leashed pets are permitted.

Reservations, fees: Reservations are not accepted. Sites are $17 per night. Open early June through mid-October, weather permitting.

Directions: On U.S. 395, drive to just south of Lee Vining and the junction with Highway

120. Turn west on Highway 120 and drive about 10 miles to the campground on the left side of the road.

From Merced, drive east on Highway 140 to the Arch Rock entrance station. Continue east to the Big Oak Flat Road junction (0.5 mile before entering Yosemite Valley). Turn left and drive 14 miles to Tioga Road. Turn right and drive about 65 miles (past Tuolumne Meadows) and through the Tioga Pass entrance station. Continue four miles to the campground entrance road on the right.

Contact: Inyo National Forest, Mono Basin Scenic Area Ranger Station and Visitor Center, 760/647-3044, fax 760/647-3046.

57 SILVER LAKE

Scenic rating: 9

in Inyo National Forest

Silver Lake is set at 7,200 feet elevation, an 80-acre lake in the June Lake Loop with Carson Peak looming in the background. Boat rentals, fishing for trout at the lake, a beautiful trout stream (Rush Creek) next to the camp, and a nearby trailhead for wilderness hiking and horseback riding (rentals available) are the highlights. The camp is largely exposed and vulnerable to winds, the only downer. Within walking distance to the south is Silver Lake, always a pretty sight, especially when afternoon winds cause the lake surface to sparkle in crackling silvers. The lake speed limit is 10 mph. Swimming is not recommended because of the rocky shoreline. Just across the road from the camp is a great trailhead for the Ansel Adams Wilderness, with a two-hour hike that climbs to pretty Agnew Lake overlooking the June Lake basin; wilderness permit required for overnight use.

Campsites, facilities: There are 63 sites for tents or RVs up to 32 feet (no hookups). Picnic tables, food lockers, and fire rings are provided. Drinking water, flush toilets, and horseback-riding facilities are available. A grocery store, coin laundry, motorboat rentals, boat ramp, bait, café, boat fuel, and propane gas are nearby. Some facilities are wheelchair-accessible. Leashed pets are permitted.

Reservations, fees: Reservations are accepted at 877/444-6777 or www.recreation.gov ($10 reservation fee). Sites are $18 per night. A 14-day limit is enforced. Open late April through early November, weather permitting.

Directions: From Lee Vining on U.S. 395, drive south for six miles to the first Highway 158 north/June Lake Loop turnoff. Turn west (right) and drive nine miles (past Grant Lake) to Silver Lake. Just as you arrive at Silver Lake (a small store is on the right), turn left at the campground entrance.

Contact: Inyo National Forest, Mono Basin Scenic Area Ranger Station and Visitor Center, 760/647-3044, fax 760/647-3046.

58 OH! RIDGE

Scenic rating: 8

on June Lake in Inyo National Forest

This is the largest of the campgrounds on June Lake. However, it is not the most popular since it is not right on the lakeshore, but back about a quarter mile or so from the north end of the lake. Regardless, it has the best views of the lake, with the ridge of the high Sierra providing a backdrop. The lake is a good one for trout fishing. The elevation is 7,600 feet.

Campsites, facilities: There are 148 sites for tents or RVs up to 40 feet (no hookups). Picnic tables and fire grills are provided. Drinking water, flush toilets, and a swimming beach are available. A grocery store, coin laundry, volleyball, amphitheater, boat ramp, boat and tackle rentals, moorings, and propane gas are nearby. Some facilities are wheelchair-accessible. Leashed pets are permitted.

Reservations, fees: Reservations are accepted

at 877/444-6777 or www.recreation.gov ($10 reservation fee). Sites are $15–18 per night. Open late April through early November, weather permitting.

Directions: From Lee Vining, drive south on U.S. 395 (past the first Highway 158/June Lake Loop turnoff) to June Lake Junction (a gas station/store is on the west side of the road) and Highway 158 south. Turn west on Highway 158 south and drive two miles to Oh! Ridge Road. Turn right and drive a mile to the campground access road (signed). Turn left and drive to the campground.

Contact: Inyo National Forest, Mono Basin Scenic Area Ranger Station and Visitor Center, 760/647-3044, fax 760/647-3046.

59 PINE CLIFF RESORT

Scenic rating: 7

at June Lake

You'll find "kid heaven" at Pine Cliff Resort. This camp is in a pretty setting along the north shore of June Lake (7,600 feet elevation), the feature lake among four in the June Lake Loop. The campsites are nestled in pine trees, designed so each site accommodates different-sized rigs and families, and the campground is set about a quarter mile from June Lake. This is the only camp at June Lake Loop that has a swimming beach. The landscape is a pretty one, with the lake set below snowcapped peaks. The bonus is that June Lake gets large numbers of trout plants each summer, making it extremely popular with anglers. Of the lakes in the June Lake Loop, this is the one that has the most of everything—the most beauty, the most fish, the most developed accommodations, and, alas, the most people. This resort has been operated as a family business for more than 50 years.

Campsites, facilities: There are 154 sites with full hookups (20 and 30 amps) for RVs, 17 sites with partial hookups (20 and 30 amps) for tents or RVs, and 55 sites for tents; a few sites are pull-through. There are also 14 rental trailers. Picnic tables and fire rings are provided. Restrooms with flush toilets and coin showers, drinking water, coin laundry, basketball, volleyball, tetherball, horseshoes, convenience store, and propane gas are available. Some facilities are wheelchair-accessible. A primitive boat ramp, fish-cleaning facilities, and fuel are nearby. Leashed pets are permitted, with a maximum of two pets per site.

Reservations, fees: Reservations are recommended. Sites are $16–26 per night, $5 per night for each additional vehicle, $1 per person per night for more than four people. The first pet is free, and the second pet is $1 per night. Open mid-April through October.

Directions: From Lee Vining, drive south on U.S. 395 (passing the first Highway 158 north/June Lake Loop turnoff) to June Lake Junction (a sign is posted for "June Lake Village") and Highway 158 south. Turn right (west) on Highway 158 south and drive two miles to North Shore Drive (a sign is nearby for Pine Cliff Resort). Turn right and drive 0.5 mile to Pine Cliff Road. Turn left and drive 0.5 mile to the resort store on the right (route is well signed).

Contact: Pine Cliff Resort, 760/648-7558.

60 GULL LAKE

Scenic rating: 8

in Inyo National Forest

Little Gull Lake, just 64 acres, is the smallest of the lakes on the June Lake Loop, but to many it is the prettiest. It is set at 7,600 feet, just west of June Lake and, with Carson Peak looming on the Sierra crest to the west, it is a dramatic and intimate setting. The lake is stocked with trout each summer, providing good fishing. A boat ramp is on the lake's southwest corner. Insider's tip: There is a rope swing at Gull Lake that youngsters love.

Campsites, facilities: There are 11 sites for tents or RVs up to 30 feet (no hookups). Drinking water, fire grills, and picnic tables are provided, and flush toilets are available. A grocery store, coin laundry, boat ramp, and propane gas are nearby. Some facilities are wheelchair-accessible. Leashed pets are permitted.

Reservations, fees: Reservations are not accepted. Sites are $18 per night. Open late April through early November, weather permitting.

Directions: From Lee Vining, drive south on U.S. 395 (past the first Highway 158/June Lake Loop turnoff) to June Lake Junction (a gas station/store is on the west side of the road) and Highway 158. Turn west on Highway 158 and drive three miles to the campground entrance on the right side of the road.

Contact: Inyo National Forest, Mono Basin Scenic Area Ranger Station and Visitor Center, 760/647-3044, fax 760/647-3046.

61 REVERSED CREEK

Scenic rating: 6

in Inyo National Forest

This camp is set at 7,600 feet elevation near pretty Reversed Creek, the only stream in the region that flows toward the mountains, not away from them. It is a small, tree-lined stream that provides decent trout fishing. The campsites are sheltered and set in a grove of aspen, but close enough to the road so you can still hear highway traffic. There are also cabins available for rent near here. Directly opposite the camp, on the other side of the road, is Gull Lake and the boat ramp. Two miles to the west, on the west side of the road, is the trailhead for the hike to Fern Lake on the edge of the Ansel Adams Wilderness, a little butt-kicker of a climb.

Campsites, facilities: There are 17 sites for tents or RVs up to 30 feet (no hookups). Picnic tables and fire grills are provided. Drinking water and flush toilets are available. A grocery store, coin laundry, and propane gas are nearby. Boating is available at nearby Silver Lake, two miles away. Some facilities are wheelchair-accessible. Leashed pets are permitted.

Reservations, fees: Reservations are not accepted. Sites are $18 per night. Open mid-May through October, weather permitting.

Directions: From Lee Vining, drive south on U.S. 395 (past the first Highway 158/June Lake Loop turnoff) to June Lake Junction (a gas station/store is on the west side of the road) and Highway 158 south. Turn right (west) on Highway 158 south and drive three miles to the campground on the left side of the road (across from Gull Lake).

Contact: Inyo National Forest, Mono Basin Scenic Area Ranger Station and Visitor Center, 760/647-3044, fax 760/647-3046.

62 JUNE LAKE

Scenic rating: 9

in Inyo National Forest

June Lake gets the highest use of all the lakes in the June Lakes Loop, and it has the best swimming, best fishing, and best sailboarding. There are three campgrounds at pretty June Lake; this is one of the two operated by the Forest Service (the other is Oh! Ridge). This one is on the northeast shore of the lake at 7,600 feet elevation, a pretty spot with all supplies available just two miles to the south in the town of June Lake. The nearest boat launch is north of town. This is a good lake for trout fishing, receiving high numbers of stocked trout each year. A 10-mph speed limit is enforced.

Campsites, facilities: There are 28 sites for tents or RVs up to 32 feet (no hookups). Picnic tables, food lockers, and fire grills are provided. Drinking water, restrooms with flush toilets and coin showers, and boat ramp are available. A grocery store, coin laundry, boat and tackle rentals, moorings, and propane gas are nearby. Leashed pets are permitted.

Reservations, fees: Reservations are accepted at 877/444-6777 or www.recreation.gov ($10 reservation fee). Sites are $18 per night. Open late April through early November, weather permitting.

Directions: From Lee Vining, drive south on U.S. 395 (passing Highway 158 North) for 20 miles (six miles past Highway 158 north) to June Lake Junction (signed "June Lake Village") and Highway 158 south. Turn west (right) on Highway 158 south and drive two miles to June Lake. Turn right (signed) and drive a short distance to the campground.

Contact: Inyo National Forest, Mono Basin Scenic Area Ranger Station and Visitor Center, 760/647-3044, fax 760/647-3046.

63 HARTLEY SPRINGS

Scenic rating: 8

in Inyo National Forest

Even though this camp is only a five-minute drive from U.S. 395, those five minutes will take you into another orbit. It is set in a forest of Jeffrey pine and has the feel of a remote, primitive camp, set in a high-mountain environment at an elevation of 8,400 feet. About two miles to the immediate north, at 8,611 feet, is Obsidian Dome "Glass Flow," a craggy geologic formation that some people enjoy scrambling around and exploring; pick your access point carefully.

Campsites, facilities: There are 20 sites for tents or RVs up to 40 feet (no hookups). Picnic tables and fire grills are provided. Vault toilets are available. No drinking water is available. Garbage must be packed out. Leashed pets are permitted.

Reservations, fees: Reservations are not accepted. There is no fee for camping. (Note: This is one of four campgrounds in the Mono Basin Scenic Area that may impose a camping fee.) Open late May through early November, weather permitting.

Directions: From Lee Vining, drive south on U.S. 395 (passing the first Highway 158/June Lake Loop turnoff) for 10 miles to June Lake Junction. Continue south on U.S. 395 for six miles to Glass Creek Road (a dirt road on the west side of the highway). Turn west (right) and drive two miles to the campground entrance road on the left.

Contact: Inyo National Forest, Mono Basin Scenic Area Ranger Station and Visitor Center, 760/647-3044, fax 760/647-3046.

64 AGNEW MEADOWS AND EQUESTRIAN CAMP

Scenic rating: 9

in Inyo National Forest

BEST

This is a perfect camp to use as a launching pad for a backpacking trip or day of fly-fishing for trout. It is set along the Upper San Joaquin River at 8,400 feet, with a trailhead for the Pacific Crest Trail available near the camp. From here you can hike seven miles to the gorgeous Thousand Island Lake, a beautiful lake sprinkled with islands set below Banner and Ritter Peaks in the spectacular Minarets. For day hiking, walk the River Trail, which is routed from Agnew Meadows along the San Joaquin. The trail provides access to excellent fishing with a chance at the grand slam of California trout—four species in a single day (though the trout are small).

Campsites, facilities: There are 21 sites for tents or RVs up to 45 feet, and four group sites for tents or RVs that can accommodate 10–20 people each. No hookups. Picnic tables and fire grills are provided. Drinking water, vault toilets, and horseback-riding facilities are available (three family sites have hitching racks where horse camping is permitted). Supplies can be obtained at Red's Meadow store. Leashed pets are permitted.

Reservations, fees: Reservations are not accepted for individual sites, but are required for equestrian sites and group sites at 877/444-6777 or www.recreation.gov ($10 reservation fee). Sites are $18 per night for individual sites, $15–30 per night group sites, $22 per night for equestrian site, plus $4–7 per person Reds Meadow/Agnew Meadows access fee. Open mid-June through mid-September, weather permitting.

Directions: On U.S. 395, drive to Mammoth Junction/Highway 203. Turn west on Highway 203 and drive four miles, through the town of Mammoth Lakes to Minaret Road (still Highway 203). Turn right and drive five miles to Minaret Station (past the Mammoth Mountain Ski Area). Continue for 2.6 miles to the campground entrance road on the right. Turn right and drive just under a mile to the campground. Note: The access road to the group sites is steep and narrow.

Note: Noncampers are required to use a shuttle bus (fee) from the shuttle bus terminal at Mammoth Mountain Main Lodge Gondola Station 7 A.M.–7:30 P.M. Space is available for leashed dogs, bikes, and backpacks.

Contact: Inyo National Forest, Mammoth Ranger Station and Visitor Center, 760/924-5500, fax 760/924-5547.

65 PUMICE FLAT

Scenic rating: 8

on the San Joaquin River in Inyo National Forest

Pumice Flat (7,700 feet elevation) provides roadside camping within short range of several adventures. A trail out of camp links with the Pacific Crest Trail, where you can hike along the Upper San Joaquin River for miles, with excellent access for fly-fishing, and head north into the Ansel Adams Wilderness. Devils Postpile National Monument is just two miles south, along with the trailhead for Rainbow Falls.

Campsites, facilities: There are 17 sites for tents or RVs up to 45 feet (no hookups). Picnic tables and fire grills are provided. Drinking water, vault toilets, and horseback-riding facilities are available. Limited supplies are available at a small store, or buy full supplies in Mammoth Lakes. Leashed pets are permitted.

Reservations, fees: Reservations are not accepted. Sites are $18 per night, plus $4–7 per person Reds Meadow/Agnew Meadows access fee. Open mid-June through mid-September, weather permitting.

Directions: On U.S. 395, drive to Mammoth Junction/Highway 203. Turn west on Highway 203 and drive four miles, through the town of Mammoth Lakes to Minaret Road (still Highway 203). Turn right and drive five miles to Minaret Station (past the Mammoth Mountain Ski Area). Continue for 5.1 miles to the campground on the right.

Note: Noncampers are required to use a shuttle bus (fee) from the shuttle bus terminal at Mammoth Mountain Main Lodge Gondola Station 7 A.M.–7:30 P.M. Space is available for leashed dogs, bikes, and backpacks.

Contact: Inyo National Forest, Mammoth Ranger Station and Visitor Center, 760/924-5500, fax 760/924-5547.

66 UPPER SODA SPRINGS

Scenic rating: 8

on the San Joaquin River in Inyo National Forest

This is a premium location within earshot of the Upper San Joaquin River and within minutes of many first-class recreation options. The river is stocked with trout at this camp, with several good pools within short walking distance. Farther upstream, accessible by an excellent trail, are smaller wild trout that provide good fly-fishing prospects. Devils Postpile National Monument, a massive formation of ancient columnar jointed rock, is only three miles to the south. The Pacific Crest Trail passes right by the camp, providing a trailhead for access to numerous lakes in the Ansel Adams Wilderness. The elevation is 7,700 feet.

Campsites, facilities: There are 29 sites for tents or RVs up to 36 feet (no hookups). Picnic tables and fire grills are provided. Drinking water, flush toilets, and horseback-riding facilities are available. Limited supplies can be obtained at Red's Meadow store. Leashed pets are permitted.

Reservations, fees: Reservations are not accepted. Sites are $18 per night, plus $4–7 per person Reds Meadow/Agnew Meadows access fee. Open mid-June through mid-September, weather permitting.

Directions: On U.S. 395, drive to Mammoth Junction/Highway 203. Turn west on Highway 203 and drive four miles, through the town of Mammoth Lakes to Minaret Road (still Highway 203). Turn right and drive five miles to Minaret Station (past the Mammoth Mountain Ski Area). Continue for 5.1 miles to the campground entrance road on the right. Turn right and drive 0.25 mile to the campground.

Note: Noncampers are required to use a shuttle bus (fee) from the shuttle bus terminal at Mammoth Mountain Main Lodge Gondola Station 7 A.M.–7:30 P.M. Space is available for leashed dogs, bikes, and backpacks.

Contact: Inyo National Forest, Mammoth Ranger Station and Visitor Center, 760/924-5500, fax 760/924-5547.

67 PUMICE FLAT GROUP CAMP

Scenic rating: 6

on the San Joaquin River in Inyo National Forest

Pumice Flat Group Camp is set at 7,700 feet elevation near the Upper San Joaquin River, adjacent to Pumice Flat. (For recreation information, see the *Pumice Flat* listing in this chapter.)

Campsites, facilities: There are four group sites for tents or RVs up to 45 feet (no hookups) that can accommodate 20–50 people each. Picnic tables and fire grills are provided. Drinking water, flush toilets, and horseback-riding facilities are available. You can buy supplies in Mammoth Lakes. Leashed pets are permitted.

Reservations, fees: Reservations are accepted at 877/444-6777 or www.recreation.gov ($10 reservation fee). Sites are $40–110 per night per group, plus $4–7 per person Reds Meadow/Agnew Meadows access fee. Open mid-June through mid-September, weather permitting.

Directions: On U.S. 395, drive to Mammoth Junction/Highway 203. Turn west on Highway 203 and drive four miles, through the town of Mammoth Lakes to Minaret Road (still Highway 203). Turn right and drive five miles to Minaret Station (past the Mammoth Mountain Ski Area). Continue for 5.1 miles to the campground on the left side of the road.

Note: Noncampers are required to use a shuttle bus (fee) from the shuttle bus terminal at Mammoth Mountain Main Lodge Gondola Station 7 A.M.–7:30 P.M. Space is available for leashed dogs, bikes, and backpacks.

Contact: Inyo National Forest, Mammoth Ranger Station and Visitor Center, 760/924-5500, fax 760/924-5547.

68 MINARET FALLS

Scenic rating: 8

on the San Joaquin River in Inyo National Forest

This camp has one of the prettiest settings of the series of camps along the Upper San Joaquin River and near Devils Postpile

National Monument. It is set at 7,600 feet elevation near Minaret Creek, across from where beautiful Minaret Falls pours into the San Joaquin River. Devils Postpile National Monument, one of the best examples in the world of hexagonal, columnar jointed rock, is less than a mile from camp, where there is also a trail to awesome Rainbow Falls. The Pacific Crest Trail runs right through this area as well, and if you hike to the south, there is excellent streamside fishing access.

Campsites, facilities: There are 28 sites for tents or RVs up to 47 feet (no hookups). Picnic tables and fire grills are provided. Drinking water and vault toilets are available. Horseback-riding facilities are nearby. You can buy limited supplies at Red's Meadow store, or all supplies in Mammoth Lakes. Some facilities are wheelchair-accessible. Leashed pets are permitted.

Reservations, fees: Reservations are not accepted. Sites are $18 per night, plus $4–7 per person Reds Meadow/Agnew Meadows access fee. Open mid-June through mid-September, weather permitting.

Directions: On U.S. 395, drive to Mammoth Junction/Highway 203. Turn west on Highway 203 and drive four miles, through the town of Mammoth Lakes to Minaret Road (still Highway 203). Turn right and drive five miles to Minaret Station (past the Mammoth Mountain Ski Area). Continue for six miles to the campground entrance road on the right. Turn right and drive 0.25 mile to the campground.

Note: Noncampers are required to use a shuttle bus from the shuttle bus terminal at Mammoth Mountain Main Lodge Gondola Station 7 A.M.–7:30 P.M. Space is available for leashed dogs, bikes, and backpacks.

Contact: Inyo National Forest, Mammoth Ranger Station and Visitor Center, 760/924-5500, fax 760/924-5547.

69 DEVILS POSTPILE NATIONAL MONUMENT

Scenic rating: 9

near the San Joaquin River

Devils Postpile is a spectacular and rare example of hexagonal, columnar jointed rock that looks like posts, hence the name. The camp is set at 7,600 feet elevation and provides nearby access for the easy hike to the Postpile. Guided walks are offered during the summer; call for details. If you keep walking, it is a 2.5-mile walk to Rainbow Falls, a breathtaking 101-foot cascade that produces rainbows in its floating mist, seen only from the trail alongside the waterfall looking downstream. The camp is also adjacent to the Middle Fork San Joaquin River and the Pacific Crest Trail.

Campsites, facilities: There are 21 sites for tents or RVs up to 25 feet (no hookups). Picnic tables, food lockers, and fire grills are provided. Drinking water and flush toilets are available. Some facilities are wheelchair-accessible. Leashed pets are permitted.

Reservations, fees: Reservations are not accepted. Sites are $18 per night, plus $4–7 per person Reds Meadow/Devils Postpile access fee. Open mid-June through mid-October, weather permitting, with a two-week maximum stay. Note: National Parks Pass and Golden Passport are not accepted.

Directions: On U.S. 395, drive to Mammoth Junction/Highway 203. Turn west on Highway 203 and drive four miles, through the town of Mammoth Lakes to Minaret Road (still Highway 203). Turn right and drive five miles to Minaret Station (past the Mammoth Mountain Ski Area). Continue for nine miles to the campground entrance road on the right.

Note: Noncampers are required to use a shuttle bus from the shuttle bus terminal at Mammoth Mountain Main Lodge Gondola Station 7 A.M.–7:30 P.M. Space is available for leashed dogs, bikes, and backpacks.

Contact: Devils Postpile National Monument, 760/934-2289, www.nps.gov/depo.

70 RED'S MEADOW

Scenic rating: 6

in Inyo National Forest

Red's Meadow has long been established as one of the best outfitters for horseback-riding trips. To get the feel of it, three-mile round-trip rides are available to Rainbow Falls. Multiday trips into the Ansel Adams Wilderness on the Pacific Crest Trail are also offered. A small restaurant is a bonus here, always a must-stop for long-distance hikers getting a shot to chomp their first hamburger in weeks, something like a bear finding a candy bar, quite a sight for the drive-in campers. The nearby Devils Postpile National Monument, Rainbow Falls, Minaret Falls, and San Joaquin River provide recreation options. The elevation is 7,600 feet.

Campsites, facilities: There are 56 sites for tents or RVs up to 30 feet (no hookups). Picnic tables, food lockers, and fire grills are provided. Drinking water, flush toilets, horseback riding, and natural hot springs are available. You can buy limited supplies at a small store. Leashed pets are permitted.

Reservations, fees: Reservations are not accepted. Sites are $18 per night, plus $4–7 per person Reds Meadow/Agnew Meadows access fee. Open mid-June through mid-September, weather permitting.

Directions: On U.S. 395, drive to Mammoth Junction/Highway 203. Turn west on Highway 203 and drive four miles, through the town of Mammoth Lakes to Minaret Road (still Highway 203). Turn right and drive five miles to Minaret Station (past the Mammoth Mountain Ski Area). Continue for 7.4 miles to the campground entrance on the left.

Note: Noncampers are required to use a shuttle bus from the shuttle bus terminal at Mammoth Mountain Main Lodge Gondola Station 7 A.M.–7:30 P.M. Space is available for leashed dogs, bikes, and backpacks.

Contact: Inyo National Forest, Mammoth Ranger Station and Visitor Center, 760/924-5500, fax 760/924-5547.

71 LAKE GEORGE

Scenic rating: 8

in Inyo National Forest

The sites here have views of Lake George, a beautiful lake in a rock basin set below the spectacular Crystal Crag. Lake George is at 9,000 feet elevation, a small lake fed by creeks coming from both Crystal Lake and TJ Lake. TJ Lake is only about a 20-minute walk from the campground, and Crystal Lake is about a 45-minute romp; both make excellent short hiking trips. Trout fishing at Lake George is decent—not great, not bad, but decent. Swimming is not allowed, but boats with small motors are permitted.

Campsites, facilities: There are 16 sites for tents or RVs up to 25 feet (no hookups). Picnic tables and fire grills are provided. Drinking water and flush toilets are available. A grocery store, coin laundry, coin showers, primitive boat launch, and propane gas are nearby. Leashed pets are permitted.

Reservations, fees: Reservations are not accepted. Sites are $19 per night with a seven-day limit. Open mid-June through mid-September, weather permitting.

Directions: From Lee Vining on U.S. 395, drive south for 25 miles to Mammoth Junction and Highway 203/Minaret Summit Road. Turn west on Highway 203 and drive four miles to Lake Mary Road. Continue straight through the intersection and drive four miles to Lake Mary Loop Drive. Turn left and drive 0.3 mile to Lake George Road. Turn right and drive 0.5 mile to the campground.

Contact: Inyo National Forest, Mammoth Ranger Station and Visitor Center, 760/924-5500, fax 760/924-5547.

72 GLASS CREEK

Scenic rating: 5

in Inyo National Forest

This primitive camp is set along Glass Creek at 7,600 feet elevation, about a mile from Obsidian Dome to the nearby west. A trail follows Glass Creek past the southern edge of the dome, a craggy, volcanic formation that tops out at 8,611 feet elevation. That trail continues along Glass Creek, climbing to the foot of San Joaquin Mountain for a great view of the high desert to the east. Insider's tip: The Department of Fish and Game stocks Glass Creek with trout just once each June, right at the camp.

Campsites, facilities: There are 50 sites for tents or RVs up to 40 feet (no hookups). Picnic tables and fire grills are provided. Vault toilets are available. No drinking water is available. Some facilities are wheelchair-accessible. Leashed pets are permitted.

Reservations, fees: Reservations are not accepted. There is no fee for camping. (Note: This is one of four campgrounds in the Mono Basin Scenic Area that may impose a camping fee.) A 42-day limit is enforced. Open late April through early November, weather permitting.

Directions: From Lee Vining, drive south on U.S. 395 (past the first Highway 158/June Lake Loop turnoff) for 11 miles to June Lake Junction. Continue south on U.S. 395 for six miles to a Forest Service road (Glass Creek Road). Turn west (right) and drive 0.25 mile to the camp access road on the right. Turn right and continue 0.5 mile to the main camp at the end of the road. Two notes: 1. A primitive area with large RV sites can be used as an overflow area on the right side of the access road. 2. If arriving from the south on U.S. 395, a direct left turn to Glass Creek Road is impossible. Heading north you will pass the CalTrans Crestview Maintenance Station on the right. Continue north, make a U-turn when possible, and follow the above directions.

Contact: Inyo National Forest, Mono Basin Scenic Area Ranger Station and Visitor Center, 760/647-3044, fax 760/647-3046.

73 BIG SPRINGS

Scenic rating: 5

on Deadman Creek in Inyo National Forest

Big Springs, at 7,300 feet elevation, is set on the edge of the high desert on the east side of U.S. 395. The main attractions are Deadman Creek, which runs right by the camp, and Big Springs, which is set just on the opposite side of the river. There are several hot springs in the area, best reached by driving south on U.S. 395 to the Mammoth Lakes Airport and turning left on Hot Creek Road. As with all hot springs, use at your own risk.

Campsites, facilities: There are 26 sites for tents or RVs up to 40 feet (no hookups). Picnic tables and fire grills are provided. Vault toilets are available. No drinking water is available. Leashed pets are permitted.

Reservations, fees: Reservations are not accepted. There is no fee for camping. (Note: This is one of four campgrounds in the Mono Basin Scenic Area that may impose a camping fee.) A 21-day limit is enforced. Open late April through early November, weather permitting.

Directions: From Lee Vining, drive south on U.S. 395 (past the first Highway 158/June Lake Loop turnoff) to June Lake Junction. Continue south for about seven miles to Owens River Road. Turn east (left) and drive two miles to a fork. Bear left at the fork and drive 0.25 mile to the camp on the left side of the road.

Contact: Inyo National Forest, Mono Basin Scenic Area Ranger Station and Visitor Center, 760/647-3044, fax 760/647-3046.

74 DEADMAN

Scenic rating: 5

on Deadman Creek in Inyo National Forest

This little-known camp is set at 7,800 feet elevation along little Deadman Creek. It is primitive and dusty in the summer, cold in the early summer and fall. From camp, hikers can drive west for three miles to the headwaters of Deadman Creek and to a trailhead for a route that runs past San Joaquin Mountain and beyond to little Yost Lake, a one-way hike of four miles.

Campsites, facilities: There are 30 sites for tents or RVs up to 30 feet. Nearby Obsidian Flat Group Camp can accommodate tents or RVs of any length and up to 50 people (no hookups). Picnic tables and fire grills are provided. Vault toilets are available. No drinking water is available. Garbage must be packed out. Leashed pets are permitted.

Reservations, fees: Reservations are not accepted. There is no camping fee for individual sites. (Note: This is one of four campgrounds in the Mono Basin Scenic Area that may impose a camping fee.) Obsidian Group is $20 per night; reservations are required at 877/444-6777 or www.recreation.gov. Open late May through early November, weather permitting.

Directions: From Lee Vining, drive south on U.S. 395 (past the first Highway 158/June Lake Loop turnoff) to June Lake Junction. Continue south for 6.5 miles to a Forest Service road (Deadman Creek Road) on the west (right) side of the road. Turn west (right) and drive two miles to the camp access road on the right. Turn right and drive 0.5 mile to the camp. Note: If you are arriving from the south on U.S. 395 and you reach the CalTrans Crestview Maintenance Station on the right, you have gone one mile too far; make a U-turn when possible and return for access.

Contact: Inyo National Forest, Mono Basin Scenic Area and Visitor Center, 760/647-3044, fax 760/647-3046.

75 BROWN'S OWENS RIVER CAMPGROUND

Scenic rating: 7

near the Owens River

This camp is located along the upper Owens River, and is well situated for hiking, mountain biking, fishing, and swimming. The campground landscape is fairly sparse, so the campground can seem less intimate than those set in a forest. But this makes for great long-distance views of the White Mountains and for taking in those sunsets.

Campsites, facilities: There are 75 sites for tents or RVs up to any feet (no hookups). Some trailer rentals with full hookups are available. Picnic tables and fire rings are provided. Drinking water, flush and pit toilets, coin showers, coin laundry, a convenience store and cafe are available. Some facilities are wheelchair-accessible. Leashed pets are permitted.

Reservations, fees: Reservations are accepted. Sites are $17-20 per night.

Directions: From Mammoth Lakes on Highway 395/203, drive south on Highway 395 to Benton Crossing Road. Turn left and drive five miles to campground.

Contact: Brown's Owens River Campground, 760/920-0975, www.brownscampgrounds.com.

76 PINE GLEN

Scenic rating: 6

in Inyo National Forest

This is a well-situated base camp for several side trips. The most popular is the trip to Devils Postpile National Monument, with a shuttle ride from the Mammoth Ski Area. Other nearby trips include exploring Inyo Craters and Mammoth Lakes. The elevation is 7,800 feet.

Campsites, facilities: There are 11 sites (used as overflow from Old Shady Rest and New Shady Rest campgrounds) and five group sites for tents or RVs up to 55 feet (no hookups) that can accommodate 25–30 people each. Picnic tables and fire grills are provided. Drinking water, flush toilets, and a dump station are available. A grocery store, coin laundry, propane gas, and horseback-riding facilities are nearby in Mammoth Lakes. Leashed pets are permitted.

Reservations, fees: Reservations are not accepted for individual sites but are required for group sites at 877/444-6777 or www.recreation.gov ($10 reservation fee). Sites are $18 per night, and group sites are $35–50 per night. Open late May through September, weather permitting.

Directions: From Lee Vining on U.S. 395, drive south for 25 miles to Mammoth Junction and Highway 203/Minaret Summit Road. Turn west on Highway 203 and drive about three miles to the Mammoth Lakes Visitor Center. Just past the visitor center, turn right on Old Sawmill Road and drive a short distance to the campground on the right.

Contact: Inyo National Forest, Mammoth Ranger Station and Visitor Center, 760/924-5500, fax 760/924-5547.

77 NEW SHADY REST

Scenic rating: 6

in Inyo National Forest

This easy-to-reach camp is set at 7,800 feet elevation, not far from the Mammoth Mountain Ski Area. The surrounding Inyo National Forest provides many side-trip opportunities, including Devils Postpile National Monument (by shuttle available from near the Mammoth Mountain Ski Area), Upper San Joaquin River, and the Inyo National Forest backcountry trails, streams, and lakes.

Campsites, facilities: There are 95 sites for tents or RVs up to 38 feet (no hookups). Picnic tables and fire grills are provided. Drinking water and flush toilets are available. A dump station, playground, grocery store, coin laundry, and propane gas are nearby. Leashed pets are permitted.

Reservations, fees: Reservations are accepted at 877/444-6777 or www.recreation.gov ($10 reservation fee). Sites are $18 per night with a 14-day limit. Open mid-May through October, weather permitting.

Directions: From Lee Vining on U.S. 395, drive south for 25 miles to Mammoth Junction and Highway 203/Minaret Summit Road. Turn west on Highway 203 and drive about three miles to the Mammoth Lakes Visitor Center. Just past the visitors center, turn right on Old Sawmill Road and drive a short distance to the campground on the right.

Contact: Inyo National Forest, Mammoth Ranger Station and Visitor Center, 760/924-5500, fax 760/924-5547.

78 OLD SHADY REST

Scenic rating: 6

in Inyo National Forest

Names such as "Old Shady Rest" are usually reserved for mom-and-pop RV parks. The Forest Service respected tradition in officially naming this park what the locals have called it all along. Like New Shady Rest, this camp is near the Mammoth Lakes Visitor Center, with the same side trips available. It is one of three camps in the immediate vicinity. The elevation is 7,800 feet.

Campsites, facilities: There are 51 sites for tents or RVs up to 55 feet (no hookups). Picnic tables and fire grills are provided. Drinking water and flush toilets are available. A dump station, playground, grocery store, coin laundry, and propane gas are nearby. Leashed pets are permitted.

Reservations, fees: Reservations are accepted

at 877/444-6777 or www.recreation.gov ($10 reservation fee). Sites are $18 per night with a 14-day limit. Open mid-June through early September, weather permitting.

Directions: From Lee Vining on U.S. 395, drive south for 25 miles to Mammoth Junction and Highway 203/Minaret Summit Road. Turn west on Highway 203 and drive about three miles to the Forest Service Visitor Center. Just past the visitors center, turn right and drive 0.3 mile to the campground on the left.

Contact: Inyo National Forest, Mammoth Ranger Station and Visitor Center, 760/924-5500, fax 760/924-5547.

79 MAMMOTH MOUNTAIN RV PARK

Scenic rating: 6

near Mammoth Lakes

This RV park is just across the street from the Forest Service Visitor Center. Got a question? Someone there has got an answer. This camp is open year-round, making it a great place to stay for a ski trip.

Campsites, facilities: There are 185 sites, some with full hookups (50 amps), for tents or RVs up to 45 feet. Two cabins are also available. Picnic tables are provided. Fire pits are provided at some sites. Restrooms with showers, drinking water, cable TV, modem access, dump station, coin laundry, heated year-round swimming pool, seasonal recreation room, playground, RV supplies, and a spa are available. Some facilities are wheelchair-accessible. Supplies can be obtained in Mammoth Lakes, 0.25 mile away. Leashed pets are permitted, with certain restrictions.

Reservations, fees: Reservations are accepted at 800/582-4603. Sites are $21–40 per night, $3 per person per night for more than two people, $2 per night for each additional vehicle, $3 per pet per night. Some credit cards accepted. Open year-round.

Directions: From Lee Vining on U.S. 395, drive south for 25 miles to Mammoth Junction and Highway 203. Turn west on Highway 203 and drive three miles to the park on the left.

From Bishop, drive 40 miles north on Highway 395 to Mammoth Lakes exit. Turn west on Highway 203, go under the overpass, and drive three miles to the park on the left.

Contact: Mammoth Mountain RV Park, 760/934-3822, fax 760/934-1896, www.mammothrv.com.

80 TWIN LAKES

Scenic rating: 8

in Inyo National Forest

From Twin Lakes, you can look southwest and see pretty Twin Falls, a wide cascade that runs into the head of upper Twin Lake. There are actually two camps here, one on each side of the access road, at 8,600 feet. Lower Twin Lake is a favorite for fly fishers in float tubes. Powerboats, swimming, and sailboarding are not permitted. Use is heavy at the campground. Often there will be people lined up waiting for another family's weeklong vacation to end so theirs can start. Excellent hiking trails are in the area.

Campsites, facilities: There are 94 sites for tents or RVs up to 40 feet (no hookups). Picnic tables and fire grills are provided. Drinking water, flush toilets, and a boat launch are available. A grocery store, coin laundry, coin showers, and propane gas are nearby. Some facilities are wheelchair-accessible. Leashed pets are permitted.

Reservations, fees: Reservations are accepted at 877/444-6777 or www.recreation.gov ($10 reservation fee). Sites are $19 per night. Open mid-May through late October, weather permitting.

Directions: From Lee Vining on U.S. 395, drive south for 25 miles to Mammoth Junction and Highway 203/Minaret Summit Road.

Turn west on Highway 203 and drive four miles to Lake Mary Road. Continue straight through the intersection and drive 2.3 miles to Twin Lakes Loop Road. Turn right and drive 0.5 mile to the campground.
Contact: Inyo National Forest, Mammoth Ranger Station and Visitor Center, 760/924-5500, fax 760/924-5547.

81 SHERWIN CREEK

Scenic rating: 7

in Inyo National Forest

This camp is set along little Sherwin Creek, at 7,600 feet elevation, a short distance from the town of Mammoth Lakes. If you drive a mile east on Sherwin Creek Road, then turn right at the short spur road, you will find a trailhead for a hike that is routed up six miles to Valentine Lake in the John Muir Wilderness, set on the northwest flank of Bloody Mountain.
Campsites, facilities: There are 87 sites for tents or RVs up to 34 feet (no hookups), and 15 walk-in sites for tents only. Picnic tables and fire grills are provided. Drinking water and flush toilets are available. Leashed pets are permitted.
Reservations, fees: Reservations are accepted at 877/444-6777 or www.recreation.gov ($10 reservation fee). Sites are $18 per night. Open early May through mid-September, weather permitting.
Directions: From Lee Vining on U.S. 395, drive south for 25 miles to Mammoth Junction and Highway 203/Minaret Summit Road. Turn west on Highway 203 and drive about three miles to the Mammoth Lakes Visitor Center and continue a short distance to Old Mammoth Road. Turn left and drive about a mile to Sherwin Creek. Turn south and drive two miles on largely unpaved road to the campground on the left side of the road.
Contact: Inyo National Forest, Mammoth Lakes Visitor Center, 760/924-5500, fax 760/924-5547.

82 LAKE MARY

Scenic rating: 9

in Inyo National Forest

Lake Mary is the star of the Mammoth Lakes region. Of the 11 lakes in the area, this is the largest and most developed. It provides a resort, boat ramp, and boat rentals, and it receives the highest number of trout stocks. No water/body contact, including swimming, is allowed, and the speed limit is 10 mph. It is set at 8,900 feet elevation in a place of incredible natural beauty, one of the few spots that literally has it all. Of course, that often includes quite a few other people. If there are too many for you, an excellent trailhead is available at nearby Coldwater camp that routes you up to Emerald Lake.
Campsites, facilities: There are 48 sites for tents or RVs up to 30 feet (no hookups). Picnic tables, food lockers, and fire grills are provided. Drinking water and flush toilets are available. A grocery store, coin laundry, and propane gas are nearby. Leashed pets are permitted.
Reservations, fees: Reservations are not accepted. Sites are $19 per night with a 14-day limit. Open early June through mid-September, weather permitting.
Directions: Take U.S. 395 to Mammoth Junction and Highway 203. Turn west on Highway 203 and drive through the town of Mammoth Lakes to the junction of Minaret Road/Highway 203 and Lake Mary Road. Continue straight through the intersection and drive 3.6 miles to Lake Mary Loop Drive. Turn right and drive 0.5 mile to the campground entrance.
Contact: Inyo National Forest, Mammoth Ranger Station and Visitor Center, 760/924-5500, fax 760/924-5547.

83 PINE CITY

Scenic rating: 7

near Lake Mary in Inyo National Forest

This camp is at the edge of Lake Mary at an elevation of 8,900 feet. It's popular for both families and fly fishers with float tubes. Swimming is not permitted.

Campsites, facilities: There are 10 sites for tents or RVs up to 40 feet (no hookups). Picnic tables and fire grills are provided. Drinking water and flush toilets are available. A grocery store, coin laundry, boat launch, boat rentals, and propane gas are nearby. Some facilities are wheelchair-accessible. Leashed pets are permitted.

Reservations, fees: Reservations are not accepted. Sites are $19 per night. Open early June through mid-September.

Directions: Take U.S. 395 to Mammoth Junction and Highway 203. Turn west on Highway 203 and drive through the town of Mammoth Lakes to the junction of Minaret Road/Highway 203 and Lake Mary Road. Continue straight through the intersection and drive 3.6 miles to Lake Mary Loop Drive. Turn left and drive 0.25 mile to the campground.

Contact: Inyo National Forest, Mammoth Ranger Station and Visitor Center, 760/924-5500, fax 760/924-5547.

84 COLDWATER

Scenic rating: 7

on Coldwater Creek in Inyo National Forest

While this camp is not the first choice of many simply because there is no lake view, it has a special attraction all its own. First, it is a two-minute drive from the campground to Lake Mary, where there is a boat ramp, rentals, and good trout fishing. Second, at the end of the campground access road is a trailhead for two outstanding hikes. From the Y at the trailhead, if you head right, you will be routed up Coldwater Creek to Emerald Lake, a great little hike. If you head to the left, you will have a more ambitious trip to Arrowhead, Skelton, and Red Lakes, all within three miles. The elevation is 8,900 feet.

Campsites, facilities: There are 78 sites for tents or RVs up to 50 feet (no hookups). Picnic tables and fire grills are provided. Drinking water, flush toilets, and horse facilities are available. You can buy supplies in Mammoth Lakes. Leashed pets are permitted.

Reservations, fees: Reservations are accepted at 877/444-6777 or www.recreation.gov ($10 reservation fee). Sites are $19 per night, with a 14-day limit. Open mid-June through mid-September.

Directions: From Lee Vining on U.S. 395, drive south for 25 miles to Mammoth Junction and Highway 203/Minaret Summit Road. Turn west on Highway 203 and drive four miles to Lake Mary Road. Continue straight through the intersection and drive 3.6 miles to Lake Mary Loop Drive. Turn left and drive 0.6 mile to the camp entrance road.

Contact: Inyo National Forest, Mammoth Ranger Station and Visitor Center, 760/924-5500, fax 760/924-5547.

85 CONVICT LAKE

Scenic rating: 7

in Inyo National Forest

BEST

This is the most popular camp in the Mammoth area and it is frequently full. While the lake rates a 10 for scenic beauty, the camp itself is in a stark desert setting, out of sight of the lake, and it can get windy and cold due to the exposed sites. After driving on U.S. 395 to get here, it is always astonishing to clear the rise and see Convict Lake (7,583 feet) and its gem-like waters set in a mountain bowl beneath a back wall of high, jagged wilderness peaks. The camp is right beside Convict Creek, about a quarter mile from Convict Lake. Both provide very good trout fishing, including some rare monster-sized brown trout below the Convict Lake outlet. Fishing is often outstanding in Convict Lake, with a chance of hooking a 10- or 15-pound trout. The lake speed limit is 10 mph, and although swimming is allowed, it is not popular because of the cold, often choppy water. A trail is routed around the lake, providing a nice day hike. A bonus is an outstanding resort with a boat launch, boat rentals, cabin rentals, small store, restaurant, and bar. Horseback rides and hiking are also available, with a trail routed along the north side of the lake, then along upper Convict Creek (a stream crossing is required about three miles in), and into the John Muir Wilderness.

Campsites, facilities: There are 88 sites for tents or RVs up to 40 feet (no hookups). Rental cabins are also available through the Convict Lake Resort. Picnic tables and fire grills are provided. Drinking water and flush toilets are available. A dump station, boat ramp, store, restaurant, and horseback-riding facilities are available nearby. Some facilities are wheelchair-accessible. Leashed pets are permitted.

Reservations, fees: Reservations are accepted at 877/444-6777 or www.recreation.gov ($10 reservation fee). Sites are $18 per night. For cabin reservations, phone 760/934-3880 or 800/992-2260. Open mid-April through October, weather permitting; cabins open year-round.

Directions: From Lee Vining on U.S. 395, drive south for 31 miles (five miles past Mammoth Junction) to Convict Lake Road (adjacent to Mammoth Lakes Airport). Turn west (right) on Convict Lake Road and drive three miles to Convict Lake. Cross the dam and drive a short distance to the campground entrance road on the left. Turn left and drive 0.25 mile to the campground.

From Bishop, drive north on U.S. 395 for 35 miles to Convict Lake Road. Turn west (left) and drive three miles to the lake and campground.

Contact: Inyo National Forest, Mammoth Ranger Station and Visitor Center, 760/924-5500, fax 760/924-5547; Convict Lake Resort and Cabins, 800/992-2260.

86 McGEE CREEK RV PARK

Scenic rating: 6

near Crowley Lake

This is a popular layover spot for folks visiting giant Crowley Lake. Crowley Lake is still one of the better lakes in the Sierra for trout fishing, with good prospects for large rainbow trout and brown trout, though the 20-pound brown trout that once made this lake famous are now mainly a legend. McGee Creek runs through the campground, and trout fishing is popular. Several trout ponds are also available; call for fees. Beautiful Convict Lake provides a nearby side-trip option. It is also about nine miles to Rock Creek Lake, a beautiful high-mountain destination. The elevation is 7,000 feet.

Campsites, facilities: There are 40 sites with full, partial, or no hookups (50 amps) for tents or RVs up to 40 feet; some sites are pull-through. Picnic tables and fire pits are provided. Drinking water and restrooms with showers and vault toilets are available. Leashed pets are permitted.

Reservations, fees: Reservations are accepted. Sites are $20–30 per night, $3 per person per night for more than two people. Weekly and monthly rates available. Open late April through September, weather permitting.

Directions: From the junction of U.S. 395 and Highway 203 (the Mammoth Lakes turnoff), drive south on U.S. 395 for eight miles to the turnoff for McGee Creek Road. Take that exit and look for the park entrance on the left.

Contact: McGee Creek RV Park, 760/935-4233, www.mcgeecreekrv-campground.com.

87 McGEE CREEK

Scenic rating: 7

in Inyo National Forest

This is a Forest Service camp at an elevation of 7,600 feet, set along little McGee Creek, a good location for fishing and hiking. There are few trees here. The stream is stocked with trout, and a trailhead is just up the road. From here you can hike along upper McGee Creek and into the John Muir Wilderness.

Campsites, facilities: There are 28 sites for tents or RVs up to 25 feet (no hookups). Picnic tables and fire grills are provided. Drinking water, vault toilets, and shade structures are available. Horseback-riding facilities are available nearby. Some facilities are wheelchair-accessible. Leashed pets are permitted.

Reservations, fees: Reservations are accepted at 877/444-6777 or www.recreation.gov ($10 reservation fee). Sites are $18 per night. Open mid-May through mid-October, weather permitting.

Directions: From Mammoth Lakes at the junction of U.S. 395 and Highway 203, drive south on U.S. 395 for 8.5 miles to McGee Creek Road (signed). Turn right (toward the Sierra) and drive 1.5 miles on a narrow, windy road to the campground.

Contact: Inyo National Forest, White Mountain Ranger District, 760/873-2500, fax 760/873-2563; McGee Creek Pack Station, 760/935-4324.

88 CROWLEY LAKE

Scenic rating: 5

near Crowley Lake

This large BLM camp is across U.S. 395 from the south shore of Crowley Lake. For many, Crowley is the trout-fishing capital of the eastern Sierra, with the annual opener (the last Saturday in April) a great celebration. Though the trout fishing can go through a lull in midsummer, it can become excellent again in the fall when the lake's population of big brown trout heads up to the top of the lake at the mouth of the Owens River. This is a large lake with 45 miles of shoreline. In the summer, water sports include swimming, waterskiing, wakeboarding, personal watercraft riding, and sailboarding. The surroundings are fairly stark; the elevation is 6,800 feet.

Campsites, facilities: There are 47 sites for tents or RVs of any length (no hookups). Picnic tables and fire grills are provided. Vault toilets are available. No drinking water is available. A grocery store, boat ramp, boat rentals, and horseback-riding facilities are nearby. Floating chemical toilets are available on the lake. Leashed pets are permitted.

Reservations, fees: Reservations are not accepted. Sites are $5 per night, and season passes are available for $300. Open late April through October, weather permitting.

Directions: Drive on U.S. 395 to the Crowley Lake Road exit (30 miles north of Bishop). Take that exit west (toward the Sierra) to Crowley Lake Road. Turn right on Crowley Lake Road and drive northwest for three miles to the campground entrance on the left (well signed).

Contact: Bureau of Land Management, Bishop Field Office, 760/872-4881, fax 760/872-5050; McGee Creek Pack Station, 760/935-4324.

89 TUFF

Scenic rating: 5

near Crowley Lake in Inyo National Forest

Easy access off U.S. 395 makes this camp a winner, though it is not nearly as pretty as those up Rock Creek Road to the west of Tom's Place. The fact that you can get in and out of here quickly makes it ideal for campers planning fishing trips to nearby Crowley Lake. The elevation is 7,000 feet.

Campsites, facilities: There are 34 sites for tents or RVs up to 45 feet (no hookups). Picnic tables and fire grills are provided. Drinking water and flush toilets are available. Some facilities are wheelchair-accessible. Leashed pets are permitted.

Reservations, fees: Reservations are accepted at 877/444-6777 or www.recreation.gov ($10 reservation fee). Sites are $18 per night. A 21-day limit is enforced. Open late April through mid-October, weather permitting.

Directions: From Mammoth Lakes at the junction of U.S. 395 and Highway 203, drive south on U.S. 395 for 15.5 miles (one mile north of Tom's Place) to Rock Creek Road. Turn left (east) on Rock Creek Road and drive 0.5 mile to the campground.

Contact: Inyo National Forest, White Mountain Ranger District, 760/873-2500, fax 760/873-2563.

90 FRENCH CAMP

Scenic rating: 5

on Rock Creek near Crowley Lake in Inyo National Forest

French Camp is just a short hop from U.S. 395 and Tom's Place, right where the high Sierra turns into high plateau country. Side-trip opportunities include boating and fishing on giant Crowley Lake and, to the west on Rock Creek Road, visiting little Rock Creek Lake 10 miles away. The elevation is 7,500 feet.

Campsites, facilities: There are 86 sites for tents or RVs up to 40 feet (no hookups). Picnic tables and fire grills are provided. Drinking water, flush toilets, and dump station are available. Leashed pets are permitted.

Reservations, fees: Reservations are accepted at 877/444-6777 or www.recreation.gov ($10 reservation fee). Sites are $18 per night. Open early May through October, weather permitting.

Directions: From Mammoth Lakes at the junction of U.S. 395 and Highway 203, drive south on U.S. 395 for 15 miles to Tom's Place and Rock Creek Road. Turn right (toward the Sierra) at Rock Creek Road and drive 0.25 mile to the campground on the right.

Contact: Inyo National Forest, White Mountain Ranger District, 760/873-2500, fax 760/873-2563.

91 HOLIDAY GROUP CAMP

Scenic rating: 5

near Crowley Lake in Inyo National Forest

There's a story behind every name. Holiday is a group camp that is opened as an overflow camp unless reserved on holiday weekends. It is near Rock Creek, not far from Crowley Lake, with surroundings far more stark than the camps to the west on Rock Creek Road. The elevation is 7,500 feet.

Campsites, facilities: There are 35 sites for tents or RVs up to 16 feet (no hookups) or groups up to 100 people. Picnic tables and fire grills are provided. Drinking water and vault toilets are available. Some facilities are wheelchair-accessible. Leashed pets are permitted.

Reservations, fees: Reservations are required at 760/935-4339. As a group site, it is $135 per night. Open only when reserved by groups.

Directions: From Mammoth Lakes at the junction of U.S. 395 and Highway 203, drive south on U.S. 395 for 15 miles south to Tom's Place and Rock Creek Road. Turn right (toward the Sierra) and drive 0.5 mile to the campground on the left.

Contact: Inyo National Forest, White Mountain Ranger District, 760/873-2500, fax 760/873-2563.

92 ASPEN GROUP CAMP

Scenic rating: 7

near Crowley Lake in Inyo National Forest

This small group campground set on Rock Creek is used primarily as a base camp for anglers and campers heading to nearby Crowley Lake or venturing west to Rock Creek Lake. The elevation at the camp is 8,100 feet.

Campsites, facilities: There is one group camp for tents or RVs up to 25 feet (no hookups) that can accommodate up to 25 people. Picnic tables and fire grills are provided. Drinking water and flush toilets are available. Limited supplies are available in Tom's Place, three miles away. Some facilities are wheelchair-accessible. Leashed pets are permitted.

Reservations, fees: Reservations are required at 877/444-6777 or www.recreation.gov ($10 reservation fee). The group fee is $65 per night. Open mid-May through mid-October, weather permitting.

Directions: From Mammoth Lakes at the junction of U.S. 395 and Highway 203, drive south on U.S. 395 for 15 miles south to Tom's Place and Rock Creek Road. Turn right (toward the Sierra) at Rock Creek Road and drive three miles to the campground.

Contact: Inyo National Forest, White Mountain Ranger District, 760/873-2500, fax 760/873-2563; Recreation Resource Management, 760/935-4321.

93 IRIS MEADOW

Scenic rating: 5

near Crowley Lake in Inyo National Forest

Iris Meadow, at 8,300 feet elevation on the flank of Red Mountain (11,472 feet), is the first in a series of five Forest Service camps set near Rock Creek Canyon on the road leading from Tom's Place up to pretty Rock Creek Lake. A bonus is that some of the campsites are next to the creek. Rock Creek is stocked with trout, and nearby Rock Creek Lake also provides fishing and boating for hand-launched boats. This camp also has access to a great trailhead for wilderness exploration.

Campsites, facilities: There are 14 sites for tents or RVs up to 40 feet (no hookups). Picnic tables and fire grills are provided. Drinking water and flush toilets are available. Limited supplies are available in Tom's Place, three miles away. Some facilities are wheelchair-accessible. Leashed pets are permitted.

Reservations, fees: Reservations are not accepted. Sites are $18 per night. Open late May through mid-September, weather permitting.

Directions: From Mammoth Lakes at the junction of U.S. 395 and Highway 203, drive south on U.S. 395 for 15 miles to Tom's Place and Rock Creek Road. Turn right (toward the Sierra) at Rock Creek Road and drive three miles to the campground.

Contact: Inyo National Forest, White Mountain Ranger District, 760/873-2500, fax 760/873-2563.

94 BIG MEADOW

Scenic rating: 8

near Crowley Lake in Inyo National Forest

This is a smaller, quieter camp in the series of campgrounds along Rock Creek. Some of the campsites are along the creek. Beautiful Rock Creek Lake provides a nearby side trip. The elevation is 8,600 feet. In the fall, turning aspens make for spectacular colors.

Campsites, facilities: There are 11 sites for tents or RVs up to 22 feet (no hookups). Picnic tables and fire grills are provided. Drinking water and flush toilets are available. Limited supplies are available in Tom's Place, four miles

away. Some facilities are wheelchair-accessible. Leashed pets are permitted.
Reservations, fees: Reservations are not accepted. Sites are $18 per night. Open early May through late October.
Directions: From Mammoth Lakes at the junction of U.S. 395 and Highway 203, drive south on U.S. 395 for 15 miles south to Tom's Place and Rock Creek Road. Turn right (toward the Sierra) at Rock Creek Road and drive four miles to the campground.
Contact: Inyo National Forest, White Mountain Ranger District, 760/873-2500, fax 760/873-2563.

95 PALISADE

Scenic rating: 8

near Crowley Lake in Inyo National Forest

This shoe might just fit. Palisade, a tiny campground, provides a pretty spot along Rock Creek at 8,600 feet elevation, with many side-trip options. The closest is fishing for small trout on Rock Creek and at pretty Rock Creek Lake up the road to the west. Another option is horseback riding, and horse rentals are in the area. The area is loaded with aspens. Some of the campsites are directly on the creek.
Campsites, facilities: There are five sites for tents or RVs up to 30 feet (no hookups); this campground can also be used as a group site for up to 30 people. Picnic tables and fire grills are provided. Drinking water and flush toilets are available. Horseback-riding facilities are nearby. Limited supplies are available in Tom's Place, five miles away. Leashed pets are permitted.
Reservations, fees: Reservations are accepted at 760/935-4339. Sites are $18 per night. The group price is $90 per night. Open mid-May through mid-September, weather permitting.
Directions: From Mammoth Lakes at the junction of U.S. 395 and Highway 203, drive south on U.S. 395 for 15 miles south to Tom's Place and Rock Creek Road. Turn right (toward the Sierra) at Rock Creek Road and drive five miles to the campground.
Contact: Inyo National Forest, White Mountain Ranger District, 760/873-2500, fax 760/873-2563; Rock Creek Pack Station, 760/935-4493; Recreation Resource Management, 760/935-4339.

96 EAST FORK

Scenic rating: 8

near Crowley Lake in Inyo National Forest

This is a beautiful, popular campground set along East Fork Rock Creek at 9,000 feet elevation. The camp is only three miles from Rock Creek Lake, where there's an excellent trailhead. Mountain biking is popular in this area, and Lower Rock Creek and Sand Canyon have two of the most difficult and desirable trails around; they're suggested for experienced riders only.
Campsites, facilities: There are 138 sites for tents or RVs up to 40 feet (no hookups). Picnic tables and fire grills are provided. Drinking water and flush toilets are available. Limited supplies are available in Tom's Place and at Rock Creek Lakes Resort. Leashed pets are permitted.
Reservations, fees: Reservations are accepted at 877/444-6777 or www.recreation.gov ($10 reservation fee). Sites are $18 per night. Open early May through October.
Directions: From Mammoth Lakes at the junction of U.S. 395 and Highway 203, drive south on U.S. 395 for 15 miles south to Tom's Place and Rock Creek Road. Turn right (toward the Sierra) at Rock Creek Road and drive five miles to the campground access road on the left.
Contact: Inyo National Forest, White Mountain Ranger District, 760/873-2500, fax 760/873-2563.

97 PINE GROVE UPPER AND LOWER

Scenic rating: 8

near Crowley Lake in Inyo National Forest

Pine Grove is one of the smaller camps in the series of campgrounds along Rock Creek. Of the five camps in this canyon, this one is the closest to Rock Creek Lake, just a two-mile drive away (Rock Creek Lake Campground is closer, of course). The aspens here are stunning in September, when miles of mountains turn to shimmering golds. Some of the campsites are along the creek. The elevation is 9,300 feet.

Campsites, facilities: There are 19 sites for tents or RVs up to 16 feet (no hookups). Picnic tables and fire grills are provided. Drinking water and flush toilets are available. Horseback-riding facilities are nearby. Limited supplies can be obtained in Tom's Place and at Rock Creek Lakes Resort. Leashed pets are permitted.

Reservations, fees: Reservations are not accepted. Sites are $18 per night. Open mid-May through mid-October.

Directions: From Mammoth Lakes at the junction of U.S. 395 and Highway 203, drive south on U.S. 395 for 15 miles south to Tom's Place and Rock Creek Road. Turn right (toward the Sierra) at Rock Creek Road and drive seven miles to the campground.

Contact: Inyo National Forest, White Mountain Ranger District, 760/873-2500, fax 760/873-2563.

98 ROCK CREEK LAKE

Scenic rating: 9

in Inyo National Forest

Rock Creek Lake, set at an elevation of 9,600 feet, is a small but beautiful lake that features cool, clear water, small trout, and a great trailhead for access to the adjacent John Muir Wilderness, with 50 other lakes within a two-hour hike. The setting is drop-dead beautiful, hence the high rating for scenic beauty, but note that the campsites are set closely together, side by side, in a paved parking area. This 63-acre lake has a 5-mph speed limit and swimming is allowed. The lake is stocked with Alpers trout, and they are joined by resident brown trout in the 10- to 16-pound class. At times, especially afternoons in late spring, winds out of the west can be cold and pesky at the lake. If this campground is full, the nearby Mosquito Flat walk-in campground provides an option. Note that Mosquito Flat has a limit of one night and is designed as a staging area for wilderness backpacking trips, with tent camping only. Insider's tip: Rock Creek Lakes Resort has mouth-watering homemade pie available in the café.

Campsites, facilities: There are 28 sites for tents or RVs up to 22 feet (no hookups), and one group tent site for up to 50 people; some of the sites require a short walk-in. Picnic tables and fire grills are provided. Drinking water, flush toilets, an unimproved boat launch, and boat rentals are available. Horseback-riding facilities and a café are nearby. Limited supplies can be obtained in Tom's Place and at Rock Creek Lakes Resort. Leashed pets are permitted.

Reservations, fees: Reservations are accepted for individual sites and required for group sites at 877/444-6777 or www.recreation.gov ($10 reservation fee). Sites are $18 per night, $55–65 per night for a group site. Open mid-May through October, weather permitting.

Directions: From the junction of U.S. 395 and Highway 203 (the Mammoth Lakes turnoff), drive 15 miles south on U.S. 395 to Tom's Place. Turn right (toward the Sierra) at Rock Creek Road and drive seven miles to the campground.

Contact: Inyo National Forest, White Mountain Ranger District, 760/873-2500, fax 760/873-2563; Rock Creek Pack Station, 760/935-4493.

99 PLEASANT VALLEY

Scenic rating: 7

near Pleasant Valley Reservoir

Pleasant Valley County Campground is set near long, narrow Pleasant Valley Reservoir, created by the Owens River. A 15-minute walk from camp will take you to the lake. It is east of the Sierra range in the high desert plateau country; the elevation is 4,200 feet. That makes it available for year-round fishing, and trout are stocked. The Owens River passes through the park, providing wild trout fishing, with most anglers practicing catch-and-release fly-fishing. This is also near a major jump-off point for hiking, rock-climbing, and wilderness fishing at the Bishop Pass area to the west.

Campsites, facilities: There are 200 sites for tents or RVs of any length (no hookups). Picnic tables and fire grills are provided. Drinking water (hand-pumped well water) and vault toilets are available. Groups can be accommodated. Some facilities are wheelchair-accessible. Leashed pets are permitted.

Reservations, fees: Reservations are not accepted. Sites are $10 per night per vehicle. Open year-round.

Directions: Drive on U.S. 395 to Pleasant Valley Road (seven miles north of Bishop) on the east side of the road. Turn northeast and drive one mile to the park entrance.

Contact: Inyo County Parks Department, 760/873-5577, www.395.com/inyo/campgrounds.

100 PLEASANT VALLEY PIT CAMPGROUND

Scenic rating: 6

near Bishop off US 395

This camp is set in a rocky desert area just south of Pleasant Valley Reservoir. It's a good spot for kids, with boulder scrambling the primary recreation, and is also a good area to see a variety of raptors. Few travelers on U.S. 395 know about the campground, operated by the Bureau of Land Management.

Campsites, facilities: There are 75 sites for tents or RVs (no hookups). Vault toilets and a dumpster are provided. There is a campground host, as well as law enforcement patrols, and the campground sees regular maintenance. Fires, charcoal grills, and portable stoves outside developed campgrounds require a permit, when allowed. Leashed pets are permitted.

Reservations, fees: Reservations are not accepted. The fee is $2 per night. There is a 60-day limit. Open November to early May, weather permitting.

Directions: From Bishop, drive north on U.S. 395 for about five miles to Pleasant Valley Road. Turn right on Pleasant Valley Road and proceed approximately one-half mile to the gravel road on the left (west) side of the road. Turn left on the gravel road and drive to the Pleasant Valley Pit Campground.

Contact: Bureau of Land Management, Bishop Field Office, 760/872-4881, fax 760/872-5050, www.blm.gov.

101 HIGHLANDS RV PARK

Scenic rating: 3

near Bishop

This is a privately operated RV park near Bishop that is set up for U.S. 395 cruisers. There is a casino in town. A great side trip is up two-lane Highway 168 to Lake Sabrina. The elevation is 4,300 feet. Note that a few sites are occupied by long-term renters.

Campsites, facilities: There are 103 sites with full hookups (30 and 50 amps) for RVs of any length; many sites are pull-through. No tents. Picnic tables and cable TV are provided. Drinking water, restrooms with flush toilets and showers, dump station, social room with pool table, Wi-Fi, propane gas, ice, fish-cleaning station, and coin laundry are available. Supplies are available nearby. Some facilities are wheelchair-accessible. Leashed pets are permitted.

Reservations, fees: Reservations are recommended. Sites are $39 per night, $1 per person per night for more than two people. Weekly and monthly rates available. Some credit cards accepted. Open year-round.

Directions: From Bishop, drive two miles north on U.S. 395/North Sierra Highway to the campground on the right (east side of road) at 2275 North Sierra Highway.

Contact: Highlands RV Park, 760/873-7616.

YOSEMITE & MAMMOTH LAKES HIKING

© ANN MARIE BROWN

BEST HIKES

Bird-Watching
Mono Lake South Tufa Trail, **page 102.**

Butt-Kickers
Half Dome, **page 120.**

Fall Colors
Parker Lake Trail, **page 104.**
Convict Canyon to Lake Dorothy, **page 133.**
McGee Creek to Steelhead Lake, **page 133.**

Hikes with a View
Clouds Rest, **page 85.**
Sentinel Dome, **page 124.**
Panorama Trail, **page 126.**

Kids
Pinecrest Lake National Recreation Trail, **page 69.**
Devils Postpile and Rainbow Falls, **page 110.**

Meadow Hikes
McGurk Meadow and Dewey Point, **page 122.**

Redwoods and Sequoias
Shadow of the Giants, **page 131.**

Self-Guided Nature Walks
Shadow of the Giants, **page 131.**
Methuselah Trail, **page 137.**

Short Backpack Trips
May Lake and Mount Hoffman, **page 85.**
Glen Aulin and Tuolumne Falls, **page 92.**

Summit Hikes
Mount Dana, **page 98.**
White Mountain Peak Trail, **page 137.**

Waterfalls
Waterwheel Falls, **page 91.**
Devils Postpile and Rainbow Falls, **page 110.**
Upper Yosemite Fall, **page 115.**
Mist and John Muir Loop to Nevada Fall, **page 118.**
Bridalveil Fall, **page 121.**

Wheelchair-Accessible Trails
Lower Yosemite Fall, **page 117.**

Wildflowers
Lundy Canyon Trail, **page 74.**
Hite Cove Trail, **page 114.**

Plunging waterfalls, stark granite, alpine lakes, pristine meadows, giant sequoias, and raging rivers – you'll find them all in the Yosemite and Mammoth Lakes region, which encompasses not only world-famous Yosemite National Park but also the popular recreation areas of Mammoth Lakes and the Eastern Sierra.

The centerpiece of this region, of course, is Yosemite National Park, a must-see on every hiker's itinerary. From Yosemite Valley's famous waterfalls – three of which are among the tallest in the world – to the towering granite domes and glistening meadows of Tioga Pass, Yosemite is a place that can only be described in superlatives. Hikers can choose from short-and-easy jaunts to world-class destinations such as Vernal Fall and Sentinel Dome, or exhaustive treks to the summits of Half Dome or Clouds Rest – but there's also a wealth of moderate trails in between the two extremes. One thing is certain: Every trail in Yosemite leads to a destination that is completely worth the effort to reach it.

As scenic as the national park itself are the resort areas just to the east, particularly Mammoth Lakes and June Lake on the U.S. 395 corridor, as well as the surrounding wilderness areas – Hoover, Ansel Adams, and John Muir. Best known for skiing and snowboarding in winter, the resort towns of the Eastern Sierra are ideal base camps for hiking trips in the warmer seasons.

The alpine lakes of this region are a major draw for day hikers and backpackers alike, but equally as compelling are the Eastern Sierra's alpine meadows, fir and pine forests, and sagebrush-covered plains. This is a region known for its unusual diversity – including volcanic craters, hot springs, lava flows, and the strange beauty of Mono Lake, an ancient and majestic body of water covering 60 square miles. An easy, popular hiking trail provides access to its lakeshore.

More uncommon geologic features are found nearby at Devils Postpile National Monument. This 800-acre national park preserves the Devils Postpile – a "pile" of 60-foot-high basalt columns that are remnants of an ancient lava flow – plus breathtaking 101-foot Rainbow Falls. Hikers can spend a day walking to these and other destinations within the monument, or they can hike beyond park borders into the glacially carved backcountry of the Ansel Adams Wilderness.

Key to enjoying your experience in the Yosemite and Mammoth Lakes region is planning your visit for the least crowded months of the year. Summer weekends are the busiest time and are best avoided, especially in the national park. After school starts in September, the crowds lessen substantially. Autumn is a fine time for hiking in and around Yosemite, even though most of the Valley's famous waterfalls (except for dependable Bridalveil) have run dry by midsummer. This lack of falling water is more than made up for by the show of fall colors on the Valley floor and the chance for solitude in this too-well-loved park. Another option, especially for waterfall aficionados, is to show up before school lets out in June. Although the high country is snowed in and inaccessible at this time, Yosemite Valley is in its full watery splendor in April and May.

Likewise, if there is a perfect time to visit the Eastern Sierra, it's in the transition between summer and winter. Autumn transforms the scenic canyons and pristine lakeshores into a wave of blazing color. Aspens, willows, and cottonwoods turn showy hues of orange, yellow, and red. The trees generally begin their color change early in September; peak viewing time is usually late September and early October.

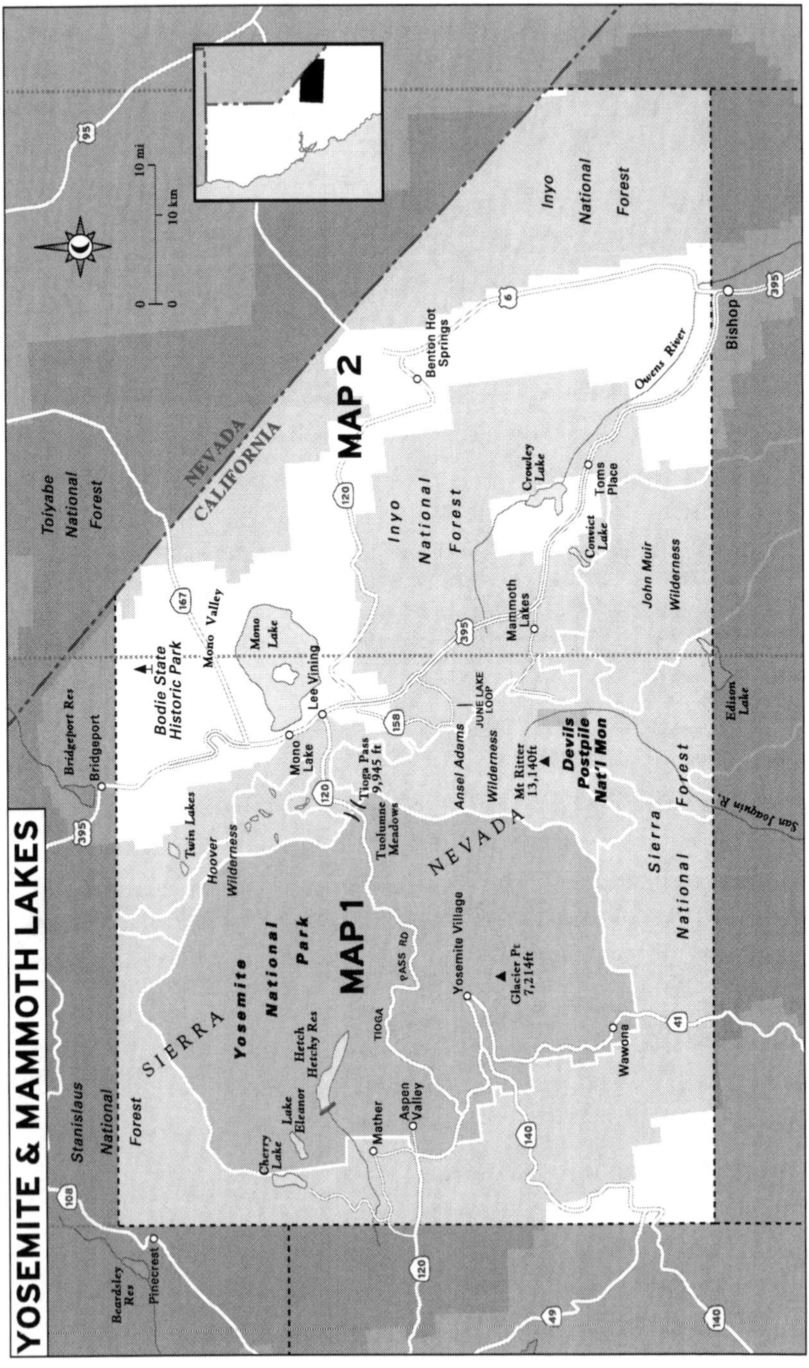
YOSEMITE & MAMMOTH LAKES
MAP 1
MAP 2
NEVADA
CALIFORNIA
Toiyabe National Forest
Stanislaus National Forest
Inyo National Forest
Sierra National Forest
Yosemite National Park
Hoover Wilderness
Ansel Adams Wilderness
John Muir Wilderness
Devils Postpile Nat'l Mon
Bodie State Historic Park
SIERRA NEVADA
TIOGA PASS RD
Bridgeport Res
Bridgeport
Twin Lakes
Mono Valley
Mono Lake
Lee Vining
Tioga Pass 9,945 ft
Tuolumne Meadows
JUNE LAKE LOOP
Mt Ritter 13,140ft
Mammoth Lakes
Convict Lake
Crowley Lake
Toms Place
Owens River
Benton Hot Springs
Bishop
Edison Lake
San Joaquin R.
Yosemite Village
Glacier Pt 7,214ft
Wawona
Hetch Hetchy Res
Lake Eleanor
Cherry Lake
Mather
Aspen Valley
Beardsley Res
Pinecrest
0 10 mi
0 10 km
395
95
6
120
167
158
41
140
108
49

Map 1

Hikes 1-94

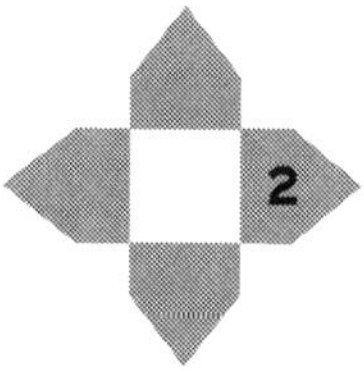

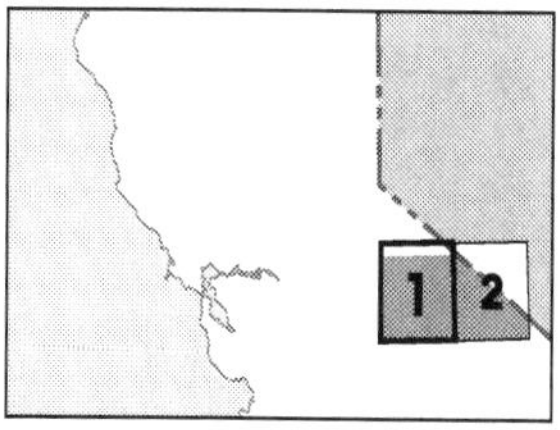

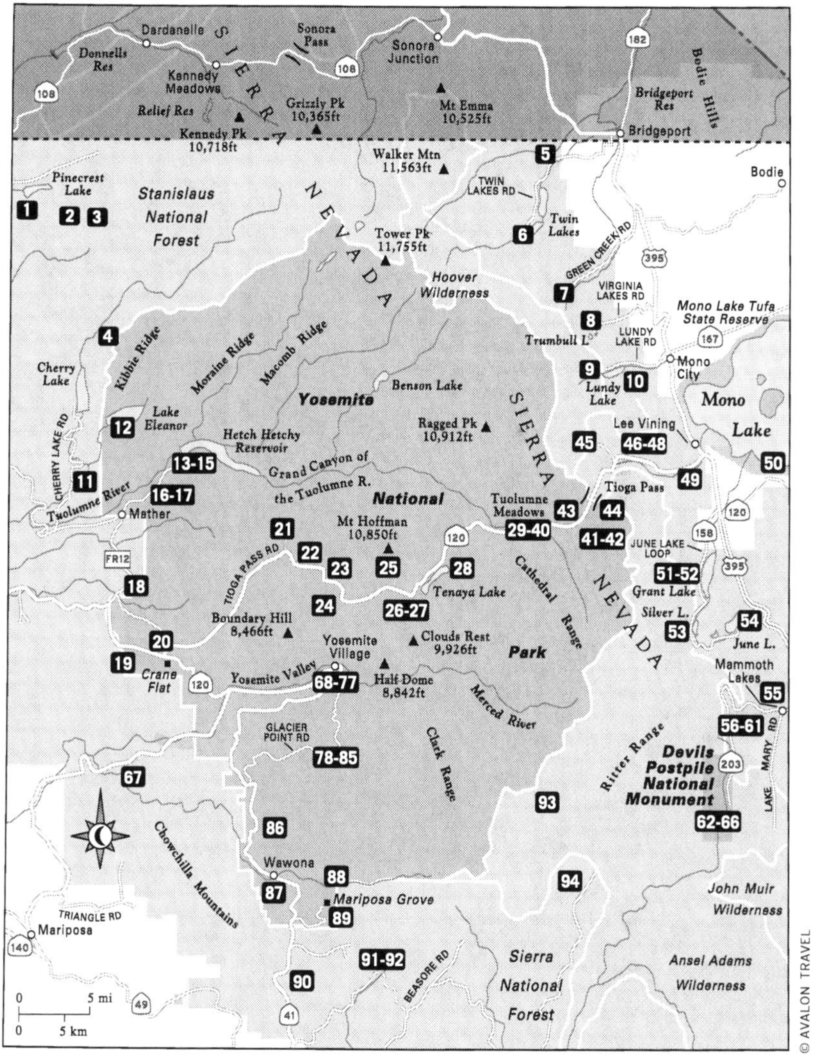

Map 2

Hikes 95-102

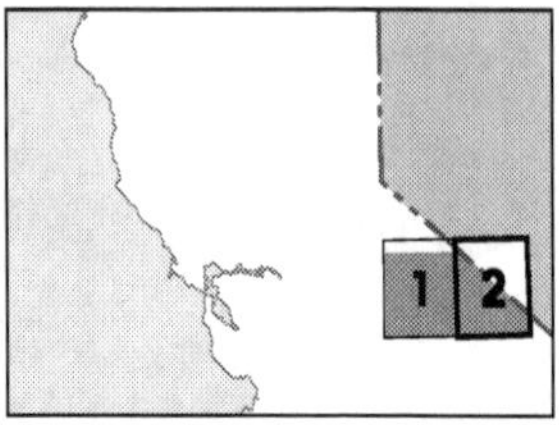

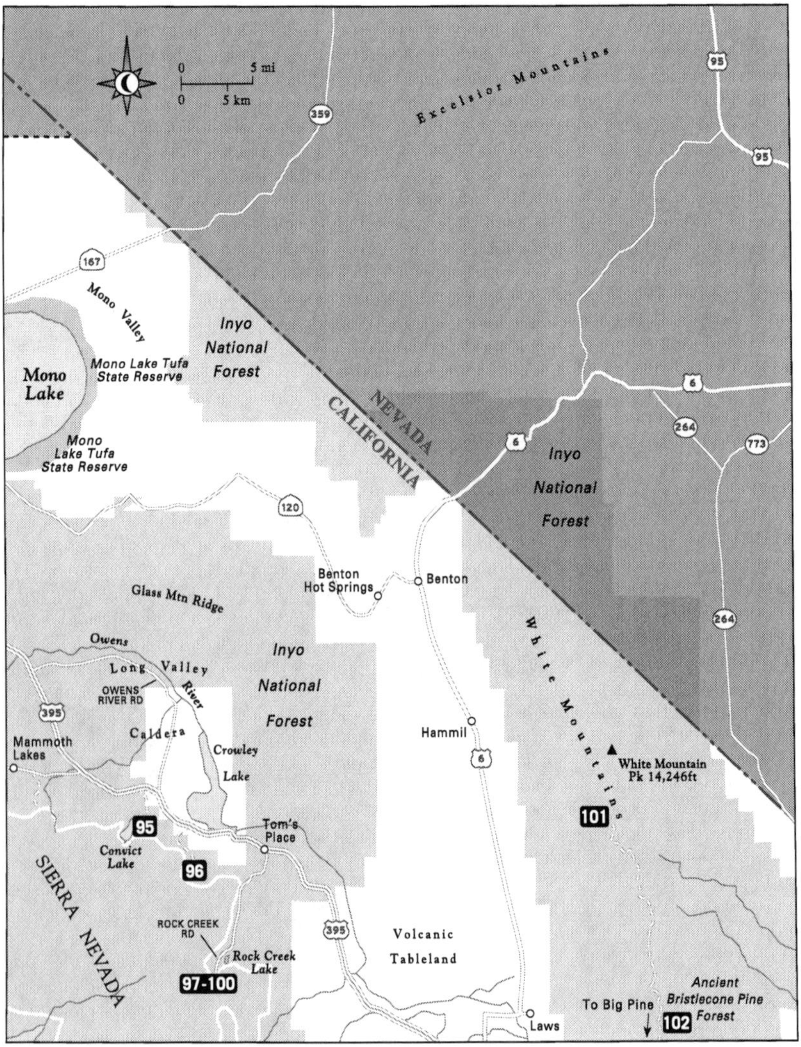

1 PINECREST LAKE NATIONAL RECREATION TRAIL

4.0 mi / 2.0 hr 1 7

on Pinecrest Lake near Strawberry in Stanislaus National Forest

BEST

Pinecrest Lake is a tremendously popular family vacation resort just off Highway 108, the kind of place that people go year after year for a week of boating, camping, and fishing. The trail that circles its shoreline is a lot like the lake itself—it's pretty, it's popular, and it's no place to go if you like solitude. However, the four-mile loop makes a pleasant early morning walk or run if you're up and at it before the crowds get out of bed. In the afternoons, you can hike to the east side of the lake and follow a spur trail along the South Fork Stanislaus River to some excellent swimming holes, called Cleo's Bath. Keep in mind that this trail is by no means a wilderness experience. The south side of the loop is littered with vacation homes, and pay telephones are located at a few points alongside the trail.

User Groups: Hikers and dogs. No horses or mountain bikes. No wheelchair facilities except at the fishing ramp and day-use area.

Permits: No permits are required. Parking and access are free.

Maps: An Emigrant Wilderness map is available from Tom Harrison Maps or Stanislaus National Forest. For a topographic map, ask the USGS for Pinecrest.

Directions: From Sonora, drive east on Highway 108 for 31 miles to the Pinecrest turnoff. Turn right on Pinecrest Lake Road and continue for another mile to the day-use parking area, on the south side of the lake. Park as close to the end of the road as possible.

Contact: Stanislaus National Forest, Summit Ranger District, 1 Pinecrest Lake Road, Pinecrest, CA 95364, 209/965-3434, www.fs.fed.us/r5/stanislaus.

2 CAMP AND BEAR LAKES

8.0 mi / 4.0 hr 2 9

in the Emigrant Wilderness near Pinecrest Lake

The Crabtree trailhead, at elevation 7,180 feet, is the trailhead of choice for most casual hikers and backpackers entering the Emigrant Wilderness. It's easy to reach and allows access to many excellent destinations with a relatively short walk. From Crabtree, it's a moderate 2.5-mile hike to Camp Lake, which is just inside the Emigrant Wilderness boundary. Despite its name, camping is not allowed at Camp Lake, so while day users may choose to linger along its shores, backpackers must continue another 1.5 miles to Bear Lake, accessible via a one-mile left spur trail. Both lakes offer stellar granite-country scenery, good (but icy) swimming, decent rainbow trout fishing, and the chance of seeing plenty of wildflowers along the route in summer. You, too, can be wowed by the wandering daisies and blue lupine. You'll face only one sustained hill climb along the route; most of the trail gently undulates. Watch for beaver evidence at Bear Lake.

User Groups: Hikers, dogs, and horses. No mountain bikes. No wheelchair facilities.

Permits: A free wilderness permit is required for overnight stays and is available from the Summit Ranger Station. Parking and access are free.

Maps: An Emigrant Wilderness map is available from Tom Harrison Maps or Stanislaus National Forest. For a topographic map, ask the USGS for Pinecrest.

Directions: From Sonora, drive east on Highway 108 for 31 miles to the Pinecrest turnoff. Turn right on Pinecrest Lake Road and continue 0.5 mile to the right fork for Dodge Ridge Ski Area. Bear right and drive 2.9 miles, then turn right at the sign for Aspen Meadow and Gianelli trailhead. Drive 0.5 mile, turn left, and drive four miles to the turnoff for the Crabtree trailhead (follow the signs). Turn right and drive 0.25 mile.

Contact: Stanislaus National Forest, Summit Ranger District, 1 Pinecrest Lake Road, Pinecrest, CA 95364, 209/965-3434, www.fs.fed.us/r5/stanislaus.

3 BURST ROCK/ POWELL LAKE

4.0 mi / 2.5 hr — 2 — 9

in the Emigrant Wilderness near Pinecrest Lake

Both Burst Rock and Powell Lake are supreme day-hike destinations, but they present a problem for first-time visitors: Neither one is located right along the trail and neither one is signed. This results in a lot of people wandering around asking, "So which rock is Burst Rock?"

The short answer is, it doesn't matter all that much. After hiking gently but steadily uphill for one mile, you'll reach an interpretive sign that details the difficulties of pioneers who tried to use this route, called the West Walker–Sonora Emigrant Trail, to cross the Sierra in the 1850s. From the wilderness boundary sign, cut off to your left for about 50 yards, and you'll witness an incredible vista and dropoff to the valley below—and who knows, you might even be standing on Burst Rock. After feeling suitably humbled, retrace your steps and continue another mile until you reach an unsigned fork. Go left for less than 0.25 mile to Powell Lake, a favorite spot of young anglers. If you miss the fork, shortly you'll catch sight of the lake, off to your left, and you'll know to go back and find it. The peninsula of rocks that juts out into the water is the perfect place to launch into a swan dive.

User Groups: Hikers, dogs, and horses. No mountain bikes. No wheelchair facilities.

Permits: A free wilderness permit is required for overnight stays and is available from the Summit Ranger Station. Parking and access are free.

Maps: An Emigrant Wilderness map is available from Tom Harrison Maps or Stanislaus National Forest. For a topographic map, ask the USGS for Pinecrest.

Directions: From Sonora, drive east on Highway 108 for 31 miles to the Pinecrest turnoff. Turn right on Pinecrest Lake Road and continue for 0.5 mile to the right fork for Dodge Ridge Ski Area. Bear right, drive 2.9 miles, and turn right at the sign for Aspen Meadow and Gianelli trailhead. Drive 0.5 mile, turn left, and drive 8.3 miles to the trailhead parking area. The route is well signed.

Contact: Stanislaus National Forest, Summit Ranger District, 1 Pinecrest Lake Road, Pinecrest, CA 95364, 209/965-3434, www.fs.fed.us/r5/stanislaus.

4 KIBBIE LAKE

8.4 mi / 1.0–2.0 days — 3 — 8

in northwest Yosemite National Park

This day hike or easy backpacking trip starts near Cherry Lake in Stanislaus National Forest and heads into the Hetch Hetchy region of Yosemite. The hike is easy enough that it makes a rewarding weekend trip for beginning backpackers, who can easily carry a pack over the 4.2-mile distance. From the trailhead, you hike the Kibbie Ridge Trail 1.2 miles to the Kibbie Lake Trail, then go right and head for the lake in another 3.0 miles. Near this main junction you leave Stanislaus National Forest and enter Yosemite National Park, so dogs are not allowed past this point. Much of the route travels through a fire-scarred lodgepole pine forest that is rapidly regenerating. Once you near the lake, the burned areas are left behind and the forest is pristine. The trail deposits you at the southern tip of the granite-bound lake, elevation 6,513 feet. Although quite large (more than 100 surface acres), Kibbie Lake is fairly shallow and supports a good population of rainbow trout. The long and narrow body of water has high rocky cliffs on some of its shoreline, so not all of it is easily accessible. On summer weekends, the lake gets visited fairly heavily, but on weekdays, you are likely to be the only soul around.

Special Note: Check your calendar before you go. The gate at Cherry Lake is closed every year one week before deer season, which is usually sometime in September, and doesn't reopen until spring. Most years, the road is open from May 1 to September 15.

User Groups: Hikers and horses. No dogs or mountain bikes. No wheelchair facilities.

Permits: There is a $20 entrance fee per vehicle at Yosemite National Park, good for seven days. Free wilderness permits are required for overnight stays. They are available on a first-come, first-served basis up to one day in advance at the Yosemite Wilderness kiosk near your chosen trailhead, or further in advance by mail, phone, or online for a $5 reservation fee per person.

Maps: A Hetch Hetchy map is available from Tom Harrison Maps. For topographic maps, ask the USGS for Kibbie Lake and Hetch Hetchy Reservoir.

Directions: From Groveland, drive east on Highway 120 for 14 miles toward Yosemite National Park. Turn left on Cherry Lake Road and drive 24 miles to Cherry Lake's dam, then cross it. On the far side of the dam, bear right and drive 0.4 mile, then turn left on Road 1N45Y and follow it for 4.5 miles to its end at the Kibbie Ridge trailhead.

Contact: Yosemite National Park, P.O. Box 577, Yosemite, CA 95389, 209/372-0200 or 209/372-0740 (permit reservations), www.nps.gov/yose or www.nps.gov/yose/wilderness (permit reservations).

5 BUCKEYE CREEK TRAIL

5.0 mi / 2.5 hr — 1 / 8

in Humboldt-Toiyabe National Forest west of Bridgeport and Highway 395

You can hike up to eight miles one-way along Buckeye Creek to the Hoover Wilderness boundary at the Buckeye Roughs. But most hikers do less than that; they just take off from Buckeye Campground (7,000 feet), maybe pack along their fishing rods, and walk a couple of miles each way up and down the stream. Brook trout are planted close to the campground all summer. It's rare to hike far in the Eastern Sierra without having to climb, but that's what you get here at the base of Buckeye Canyon. If you don't like to fish, there's plenty of other stuff to do, like admire the wildflowers in the meadows or gape at the impressive walls of glacial summits and ridges that surround you. A popular hot spring is found in Buckeye Creek less than a mile from the campground, but be forewarned: You might get an anatomy lesson there. Occasional Buckeye Creek bathers have been spotted wearing only birthday suits.

User Groups: Hikers, dogs, and horses. No mountain bikes. No wheelchair facilities.

Permits: No day-hiking permits are required. Parking and access are free.

Maps: A Hoover Wilderness map is available from Tom Harrison Maps or the U.S. Forest Service. For a topographic map, ask the USGS for Twin Lakes.

Directions: From Bridgeport on U.S. 395, drive west on Twin Lakes Road for seven miles to the Buckeye Road turnoff. Turn right on Buckeye Road and drive 3.5 miles to the Buckeye Campground and trailhead. (Buckeye Road turns to dirt at Doc and Al's Resort.)

Contact: Humboldt-Toiyabe National Forest, Bridgeport Ranger District, HCR1 Box 1000, Bridgeport, CA 93517, 760/932-7070, www.fs.fed.us/r4/htnf.

6 BARNEY LAKE TRAIL

7.8 mi / 5.0 hr — 2 / 8

in the Hoover Wilderness west of Bridgeport

Some call it Barney Lake Trail and others call it Robinson Creek Trail. Whatever you call it, you should know that this is the

HIKING

busiest trail into the Hoover Wilderness. Why? It's downright easy, gaining only 1,000 feet along its four-mile length. The remedy for the crowds? Start hiking very early in the day, before the hundreds of campers in the Twin Lakes area have risen from their sleeping bags. You must park outside Mono Village Campground and then walk due east through it to reach the trailhead, which is signed for Barney Lake. (The attendant in the camp entrance kiosk can point you to the trailhead.) The trail roughly parallels Robinson Creek, first in a pine forest and then skirting big meadows highlighted by vast stands of aspen trees. While in the wide open meadows, you are rewarded with impressive views of the jagged Sawtooth Range. The path passes a Hoover Wilderness sign at 2.6 miles, then climbs a bit more steeply and reaches the lake at 3.9 miles. If you get there before everyone else, you are one lucky hiker. Ambitious day hikers and backpackers can continue another 3.5 miles to larger Peeler Lake. Because of the amount of aspens seen along this trail, it's a real treat to hike here from late September to mid-October when the color show happens.

User Groups: Hikers, dogs, and horses. No mountain bikes. No wheelchair facilities.

Permits: A free wilderness permit is required for overnight stays and is available from the Bridgeport Ranger Station. Quotas are in effect from the end of June to mid-September; permits are available in advance by mail for this period for a $3 fee per person.

Maps: A Hoover Wilderness map is available from Tom Harrison Maps or the U.S. Forest Service. For a topographic map, ask the USGS for Twin Lakes.

Directions: From Bridgeport on U.S. 395, drive west on Twin Lakes Road for 13.2 miles to the signed parking area, on the west end of the lakes, near Mono Village Campground.

Contact: Humboldt-Toiyabe National Forest, Bridgeport Ranger District, HCR1 Box 1000, Bridgeport, CA 93517, 760/932-7070, www.fs.fed.us/r4/htnf.

7 GREEN, EAST, AND WEST LAKES

8.6–11.6 mi / 5.0 hr — 3 / 9

in the Hoover Wilderness west of Bridgeport

Three beautiful lakes—Green, East, and West—are situated right around 9,000 feet in elevation in the spectacular Hoover Wilderness. They offer fair trout fishing and are accessible via Green Creek Trail (sometimes called Green Lake Trail). It's only 4.6 miles round-trip to Green Lake, but you can go two miles farther for an 8.6-mile round-trip that includes East Lake as well. Or, you can take a 1.5-mile spur off the main trail for a much steeper (but well worth it) jaunt to stark, rockbound West Lake. Some people make a short backpacking trip out of it and see all three lakes. If you do, note that Green Lake is the only one of the three that is just below 9,000 feet in elevation, which means it is the only one where campfires are permitted. (You must use the established campfire rings.) At the other, higher lakes, only backpacking stoves are allowed. The fishing is generally better at East and West Lakes than at Green Lake, although it's nothing to write home about. The high mountain scenery, on the other hand, will knock your socks off.

The Green Creek Trail climbs, of course—but not so much that you'll be worn out when you reach Green Lake; just enough to provide you with expansive valley views most of the way. The path closely parallels the tumbling cascades of the west fork of Green Creek, and the July wildflower show is outstanding here. (The autumn aspen show is also noteworthy.) The turnoff for West Lake is on the right at 2.2 miles. This trail makes a memorably steep 1,000-foot ascent over 1.5 miles, climbing high above Green Lake. After the easy grade of the first two miles of trail, this last stretch can really take you by surprise. For solitude lovers, West Lake is your best bet. The main trail reaches the shore of Green Lake 200 yards past the West Lake turnoff. East Lake can be reached by heading left off the main trail and gaining another 500 feet in elevation over two miles. All three lakes are sparkling, rock-bound gems, so you can't go wrong here no matter which one you choose to visit.

User Groups: Hikers, dogs, and horses. No mountain bikes. No wheelchair facilities.

Permits: A free wilderness permit is required for overnight stays and is available from the Bridgeport Ranger Station. Quotas are in effect from the end of June to mid-September; permits are available in advance by mail for this period for a $3 fee per person.

Maps: A Hoover Wilderness map is available from Tom Harrison Maps or the U.S. Forest Service. For a topographic map, ask the USGS for Twin Lakes.

Directions: From Bridgeport, drive south on U.S. 395 for 4.5 miles to Green Creek Road (dirt). Turn west and drive 8.2 miles to the signed trailhead parking area, shortly before Green Creek Campground.

Contact: Humboldt-Toiyabe National Forest, Bridgeport Ranger District, HCR1 Box 1000, Bridgeport, CA 93517, 760/932-7070, www.fs.fed.us/r4/htnf.

8 VIRGINIA LAKES TRAIL

6.2-10.2 mi / 3.0 hr-2.0 days 3 9

in the Hoover Wilderness south of Bridgeport

Virginia Lakes form the gateway to a beautiful high-mountain basin that contains eight small alpine lakes within a two-mile radius. The trailhead is at the Big Virginia Lake day-use area, set at 9,500 feet between mountain peaks that jut 12,000 feet into the sky. From here, you hike west past Blue Lake to Cooney Lake and on to Frog Lakes (a very easy 1.4 miles), then start climbing seriously, continuing 1.8 more miles to 11,100-foot Summit Pass (sometimes called Burro Pass). The landscape here is windswept, barren, and beautiful—a mix of rock, occasional whitebark pines, and high alpine wildflowers. Many hikers take a look at the scene from the pass, then retreat to one of the aforementioned lakes to spend the afternoon, making a 6.2-mile day. If you continue beyond the pass, you curve downhill through dozens of switchbacks for 1.4 miles, then climb gently 0.5 mile west to Summit Lake (at 10,203 feet), on the northeast boundary of Yosemite National Park. Summit Lake is set between Camiaca Peak (11,739 feet) to the north and Excelsior Mountain (12,446 feet) to the south. This is the logical place for backpackers to make camp, and for day-trippers to turn around for a 10.2-mile day. If you want to take a longer trip into even wilder country, you can do so from this point. The trail skirts Summit Lake's north side, then enters Yosemite National Park in Virginia Canyon, one of the least-visited areas of the park. Another option is to take the fork right before Summit Lake that leads east (right) to the double Hoover Lakes, connecting with the Green Creek Trail. Some backpackers and day hikers make a one-way hike of about 11 miles out of this trip by arranging to have a shuttle car waiting for them at the Green Creek trailhead (see the previous listing).

User Groups: Hikers, dogs, and horses. No dogs on trail in the Yosemite National Park portion. No mountain bikes. No wheelchair facilities.

Permits: A free wilderness permit is required for overnight stays and is available from the Bridgeport Ranger Station. Quotas are in effect from the end of June to mid-September; permits are available in advance by mail for this period for a $3 fee per person.

Maps: A Hoover Wilderness map is available from Tom Harrison Maps or the U.S. Forest Service. For a topographic map, ask the USGS for Dunderberg Peak.

Directions: From Bridgeport, drive 13.5 miles south on U.S. 395 (or from Lee Vining, drive 12 miles north on U.S. 395) to Conway Summit. Turn west on Virginia Lakes Road and drive 6.5 miles to the trailhead, at the Big Virginia Lake day-use area.

Contact: Humboldt-Toiyabe National Forest, Bridgeport Ranger District, HCR 1, Box 1000, Bridgeport, CA 93517, 760/932-7070, www.fs.fed.us/r4/htnf.

9 LUNDY CANYON TRAIL

4.4-10.0 mi / 2.0 hr-2.0 days 3 9

north of Lee Vining in the Hoover Wilderness

BEST

The Lundy Canyon Trail is the back door into the 20 Lakes Basin, a well-traveled area of the Hoover Wilderness that is most commonly accessed from Saddlebag Lake off Highway 120. The trailhead lies about two miles past Lundy Lake, a long, narrow pool set at 7,800 feet. From here, the trail rises along Mill Creek, passing several beaver ponds, a dilapidated trapper's cabin, and two small but boisterous waterfalls (Lower and Upper Lundy Falls, also called Mill Creek Falls) as it heads into the Hoover Wilderness. Most visitors hike to the first or second falls, enjoying the gorgeous Eastern Sierra scenery with a relatively mellow walk, then hike back out. Those who continue find that the trail, which climbed gently but steadily for the first 2.2 miles, suddenly reaches what appears to be the back of the canyon. But look straight up the canyon wall to your left—that's where the path continues, although it isn't much of a path. An unmaintained, marginally switchbacked route leads 0.8 mile upward through a frighteningly steep wall of shale, and the difficulty rating for this trail changes abruptly from a 3 to a 4 (and maybe a 5 on the way back downhill). Use great caution here; one slip and you could take a nasty fall. You don't want to be carrying a pack that is too heavy or unbalanced on this stretch.

When you finally make it to the top of the canyon wall, you come out to a beautiful high mountain meadow and a junction near the austere shores of Lake Helen, elevation 10,100 feet (3.3 miles from your start). By going right, you can follow the trail to Shamrock and Steelhead Lakes. Shamrock is 0.3 mile farther and dotted with many islands; Steelhead is another 0.5 mile beyond and is framed by 12,242-foot North Peak, towering above. The opposite trail goes left to Odell Lake (3.6 miles from your start). From Odell Lake, you could continue on to Hummingbird Lake, then to the north shore of Saddlebag Lake. If you can arrange a car shuttle at Saddlebag Lake, you can extend your trip into a one-way hike of seven miles, and that would save you the harrowing trip back down that shale-covered slope.

Note that one of the best times to visit here is in October, when Lundy Canyon's stands of quaking aspen turn bright gold and seem to dance in the breeze. This is one of the best places to admire fall colors in the Eastern Sierra. July is another first-rate time to visit; the canyon's wildflower displays are remarkable.

User Groups: Hikers, horses, and dogs. No mountain bikes. No wheelchair facilities.

Permits: A free wilderness permit is required for overnight stays and is available from the Mono Basin Scenic Area Visitors Center. There are no quotas on this trail, so advance reservations are not required.

Maps: A Hoover Wilderness map is available from Tom Harrison Maps or the U.S. Forest Service. For topographic maps, ask the USGS for Lundy and Dunderberg Peak.

Directions: From Lee Vining, drive north on U.S. 395 for seven miles to Lundy Lake Road. Turn west on Lundy Lake Road and drive five miles to Lundy Lake. Continue beyond the lake and Lundy Lake Resort, driving two miles farther on a dirt road that ends at the trailhead.

Contact: Inyo National Forest, Mono Basin Scenic Area Visitors Center, P.O. Box 429, Lee Vining, CA 93541, 760/647-3044, www.fs.fed.us/r5/inyo.

10 LAKE CANYON AND MAY LUNDY MINE

7.0 mi / 3.5 hr or 2.0 days 3 9

north of Lee Vining in the Hoover Wilderness

The Lundy Lake area is blessed with two first-rate day-hiking trails that lead into two separate and distinct canyons: Lundy Canyon (see previous listing) and Lake Canyon. Both paths offer so many rewards that when you drive up to Lundy Lake, it's hard to decide which one to take. History buffs and fishing-minded hikers would do well to take this trip from Lundy's dam into Lake Canyon, where they can see the remains of the May Lundy Mine. The mine was worked continuously for two decades starting in 1878, producing a total of about $2 million in gold. As a result, the surrounding community of Lundy grew to support 500 people, despite severe winters and deadly avalanches. Besides mining, a primary activity here was the operation of three sawmills along Lundy Creek, used to supply timber to the nearby bustling gold rush town of Bodie.

The hike to the May Lundy Mine is a fairly steep 3.5 miles one-way, climbing above Lundy Lake on the old mine road that was built in 1881. You can see the trail plain as day from the trailhead on the east side of Lundy Lake. The road/trail passes Blue Lake and Crystal Lake, where mining relics can be found. (Crystal Lake is 0.3 mile off the trail via a left fork.) Continue on the main trail, and you'll see the mine remains—old railcar tracks, tailings, and a closed-off mine shaft. Just beyond is Oneida Lake, whose waters were used to run the stamp mill for the mine. Even without the fascinating traces of history, this is an extraordinarily beautiful place. You'll want to linger awhile at sparkling Oneida Lake. Both the scenery and the fishing are quite rewarding.

User Groups: Hikers, horses, and dogs. No mountain bikes. No wheelchair facilities.

Permits: A free wilderness permit is required for overnight stays and is available from the Mono Basin Scenic Area Visitors Center. There are no quotas on this trail, so advance reservations are not required.

Maps: A Mono Lake map is available from Tom Harrison Maps. An Inyo National Forest map is available from the U.S. Forest Service. For a topographic map, ask the USGS for Lundy.

Directions: From Lee Vining, drive north on U.S. 395 for seven miles to Lundy Lake Road. Turn west on Lundy Lake Road and drive five miles to Lundy Lake's dam, on the east side of the lake. Turn left and drive 0.25 mile to a locked gate and trailhead.

Contact: Inyo National Forest, Mono Basin Scenic Area Visitors Center, P.O. Box 429, Lee Vining, CA 93541, 760/647-3044, www.fs.fed.us/r5/inyo.

11 PRESTON FLAT TRAIL

8.8 mi / 4.0 hr or 2.0 days 2 8

in Stanislaus National Forest

Although some day hikers choose to suffer through the nearly intolerable grade of the Poopenaut Valley Trail to reach the swimming holes and fishing spots on the Tuolumne River's free-flowing stretch west of Hetch Hetchy Dam, a much more pleasant approach is on the Preston Flat Trail. The trailhead is off Cherry Lake Road in Stanislaus National Forest, outside Yosemite's border. The path travels 4.4 miles up the north side of the Tuolumne River Canyon on a gently undulating grade. Shortly before the trail's end is a rock chimney and a few other remains of an old cabin that was built here by a homesteader named Preston. A few hundred yards farther is a photogenic vista of Preston Falls, a cascade formed where the Tuolumne River drops 15 feet over a granite ledge into a wide, clear pool. The cataract is just a half-mile downstream of Yosemite's boundary line. If you want to stay overnight, you can. Several good campsites are found along the trail, which sticks closely to the river for most of its length.

Compared to the Poopenaut Valley Trail, the Preston Flat Trail is by far the better choice for hikers who wish to reach the river. Hike it in early spring, when the raging Tuolumne River provides the most exciting viewing. Those who wish to fish or swim should wait to visit until late spring or early summer, when the river quiets down. Wintertime is another nice time to visit here; the elevation is low enough that the trail is always snow-free.

User Groups: Hikers, horses, dogs, and mountain bikes. No wheelchair facilities.
Permits: A free campfire permit is required for overnight stays and is available from the Groveland Ranger Station. Parking and access are free.
Maps: A Stanislaus National Forest map is available from the U.S. Forest Service. For a topographic map, ask the USGS for Cherry Lake South.
Directions: From Groveland drive east on Highway 120 for 14 miles toward Yosemite. Turn left on Cherry Lake Road and drive 8.5 miles to Early Intake, where you cross a bridge over the Tuolumne River. Turn right on the far side of the bridge and drive 0.8 mile to the trailhead parking area at the end of the road, just beyond Kirkwood Powerhouse.
Contact: Stanislaus National Forest, Groveland Ranger District, 24545 Highway 120, Groveland, CA 95321, 209/962-7825, www.fs.fed.us/r5/stanislaus.

12 LAKE ELEANOR

3.0 mi / 1.5 hr 1 8

in northwest Yosemite National Park

Lake Eleanor is a second, less famous reservoir in the Hetch Hetchy region of Yosemite. Originally a naturally shallow glacial lake, Lake Eleanor was "improved" by the city of San Francisco by damming Eleanor Creek in 1928, five years before O'Shaughnessy Dam at Hetch Hetchy was completed. The dam raised the lake's water level 40 feet. Today it is the second largest lake in Yosemite after Hetch Hetchy. Its waters are not used by San Francisco as a drinking supply but rather to generate power. Set at an elevation of 4,657 feet, Lake Eleanor is popular with hikers who tote along a fishing rod while traversing the trail around the three-mile-long lake's edge. The access road to Lake Eleanor ends at a gate 0.25 mile before the lake, so start your hike there, then take a mellow walk along the lake's south and west shores. Much of Lake Eleanor's western side is dotted with picturesque islands. A backcountry ranger station is located near the lake's dam and is usually staffed in the summer months.

It takes more than an hour's drive from Highway 120 to access Lake Eleanor, so people who come here to hike or fish often plan on spending the night. A first-come, first-served campground is located at nearby Cherry Lake, and several backpacking campsites are located on the northwest edge of Lake Eleanor (a wilderness permit is required). Note that the road to Lake Eleanor is open only May 1 to September 15 each year (the road is usually closed beyond Cherry Lake's dam).
User Groups: Hikers and horses. No dogs or mountain bikes. No wheelchair facilities.
Permits: No permits are required for day hiking. Parking and access are free (the trailhead is outside Yosemite National Park).
Maps: A Hetch Hetchy map is available from Tom Harrison Maps. For a topographic map, ask the USGS for Lake Eleanor.
Directions: From Groveland, drive east on Highway 120 for 14 miles toward Yosemite National Park. Turn left on Cherry Lake Road and drive 24 miles to Cherry Lake's dam, then across it. On the far side of the dam, bear right and drive 0.4 mile, then turn right on the dirt road that is signed for Lake Eleanor. Follow this road four miles to its end, at the gated Yosemite National Park boundary, 0.25 mile south of the lake.
Contact: Yosemite National Park, P.O. Box 577, Yosemite, CA 95389, 209/372-0200, www.nps.gov/yose.

13 WAPAMA FALL

4.8 mi / 2.5 hr 2 9

in northwest Yosemite National Park

The trail to this spectacular early-season waterfall starts by crossing the giant O'Shaughnessy Dam, where you may pause to curse (or admire, depending on your sensibilities) the San Francisco politicians who in 1908 believed that flooding Hetch Hetchy Valley was a good idea. In terms of geology and natural features, Hetch Hetchy is a near twin to Yosemite Valley, although somewhat smaller in scale. The valley today is filled by an immense, 400-foot-deep reservoir that supplies water and power to the city of San Francisco and environs. After walking across its impressive dam and passing through a dimly lit, 500-foot-long tunnel, the trail opens out to a mixed forest along the edge of the deep blue lake. Wildflower displays are often excellent in late spring. In 1.5 miles you reach Tueeulala Fall, a delicate wisp of a freefall that only runs during peak snowmelt, and is often dry by late May. Less than a mile farther you reach powerful Wapama Fall on Falls Creek, a Bridalveil-like plume of whitewater that makes a dramatic plunge into the reservoir. Depending on how early in the year you visit, you may get soaking wet standing on the sturdy steel bridges that cross over Wapama Fall's coursing flow. In early spring, Wapama Falls sometimes flows so furiously that the park rangers have to close this trail. In late spring and early summer, the temperature can get hot out at Hetch Hetchy, so this spray of water can be very refreshing. If this is your first trip to this part of Yosemite, be sure to stop and read the interpretive plaques at the dam that explain about the building of Hetch Hetchy Reservoir and its service to the city of San Francisco. Whatever else you may think about it, it's a fascinating story.

User Groups: Hikers only. No dogs, horses, or mountain bikes. No wheelchair facilities.

Permits: No permits are required. There is a $20 entrance fee per vehicle at Yosemite National Park, good for seven days.

Maps: A Hetch Hetchy map is available from Tom Harrison Maps. For topographic maps, ask the USGS for Lake Eleanor and Hetch Hetchy Reservoir.

Directions: From Groveland, drive east on Highway 120 for 22.5 miles to the Evergreen Road turnoff signed for Hetch Hetchy Reservoir on the left, a mile west of the Big Oak Flat entrance to Yosemite. Drive north on Evergreen Road for 7.4 miles and turn right on Hetch Hetchy Road. Drive 9.0 miles to the dam and trailhead.

Contact: Yosemite National Park, P.O. Box 577, Yosemite, CA 95389, 209/372-0200 or 209/372-0740 (permit reservations), www.nps.gov/yose or www.nps.gov/yose/wilderness (permit reservations).

14 RANCHERIA FALLS

13.0 mi / 1.0 or 2.0 days 3 9

in northwest Yosemite National Park

It's spring and you are hungering for a Yosemite backpacking trip, but Tuolumne Meadows is knee-deep in melting snow. This is a good time to hike the northern edge of Hetch Hetchy Reservoir (elevation 3,796 feet), admiring three stunning waterfalls along the way: Tueeulala, Wapama, and Rancheria. This easy backpacking trip (or long day hike, if you prefer) travels along the length of the reservoir to its far eastern edge, where the bears are some of the boldest in all of Yosemite. (Bear canisters are required for backpackers.) Whereas Tueeulala and Wapama Falls are both freefalling cataracts, Rancheria Falls is a series of rolling cascades pouring over polished granite.

To make the trip, follow the trail notes for Wapama Falls (see the previous listing), then continue onward, following the trail as it contours along the reservoir's edge. Much of the time you are high above the water, which allows fine views of Kolana Rock and its neighboring granite formations across the reservoir. The trail follows a gentle grade with many small ups and downs, gaining only 1,300 feet along its entire length. This trip is manageable even for beginning backpackers. Shoreline trout fishing in the reservoir can be good in spring and fall. And remember: Swimming in Hetch Hetchy is not allowed.

User Groups: Hikers and horses. No dogs or mountain bikes. No wheelchair facilities.
Permits: There is a $20 entrance fee per vehicle at Yosemite National Park, good for seven days. Free wilderness permits are required for overnight stays. They are available on a first-come, first-served basis up to one day in advance at the Yosemite Wilderness kiosk near your chosen trailhead, or farther in advance by mail, phone, or online for a $5 reservation fee per person.
Maps: A Hetch Hetchy map is available from Tom Harrison Maps. For topographic maps, ask the USGS for Lake Eleanor and Hetch Hetchy Reservoir.
Directions: From Groveland, drive east on Highway 120 for 22.5 miles to the Evergreen Road turnoff signed for Hetch Hetchy Reservoir on the left, a mile west of the Big Oak Flat entrance to Yosemite. Drive north on Evergreen Road for 7.4 miles and turn right on Hetch Hetchy Road. Drive 9.0 miles to the dam and trailhead.
Contact: Yosemite National Park, P.O. Box 577, Yosemite, CA 95389, 209/372-0200 or 209/372-0740 (permit reservations), www.nps.gov/yose or www.nps.gov/yose/wilderness (permit reservations).

15 LAUREL LAKE

14.6 mi / 1.0 or 2.0 days 3 9

in northwest Yosemite National Park

The Hetch Hetchy region of Yosemite is ideal for late-spring backpacking trips, with far fewer crowds than Yosemite Valley and far less snow than Tuolumne Meadows. And Laurel Lake is an ideal weekend destination in the region—just far enough to make you feel like you've gotten away, but close enough for a two-day trip (or even a one-day trip, if you're an ambitious day hiker). The trip begins at Hetch Hetchy Reservoir, and after an initial one-mile stretch along the lakeshore, you turn left and head up, up, and up on the Beehive Trail. The trail follows an old roadbed through a series of switchbacks, climbing 1,200 feet over 1.8 miles to the canyon rim and a junction with the Miguel Meadow Trail. Turn right and your trail meanders on a much easier grade through pine and incense-cedar forest. In another 2.4 miles, turn right and stroll for a mile to perennially soggy Beehive Meadow (water is found at a spring here, and a few campsites are available). From Beehive, take either of two trails to the lake (most people opt for the shorter trail on the left; both are signed). Beautiful Laurel Lake is surrounded by aspen groves, firs, and lodgepole pines, and its waters are a fair bet for rainbow trout fishing.

Those who want to add on another night or two to this trip can set out for even more scenic Lake Vernon the next day (4.5 miles distant). Whereas Laurel Lake is forested, Lake Vernon is surrounded by rock. From Lake Vernon, you can make a long loop back via Tiltill Valley, or if you are short on time, retrace your steps.
User Groups: Hikers and horses. No dogs or mountain bikes. No wheelchair facilities.
Permits: There is a $20 entrance fee per vehicle at Yosemite National Park, good for seven days. Free wilderness permits are required for overnight stays. They are available on a first-come, first-served basis up to one day in advance at the Yosemite Wilderness kiosk near your chosen trailhead, or farther in advance by mail, phone, or online for a $5 reservation fee per person.
Maps: A Hetch Hetchy map is available from Tom Harrison Maps. For topographic maps, ask the USGS for Lake Eleanor and Hetch Hetchy Reservoir.
Directions: From Groveland, drive east on Highway 120 for 22.5 miles to the Evergreen Road turnoff signed for Hetch Hetchy Reservoir (on the left), a mile west of the Big Oak Flat entrance to Yosemite. Drive north on Evergreen Road for 7.4 miles and turn right on Hetch Hetchy Road. Drive 16 miles to the dam and trailhead.

Contact: Yosemite National Park, P.O. Box 577, Yosemite, CA 95389, 209/372-0200 or 209/372-0740 (permit reservations), www.nps.gov/yose or www.nps.gov/yose/wilderness (permit reservations).

16 LOOKOUT POINT

2.6 mi / 1.2 hr — 2 — 7

in northwest Yosemite National Park

Check your calendar. Is it springtime? Are most of the high-country trails in Yosemite National Park still snowed in? Then it's time to take the easy jaunt to Lookout Point, where you can admire Hetch Hetchy Reservoir and its waterfalls from an unusual perspective, and count the plentiful wildflowers along the trail as you walk. The Lookout Point Trail begins by the Mather Ranger Station, on Hetch Hetchy Road. Begin hiking at the trail sign for Cottonwood and Smith Meadows and Hetch Hetchy (it's not signed for Lookout Point). Turn left at the first junction, then follow the trail as it roughly parallels Hetch Hetchy Road for 0.5 mile. You turn away from the road with a brief uphill stretch, then you enter a level, forested area that was severely burned in the wildfires of 1996. This is where the flowers bloom profusely in springtime. Look for a trail junction at one mile out, and bear left for Lookout Point, 0.3 mile away. The path gets rather faint in places, but rock cairns mark the way. Just head for the highest point you see atop a granite knob dotted with a few pines. You'll know you're at Lookout Point when you can see the west end of Hetch Hetchy Reservoir (including its immense dam) and two of Hetch Hetchy's beautiful waterfalls: Wapama and Tueeulala. If you visit much later than May or June, you may see only Wapama, the most robust of Hetch Hetchy's waterfalls. Tueeulala dries up early in the year. Although the vista is not perfect from Lookout Point—it would be better if it were 500 feet higher or if there weren't so many trees—this is still a fine spot to spread out a picnic. You probably won't have any company, either.

User Groups: Hikers and horses. No dogs or mountain bikes. No wheelchair facilities.

Permits: No permits are required. There is a $20 entrance fee per vehicle at Yosemite National Park, good for seven days.

Maps: A Hetch Hetchy map is available from Tom Harrison Maps. For a topographic map, ask the USGS for Lake Eleanor.

Directions: From Groveland, drive east on Highway 120 for 22.5 miles to the Evergreen Road turnoff (on the left), signed for Hetch Hetchy Reservoir (it's a mile west of the Big Oak Flat entrance to Yosemite). Drive north on Evergreen Road for 7.4 miles, then turn right on Hetch Hetchy Road. Drive 1.6 miles to the entrance kiosk by the Mather Ranger Station; the trail begins 100 yards past the entrance kiosk, just beyond the ranger station, on the right.

Contact: Yosemite National Park, P.O. Box 577, Yosemite, CA 95389, 209/372-0200, www.nps.gov/yose.

17 SMITH PEAK

15.0 mi / 1.0 or 2.0 days — 3 — 8

in northwest Yosemite National Park

If summit vistas strike your fancy, and it's too early in the summer for bagging some of Yosemite's highest peaks, head for the top of Smith Peak, elevation 7,751 feet. The route begins by the Mather Ranger Station. Follow the Lookout Point Trail for 1.2 miles, then turn right on the trail signed for Smith Meadow. You'll travel through a fire-scarred forest, then climb up a ridge to meet up with Cottonwood Creek at Lower Cottonwood Meadow, shortly followed by Upper Cottonwood Meadow. Smith Meadow lies another two miles farther, and just beyond it you'll find a junction of trails. The path on the right is another popular route to Smith

Peak leading from White Wolf Campground off Tioga Road. Campsites are found a short distance to the west at this junction. Get a good night's rest before bagging Smith Peak the next morning. (You've hiked six miles thus far; it's only 1.5 more to the summit.) The peak, like the nearby meadows, was named after a 1920s sheep rancher. It is covered with pockmarked granite boulders and offers a panoramic view of the Hetch Hetchy Reservoir and the Grand Canyon of the Tuolumne River, situated 4,000 dramatic feet below you. To the east, Yosemite's high country peaks are prominent, among them distinctive Mount Conness, Matterhorn Peak, and Mount Hoffman. Total elevation gain on this trip is 2,900 feet.

User Groups: Hikers only. No dogs, horses, or mountain bikes. No wheelchair facilities.

Permits: There is a $20 entrance fee per vehicle at Yosemite National Park, good for seven days. Free wilderness permits are required for overnight stays. They are available on a first-come, first-served basis up to one day in advance at the Yosemite Wilderness kiosk near your chosen trailhead, or farther in advance by mail, phone, or online for a $5 reservation fee per person.

Maps: A Hetch Hetchy map is available from Tom Harrison Maps. For topographic maps, ask the USGS for Hetch Hetchy Reservoir.

Directions: From Groveland, drive east on Highway 120 for 22.5 miles to the Evergreen Road turnoff (on the left), signed for Hetch Hetchy Reservoir (it's a mile west of the Big Oak Flat entrance to Yosemite). Drive north on Evergreen Road for 7.4 miles, then turn right on Hetch Hetchy Road. Drive 1.6 miles to the entrance kiosk by the Mather Ranger Station; the trail begins 100 yards past the entrance kiosk, just beyond the ranger station, on the right.

Contact: Yosemite National Park, P.O. Box 577, Yosemite, CA 95389, 209/372-0200 or 209/372-0740 (permit reservations), www.nps.gov/yose or www.nps.gov/yose/wilderness (permit reservations).

18 CARLON FALLS

3.8 mi / 2.5 hr — 2 — 8

on the border of Stanislaus National Forest and northwest Yosemite National Park

Carlon Falls is a pretty cascade on the South Fork Tuolumne River in the far western region of Yosemite. It is so far west that the trailhead is actually in Stanislaus National Forest, outside the park border. You hike about 100 feet and then you enter Yosemite National Park. This means there is no park entrance fee, no waiting in line at the entrance kiosk, and no crowds. The trailhead is across the river from Carlon Day-Use Area, a popular picnicking and fishing spot on the Tuolumne River. Follow the trail along the river's northern bank to reach the falls in just under two miles. The path is completely shaded, mostly level (except for one brief steep climb that skirts a landslide area), and fairly easy to follow, although it does require clambering over a few fallen trees. The waterfall drops in two tiers over wide granite ledges, and the riverbanks surrounding it are covered with big conifers and dense foliage. A bonus is that unlike most Yosemite waterfalls, Carlon Falls runs year-round. The waterfall's namesakes are Dan and Donna Carlon, who operated the popular Carl Inn from 1916 to 1930 near what is now the Carlon Day-Use Area. This trail is popular with swimmers and anglers in summer, but mostly deserted the rest of the year.

User Groups: Hikers only. No dogs, horses, or mountain bikes. No wheelchair facilities.

Permits: No permits are required. Parking and access are free.

Maps: For a topographic map, ask the USGS for Ackerson Mountain.

Directions: From Groveland, drive east on Highway 120 for 22.5 miles to the Evergreen Road turnoff, signed for Hetch Hetchy Reservoir, one mile west of the Big Oak Flat entrance to Yosemite. Follow Evergreen Road north for one mile to the far side of the bridge just past Carlon Day-Use Area. Park on the right at the closed-off dirt road on the north side of the bridge, signed only as No Camping. There is room for about five cars. Begin hiking on the closed road, heading upstream. The road narrows to single track after about 100 yards.

Contact: Yosemite National Park, P.O. Box 577, Yosemite, CA 95389, 209/372-0200, www.nps.gov/yose.

19 MERCED GROVE

3.0 mi / 1.5 hr 2 8

in western Yosemite National Park

There are three giant sequoia groves in Yosemite National Park—Merced, Tuolumne, and Mariposa. Because the Merced Grove is the smallest of the three groves and requires the longest walk to reach it, it is the least visited. Generally it only gets traffic from people who enter Yosemite at the Big Oak Flat entrance and drive by it on their way to Yosemite Valley. The hiking is on a closed-off dirt road that is ideal for snowshoeing in winter. The trail cuts a level course through a mixed conifer forest for the first 0.5 mile. Bear left at the only junction and head downhill through a canopy of white firs, incense cedars, ponderosa pines, and sugar pines. You reach the small sequoia grove at 1.5 miles; the first group of six trees will take your breath away. Continue another 100 yards past these beauties; the two largest sequoias of the Merced Grove are directly across from a handsome old log cabin. It was originally built as a retreat for the park superintendent but is no longer used. Retrace your steps from the cabin, hiking uphill for your return.

User Groups: Hikers only. No dogs, horses, or mountain bikes. No wheelchair facilities.

Permits: No permits are required. There is a $20 entrance fee per vehicle at Yosemite National Park, good for seven days.

Maps: A Yosemite National Park map is available from Tom Harrison Maps. For a topographic map, ask the USGS for Ackerson Mountain.

Directions: From Merced, drive 70 miles northeast on Highway 140 to Yosemite National Park. Follow the signs toward Yosemite Valley, entering through the Arch Rock entrance station. Continue 4.5 miles to the left turnoff for Highway 120, looping back out of the valley on Big Oak Flat Road. Continue straight on Big Oak Flat Road for 13.5 miles (past the Tioga Pass Road turnoff) to the Merced Grove parking area, on the left. If you enter Yosemite at the Big Oak Flat entrance station on Highway 120, drive 4.3 miles southeast to reach the trailhead, on your right.

Contact: Yosemite National Park, P.O. Box 577, Yosemite, CA 95389, 209/372-0200, www.nps.gov/yose.

20 TUOLUMNE GROVE

2.5 mi / 1.5 hr 2 8

in western Yosemite National Park

Up until 1993 you could drive right in to the Tuolumne Grove of Giant Sequoias, but now the road is closed off and visitors have to hike in. The grove is found on the old Big Oak Flat Road, a paved, six-mile historic road/trail that is open to bikes and hikers (although bikes are a rarity here). This is a popular destination, so arrive early in the morning to have the best chance at solitude. Leave your car at the parking lot near Crane Flat and hike downhill into the big trees. It's one mile to the first sequoias. The Tuolumne Grove's claim to fame is that it has one of the two remaining walk-through trees in Yosemite; this one is called the Dead Giant. It's a tall stump that was tunneled in 1878. Go ahead, walk through it—everybody does. At a small picnic area, a half-mile trail loops around the forest. Make sure you save some energy for the trip back uphill to the parking lot; the moderate grade ascends 550 feet. The old paved road continues downhill beyond the grove all the way to Hodgdon Meadow Campground. Some people hike the entire six-mile distance, then have someone pick them up at Hodgdon Meadow.

User Groups: Hikers and mountain bikes. No dogs or horses. No wheelchair facilities.
Permits: No permits are required. There is a $20 entrance fee per vehicle at Yosemite National Park, good for seven days.
Maps: A Yosemite National Park map is available from Tom Harrison Maps. For a topographic map, ask the USGS for Ackerson Mountain.
Directions: From Merced, drive 70 miles northeast on Highway 140 to Yosemite National Park. Follow the signs toward Yosemite Valley, entering through the Arch Rock entrance station. Continue 4.5 miles to the left turnoff for Highway 120, looping back out of the valley on Big Oak Flat Road. In 9.3 miles at Crane Flat, turn right on Tioga Pass Road, then drive 0.5 mile to the Tuolumne Grove parking lot, on the left, near Crane Flat. If you enter Yosemite at the Big Oak Flat entrance station on Highway 120, drive 7.7 miles southeast to the Crane Flat/Highway 120 East turnoff. Turn left and drive 0.5 mile to the Tuolumne Grove trailhead.
Contact: Yosemite National Park, P.O. Box 577, Yosemite, CA 95389, 209/372-0200, www.nps.gov/yose.

21 HARDEN LAKE

5.6 mi / 3.0 hr — 2 8

off Tioga Pass Road in Yosemite National Park

Harden Lake itself isn't a scene stealer—by late summer, it's not much more than a large pond, framed by a few stands of aspen trees on its northeast shore. But many people come here for another reason, and that's to see the wildflowers that bloom in a region known informally as Harden's Gardens, about a quarter-mile beyond the lake. July is the most dependable month for the wildflower bloom. Plus there are other rewards, including fine views of the Grand Canyon of the Tuolumne River just a half-mile north of the lake. Also, because of the small size of Harden Lake, it is dependably warm for swimming by mid-summer. The hike is simple enough. The trail follows White Wolf's gravel service road (a stretch of the original Tioga Road) past the campground entrance and across the Tuolumne River. Follow the obvious signs that point you through a few junctions to a blossom-filled marshy area. A few more steps and you're at the lake. If you haven't yet gotten your fill of the flower show, proceed a short distance farther and feast your eyes on Harden's Gardens.

User Groups: Hikers only. No dogs, horses, or mountain bikes. No wheelchair facilities.
Permits: No permits are required. There is a $20 entrance fee per vehicle at Yosemite National Park, good for seven days.
Maps: A Yosemite National Park map is available from Tom Harrison Maps. For a topographic map, ask the USGS for Tamarack Flat.
Directions: From Merced, drive 70 miles northeast on Highway 140 to Yosemite National Park. Follow the signs to Yosemite Valley, entering through the Arch Rock entrance station. Continue 4.5 miles to the left turnoff for Highway 120, looping back out of the valley on Big Oak Flat Road. In 9.3 miles at Crane Flat, turn right on Tioga Pass Road and drive 14 miles to the left turnoff for White Wolf. Turn left and drive one mile to the lodge and trailhead.
Contact: Yosemite National Park, P.O. Box 577, Yosemite, CA 95389, 209/372-0200, www.nps.gov/yose.

22 LUKENS LAKE

1.5-4.6 mi / 1.0-2.0 hr — 1 8

off Tioga Pass Road in Yosemite National Park

The Lukens Lake Trail is the perfect introductory lake hike for families in Yosemite National Park. A six-year-old could make the trip easily. A bonus is that the trailhead is on the western end of Tioga Road, so it's quickly reached from points in Yosemite Valley. The trail is 0.75 mile long, leading from Tioga Road up to a saddle, then dropping down to the lake. It winds through a dense red fir forest, filled with mammoth trees, then cuts across a corn lily–filled meadow to the edge of the shallow lake. If you time it right, you could see a spectacular wildflower show (thousands of pink shooting stars, among other flowers) in this meadow. Swimming in Lukens Lake is highly recommended; by midsummer, this is one of the warmest lakes in the park. If you want to take a longer trail to Lukens Lake, you can start from the trailhead at White Wolf Lodge and make a 4.6-mile round-trip.

User Groups: Hikers only. No dogs, horses, or mountain bikes. No wheelchair facilities.

Permits: No permits are required. There is a $20 entrance fee per vehicle at Yosemite National Park, good for seven days.

Maps: A Yosemite National Park map is available from Tom Harrison Maps. For a topographic map, ask the USGS for Tamarack Flat.

Directions: From Merced, drive 70 miles northeast on Highway 140 to Yosemite National Park. Follow the signs to Yosemite Valley, entering through the Arch Rock entrance station. Continue 4.5 miles to the left turnoff for Highway 120, looping back out of the valley on Big Oak Flat Road. In 9.3 miles at Crane Flat, turn right on Tioga Pass Road and drive 16.2 miles to the Lukens Lake trailhead parking area, on the south side of the road. The trail begins across the road.

Contact: Yosemite National Park, P.O. Box 577, Yosemite, CA 95389, 209/372-0200, www.nps.gov/yose.

23 TEN LAKES / GRANT LAKES

12.8 mi / 1.0 or 2.0 days 3 10

off Tioga Pass Road in Yosemite National Park

The Ten Lakes area is incredibly popular with backpackers, so get your wilderness permit early. Or get an early-morning start and make this trip as a day hike; just be prepared for some serious climbing and long miles. From the Ten Lakes trailhead at Tioga Pass Road (elevation 7,500 feet), the path climbs steadily for the first four miles. There's only one brutally steep stretch, which comes between miles four and five, after a pretty stroll around Half Moon Meadow. A series of tight switchbacks pulls you through a nasty 800-foot elevation gain to the top of a ridge and the Ten Lakes/Grant Lakes junction. From there, you make a choice. Turn right to reach Grant Lakes and head mostly downhill for a mile; or, to reach Ten Lakes, continue straight, soon heading steeply downhill for 1.4 miles. The Grant Lakes offer a little more solitude (good for day hikers), while the two larger of the Ten Lakes have the best campsites, with many trees along their shorelines offering protection from the wind. All of the lakes are sparkling, rock-bound beauties. Whether you go to Ten Lakes or Grant Lakes, don't miss taking a side trip to the rocky overlook above the Ten Lakes Basin. It's only 0.5 mile from the Ten Lakes/Grant Lakes junction (continue straight for Ten Lakes, then take the unsigned trail to the left of the main trail and head for the highest point). Four of the Ten Lakes are visible from this promontory, as well as a section of the Grand Canyon of the Tuolumne.

User Groups: Hikers only. No dogs, horses, or mountain bikes. No wheelchair facilities.

Permits: There is a $20 entrance fee per vehicle at Yosemite National Park, good for seven days. Free wilderness permits are required for overnight stays. They are available on a first-come, first-served basis up to one day in advance at the Yosemite Wilderness kiosk near your chosen trailhead or farther in advance by mail, phone, or online for a $5 reservation fee per person.

Maps: A Yosemite National Park map is available from Tom Harrison Maps. For topographic maps, ask the USGS for Yosemite Falls and Ten Lakes.

Directions: From Merced, drive 70 miles

northeast on Highway 140 to Yosemite National Park. Follow the signs toward Yosemite Valley, entering through the Arch Rock entrance station. Continue 4.5 miles to the left turnoff for Highway 120, looping back out of the valley on Big Oak Flat Road. In 9.3 miles at Crane Flat, turn right on Tioga Pass Road and drive 19.4 miles to the Yosemite Creek and Ten Lakes trailhead parking area, which is on the south side of the road. The trail begins on the north side of the road.

Contact: Yosemite National Park, P.O. Box 577, Yosemite, CA 95389, 209/372-0200 or 209/372-0740 (permit reservations), www.nps.gov/yose or www.nps.gov/yose/wilderness (permit reservations).

24 NORTH DOME

9.0 mi / 5.0 hr 3 9

off Tioga Pass Road in Yosemite National Park

There are those who say that climbing Half Dome is a bit of a disappointment, and not just because of the crowds. When you reach the top and check out the commanding view, the panorama of granite is not quite as awesome as you might expect, and that's because you can't see Half Dome—you're standing on it.

That's a dilemma that's easy to fix. If Half Dome is an absolute necessity in your view of Yosemite, climb North Dome instead, which offers a heart-stopping view of that big piece of granite. The route is not for the faint of heart, but when you are way up high looking down at Tenaya Canyon and across at Half Dome and Clouds Rest—well, you'll know why you came. The preferred route to North Dome begins at the Porcupine Creek trailhead on Tioga Pass Road, and has only a 1,500-foot gain to the summit. A dirt access road quickly brings you to a proper trail, signed as Porcupine Creek. Continue straight at two possible junctions near the 2.5-mile mark, heading due south for North Dome. After the third mile, your views begin to open up, providing fine vistas of North Dome and Half Dome and increasing your anticipation. At the trail junction at 4.5 miles, take the left spur for the final hike to North Dome's summit. Surprise—it's a downhill grade to reach it. Hope you brought a full supply of film or memory cards with you; the view from the top is sublime. Half Dome, just across the canyon, appears close enough to touch. Clouds Rest is a dramatic sight to the northeast. To the southwest, you can see cars crawling along the Yosemite Valley floor. On your return trip, consider taking the unsigned spur trail two miles from North Dome, at an obvious saddle. The spur leads a steep 0.25 mile to Indian Rock, the only natural arch on land in Yosemite. It's great fun to climb around on.

User Groups: Hikers only. No dogs, horses, or mountain bikes. No wheelchair facilities.

Permits: There is a $20 entrance fee per vehicle at Yosemite National Park, good for seven days. Free wilderness permits are required for overnight stays. They are available on a first-come, first-served basis up to one day in advance at the Yosemite Wilderness kiosk near your chosen trailhead or farther in advance by mail, phone, or online for a $5 reservation fee per person.

Maps: A Half Dome or Yosemite National Park map is available from Tom Harrison Maps. For a topographic map, ask the USGS for Yosemite Falls.

Directions: From Merced, drive 70 miles northeast on Highway 140 to Yosemite National Park. Follow the signs toward Yosemite Valley, entering through the Arch Rock entrance station. Continue 4.5 miles to the left turnoff for Highway 120, looping back out of the valley on Big Oak Flat Road. In 9.3 miles at Crane Flat, turn right on Tioga Pass Road and drive 24.5 miles to the Porcupine Creek trailhead parking area, on the right, a mile past Porcupine Flat Campground.

Contact: Yosemite National Park, P.O. Box 577, Yosemite, CA 95389, 209/372-0200 or 209/372-0740 (permit reservations), www.nps.gov/yose or www.nps.gov/yose/wilderness (permit reservations).

25 MAY LAKE AND MOUNT HOFFMAN

2.4-6.0 mi / 2.0-4.0 hr   1   9

off Tioga Pass Road in Yosemite National Park

BEST

Here's a hike that you can take the kids on—well, the first part, anyway. It's an easy 1.2 miles to May Lake, tucked in below 10,850-foot Mount Hoffman. The trail to the lake has a total elevation gain of only 400 feet, and better yet, it's downhill all the way home. Attaining the summit of Mount Hoffman, on the other hand, requires a challenging ascent, and is best left to more seasoned hikers. (Leave the kids at home if you are going to continue from the shores of May Lake to the top of Mount Hoffman.) The trail to both destinations begins at the Snow Flat trailhead (two miles off Tioga Pass Road), passes through a lodgepole pine forest, climbs up a granite-lined slope, then drops down to May Lake's southern shore. A High Sierra Camp is located here. Unfortunately, swimming is not allowed in May Lake, because it is the water source for the camp. Nonetheless, wandering along the scenic, granite-ringed shoreline is a pleasant way to spend the afternoon.

To turn this easy walk into a butt-kicker, follow the obvious use trail to the west, which leads around to the north side of May Lake. From the northwest shore, a fairly distinct use trail leads to Hoffman's summit. This is not an official park trail, and it requires scrambling skills and sure footing, especially as you near the top. It also requires good lungs and legs: You have to gain another 1,500 feet in about two miles. So why do it? The view from Mount Hoffman's ridgeline is first-class, with Half Dome, Clouds Rest, Tenaya Lake, and May Lake all in sight. Mount Hoffman is the exact geographical center of Yosemite National Park. The peak has two main summits; the one with the weather station on top is the highest. Explore the entire ridgeline, and visit both summits if you have the time; the view is surprisingly different.

User Groups: Hikers and horses. No dogs or mountain bikes. No wheelchair facilities.

Permits: No permits are required. There is a $20 entrance fee per vehicle at Yosemite National Park, good for seven days.

Maps: A Tuolumne Meadows or Yosemite National Park map is available from Tom Harrison Maps. For a topographic map, ask the USGS for Tenaya Lake.

Directions: From Merced, drive 70 miles northeast on Highway 140 to Yosemite National Park. Follow the signs toward Yosemite Valley, entering through the Arch Rock entrance station. Continue 4.5 miles to the left turnoff for Highway 120, looping back out of the valley on Big Oak Flat Road. In 9.3 miles at Crane Flat, turn right on Tioga Pass Road and drive 26.6 miles to the May Lake Road turnoff, on the left (near road marker T-21). Drive two miles to the trailhead parking lot.

Contact: Yosemite National Park, P.O. Box 577, Yosemite, CA 95389, 209/372-0200, www.nps.gov/yose.

26 CLOUDS REST

14.0 mi / 8.0 hr   3   10

off Tioga Pass Road in Yosemite National Park

BEST

Hiking to Clouds Rest is a trip that's as epic as climbing Half Dome, but with far fewer people elbowing you along the way. With a 2,300-foot climb and 14 miles to cover, it's not for those who are out of shape. The trail ascends steadily for the first four miles, descends steeply for 0.5 mile, then climbs again more moderately. Keep the faith—the first 2.5 miles from the trailhead are the toughest. The final summit ascent is a little dicey because of the terrifying dropoffs, but as with other Yosemite peaks, watch your footing on the granite slabs, and you'll be fine. Overall, the route is much safer than climbing Half Dome, because the final ascent is far more gradual, and there are no cables to maneuver. The view from the top of Clouds Rest—of

Tenaya Canyon, Half Dome, Yosemite Valley, Tenaya Lake, the Clark Range, and various peaks and ridges—will knock your socks off (hope you brought along an extra pair). Note that if this long hike has made you hot and sweaty, you can stop at the Sunrise Lakes for a swim on the way back—the first lake is only 0.25 mile from the Clouds Rest/Sunrise Trail junction.

User Groups: Hikers only. No dogs, horses, or mountain bikes. No wheelchair facilities.

Permits: No permits are required. There is a $20 entrance fee per vehicle at Yosemite National Park, good for seven days.

Maps: A Tuolumne Meadows or Yosemite National Park map is available from Tom Harrison Maps. For a topographic map, ask the USGS for Tenaya Lake.

Directions: From Merced, drive 70 miles northeast on Highway 140 to Yosemite National Park. Follow the signs toward Yosemite Valley, entering through the Arch Rock entrance station. Continue 4.5 miles to the left turnoff for Highway 120, looping back out of the valley on Big Oak Flat Road. In 9.3 miles at Crane Flat, turn right on Tioga Pass Road and drive 30.3 miles to the Sunrise Lakes trailhead, on the south side of the highway just west of Tenaya Lake.

Contact: Yosemite National Park, P.O. Box 577, Yosemite, CA 95389, 209/372-0200, www.nps.gov/yose.

27 SUNRISE LAKES

7.5 mi / 4.5 hr or 2.0 days 2 8

off Tioga Pass Road in Yosemite National Park

With all the people hiking to Clouds Rest, combined with all the people hiking to the Sunrise Lakes, the Sunrise trailhead can look like a mall parking lot on a Saturday. But don't be scared off; the hike to Sunrise Lakes is a great day hike or easy backpacking trip, especially during the week or off-season, with only a 1,000-foot elevation gain and a ton of stellar scenery, including great views of Clouds Rest at your back as you hike the final stretch to the lakes. You follow the trail as it climbs steeply above the edge of Tenaya Canyon. At 2.5 miles, turn left at the sign for the Sunrise High Sierra Camp. In about 10 minutes of easy walking, Lower Sunrise Lake shows up on the right, and the other lakes are shortly after it, on the left. The upper lake is the largest and by far the most popular; lots of folks like to swim and picnic there on warm summer days. Backpackers can pick a site here or continue onward for two more miles to the backpackers' camp or the High Sierra Camp, depending on where they've made their plans.

User Groups: Hikers only. No dogs, horses, or mountain bikes. No wheelchair facilities.

Permits: There is a $20 entrance fee per vehicle at Yosemite National Park, good for seven days. Free wilderness permits are required for overnight stays. They are available on a first-come, first-served basis up to one day in advance at the Yosemite Wilderness kiosk near your chosen trailhead or farther in advance by mail, phone, or online for a $5 reservation fee per person.

Maps: A Tuolumne Meadows or Yosemite National Park map is available from Tom Harrison Maps. For a topographic map, ask the USGS for Tenaya Lake.

Directions: From Merced, drive 70 miles northeast on Highway 140 to Yosemite National Park. Follow the signs toward Yosemite Valley, entering through the Arch Rock entrance station. Continue 4.5 miles to the left turnoff for Highway 120, looping back out of the valley on Big Oak Flat Road. In 9.3 miles at Crane Flat, turn right on Tioga Pass Road and drive 30.3 miles to the Sunrise Lakes trailhead, on the south side of the highway just west of Tenaya Lake.

Contact: Yosemite National Park, P.O. Box 577, Yosemite, CA 95389, 209/372-0200 or 209/372-0740 (permit reservations), www.nps.gov/yose or www.nps.gov/yose/wilderness (permit reservations).

28 TENAYA LAKE

2.0 mi / 1.0 hr 1 9

off Tioga Pass Road in Yosemite National Park

Lots of people drive east down Tioga Pass Road in a big rush to get to Tuolumne Meadows, but when they see giant Tenaya Lake right along the road, they stop short in their tire tracks. Luckily the 150-acre, sapphire-blue lake has a parking lot and picnic area at its east end, where you can leave your car and take a stroll down to the lake's edge. Although most people stop at the white-sand beach and picnic tables to watch the rock climbers on nearby Polly Dome, you can leave the crowds behind by strolling to the south side of the beach. Look for the trail there; it leads along the back side of Tenaya Lake, far from the road on the north side. When you get to the lake's west end, where the trail continues but the water views end, just turn around and walk back. It's a perfect, easy hike alongside one of the most beautiful lakes in Yosemite.

User Groups: Hikers only. No dogs, horses, or mountain bikes. No wheelchair facilities.

Permits: No permits are required. There is a $20 entrance fee per vehicle at Yosemite National Park, good for seven days.

Maps: A Tuolumne Meadows or Yosemite National Park map is available from Tom Harrison Maps. For a topographic map, ask the USGS for Tenaya Lake.

Directions: From Merced, drive 70 miles northeast on Highway 140 to Yosemite National Park. Follow the signs toward Yosemite Valley, entering through the Arch Rock entrance station. Continue 4.5 miles to the left turnoff for Highway 120, looping back out of the valley on Big Oak Flat Road. In 9.3 miles at Crane Flat, turn right on Tioga Pass Road and drive 31.7 miles to the eastern Tenaya Lake Picnic Area (another Tenaya Lake picnic area lies 0.5 mile west). The trail leads from the parking lot.

Contact: Yosemite National Park, P.O. Box 577, Yosemite, CA 95389, 209/372-0200, www.nps.gov/yose.

29 CATHEDRAL LAKES

7.4 mi / 4.0 hr or 2.0 days 3 10

near Tuolumne Meadows in Yosemite National Park

The Cathedral Lakes are a tremendously popular easy backpacking destination in Yosemite, but it's such a short hike to reach them that they also make a great day trip. Located on a 0.5-mile spur off John Muir Trail, the lakes are within a classic glacial cirque, tucked in below 10,840-foot Cathedral Peak. It's as scenic a spot as you'll find anywhere in Yosemite. Campsites are found close to the lakes, but you will need to secure your wilderness permit way in advance in order to spend the night. From the trail's start at Tioga Pass Road, you hike 3.2 miles on the John Muir Trail, with a 1,000-foot elevation gain. Much of the trail is shaded by lodgepole pines, but when the path breaks out of the trees, views of surrounding peaks (especially distinctive Cathedral Peak, which looks remarkably different from every angle) keep you oohing and ahhing the whole way. At 3.2 miles, turn right on the Cathedral Lake spur to reach the lower, larger lake in 0.5 mile. You'll follow the lake's inlet stream through a gorgeous meadow to the water's edge—then start snapping photographs like crazy. Many hikers stop here and go no farther, but it's a pity not to see Upper Cathedral Lake as well. To reach the upper lake, retrace your steps to John Muir Trail and continue another 0.5 mile. Fishing is often better in the upper lake, and the scenery is even more sublime.

User Groups: Hikers and horses. No dogs or mountain bikes. No wheelchair facilities.

Permits: There is a $20 entrance fee per vehicle at Yosemite National Park, good for seven days. Free wilderness permits are required for overnight stays. They are available on a first-come, first-served basis up to one day in advance at the Yosemite Wilderness kiosk near your chosen trailhead or farther in advance by mail, phone, or online for a $5 reservation fee per person.

HIKING

Maps: A Tuolumne Meadows or Yosemite National Park map is available from Tom Harrison Maps. For a topographic map, ask the USGS for Tenaya Lake.

Directions: From Merced, drive 70 miles northeast on Highway 140 to Yosemite National Park. Follow the signs toward Yosemite Valley, entering through the Arch Rock entrance station. Continue 4.5 miles to the left turnoff for Highway 120, looping back out of the valley on Big Oak Flat Road. In 9.3 miles at Crane Flat, turn right on Tioga Pass Road and drive 37.4 miles to the Cathedral Lakes trailhead, on the right, by Tuolumne Meadows. Park your car in the pullouts on either side of Tioga Pass Road near the trailhead; there is no formal parking lot.

Contact: Yosemite National Park, P.O. Box 577, Yosemite, CA 95389, 209/372-0200 or 209/372-0740 (permit reservations), www.nps.gov/yose or www.nps.gov/yose/wilderness (permit reservations).

30 VOGELSANG LOOP

19.0 mi / 3.0 or 4.0 days 3 9

near Tuolumne Meadows in Yosemite National Park

Although this loop is popular with hikers staying at the Vogelsang High Sierra Camp, backpackers who plan early can get a wilderness permit for their own self-designed trip. The traditional route is to head out on the western side of the loop along Rafferty Creek, then take a short spur and spend the night at Vogelsang Lake, which is without question the most visually dramatic spot seen on this trip. It's flanked by Fletcher Peak, a steep and rugged wall of glacier-carved granite. Few trees can grow in this sparse, high-alpine environment. The next day, you rejoin the loop and continue eastward to Evelyn Lake, another favorite camping spot. When it's time to return, you hike down to Lyell Fork, a 2,000-foot descent that takes a few hours, then meet up with John Muir Trail and follow it north through lush green and gorgeous Lyell Canyon, back to the trailhead at Tuolumne Meadows. The trailhead is at 8,600 feet—plenty high to start—and for the most part, the trail undulates along, never gaining or losing more than 2,000 feet.

User Groups: Hikers and horses. No dogs or mountain bikes. No wheelchair facilities.

Permits: There is a $20 entrance fee per vehicle at Yosemite National Park, good for seven days. Free wilderness permits are required for overnight stays. They are available on a first-come, first-served basis up to one day in advance at the Yosemite Wilderness kiosk near your chosen trailhead or farther in advance by mail, phone, or online for a $5 reservation fee per person.

Maps: A Tuolumne Meadows or Yosemite National Park map is available from Tom Harrison Maps. For a topographic map, ask the USGS for Vogelsang Peak.

Directions: From Merced, drive 70 miles northeast on Highway 140 to Yosemite National Park. Follow the signs toward Yosemite Valley, entering through the Arch Rock entrance station. Continue 4.5 miles to the left turnoff for Highway 120, looping back out of the valley on Big Oak Flat Road. In 9.3 miles at Crane Flat, turn right on Tioga Pass Road and drive 39.5 miles to the Tuolumne Lodge and Wilderness Permits turnoff, on the right. Turn right and drive 0.4 mile toward Tuolumne Lodge. Park in the lot on the left signed for Dog Lake and John Muir Trail. The trail begins across the road from the parking lot. Additional parking is available in the Wilderness Permit parking lot, at the turnoff from Tioga Pass Road.

Contact: Yosemite National Park, P.O. Box 577, Yosemite, CA 95389, 209/372-0200 or 209/372-0740 (permit reservations), www.nps.gov/yose or www.nps.gov/yose/wilderness (permit reservations).

31 LOWER GAYLOR LAKE

8.0 mi / 4.0 hr 2 9

near Tioga Pass in Yosemite National Park

This mellow, pretty hike starts on John Muir Trail near Tuolumne Lodge, then heads east along the south side of the Dana Fork of the Tuolumne River. After two miles, the trail crosses the river and Tioga Pass Road, and heads uphill through a dense lodgepole pine forest to Lower Gaylor Lake, elevation 10,049 feet. The shallow lake is a deep turquoise color and is surrounded by a grassy alpine meadow. From its edge, you gain wide vistas of the peaks in the Tuolumne Meadows area. This is classic high-country beauty at its finest. Note that if you wish to get to the Middle and Upper Gaylor Lakes from the lower lake, you have to go cross-country. An easier way is to drive to the Tioga Pass trailhead and follow the trail notes in this chapter for the *Middle and Upper Gaylor Lakes* hike. Elevation at this trailhead is 9,250 feet; the total gain is about 800 feet to Lower Gaylor Lake, a gentle climb the whole way.

User Groups: Hikers only. No dogs, horses, or mountain bikes. No wheelchair facilities.

Permits: No permits are required. There is a $20 entrance fee per vehicle at Yosemite National Park, good for seven days.

Maps: A Tuolumne Meadows or Yosemite National Park map is available from Tom Harrison Maps. For topographic maps, ask the USGS for Vogelsang Peak and Tioga Pass.

Directions: From Merced, drive 70 miles northeast on Highway 140 to Yosemite National Park. Follow the signs toward Yosemite Valley, entering through the Arch Rock entrance station. Continue 4.5 miles to the left turnoff for Highway 120, looping back out of the valley on Big Oak Flat Road. In 9.3 miles at Crane Flat, turn right on Tioga Pass Road and drive 39.5 miles to the Tuolumne Lodge and Wilderness Permits turnoff, on the right. Turn right and drive 0.4 mile toward Tuolumne Lodge, then park in the lot on the left signed for Dog Lake and John Muir Trail. The trail begins across the road from the parking lot. Additional parking is available in the Wilderness Permit parking lot, at the turnoff from Tioga Pass Road.

Contact: Yosemite National Park, P.O. Box 577, Yosemite, CA 95389, 209/372-0200, www.nps.gov/yose.

32 ELIZABETH LAKE

4.5 mi / 2.5 hr 2 8

near Tuolumne Meadows in Yosemite National Park

Starting at the trailhead elevation of 8,600 feet, you have a mere 850-foot elevation gain over 2.25 miles to get to lovely Elizabeth Lake, set in a basin at the foot of distinctive Unicorn Peak. It's a day hike that is attainable for almost anybody, and you can bet that every camper at Tuolumne Meadows Campground makes the trip at some point during their vacation. For noncampers, the trailhead is a bit tricky to find—it's tucked into the back of Tuolumne Meadows Campground, across from the group camp restrooms. Once you locate it, be prepared to climb steeply for the first mile, then breathe easier when the trail levels out. Fortunately the route is mostly shaded by a dense grove of lodgepole pines. Upon reaching its shore, you'll see that Elizabeth Lake is a gorgeous body of alpine water. Some visitors swim or fish here; others try to climb Unicorn Peak (10,900 feet); most are happy to sit near the lake's edge and admire the views of the sculpted peak and its neighbors in the Cathedral Range.

User Groups: Hikers only. No dogs, horses, or mountain bikes. No wheelchair facilities.

Permits: No permits are required. There is a $20 entrance fee per vehicle at Yosemite National Park, good for seven days.

Maps: A Tuolumne Meadows or Yosemite National Park map is available from Tom Harrison Maps. For a topographic map, ask the USGS for Vogelsang Peak.

Directions: From Merced, drive 70 miles northeast on Highway 140 to Yosemite National Park. Follow the signs toward Yosemite Valley, entering through the Arch Rock entrance station. Continue 4.5 miles to the left turnoff for Highway 120, looping back out of the valley on Big Oak Flat Road. In 9.3 miles at Crane Flat, turn right on Tioga Pass Road and drive 39 miles to the Tuolumne Meadows Campground. Turn right and follow the signs through the main camp to the group camp. The trail begins across from the group camp restrooms, near group site No. B49.

Contact: Yosemite National Park, P.O. Box 577, Yosemite, CA 95389, 209/372-0200, www.nps.gov/yose.

33 LYELL CANYON

6.0 mi / 3.0 hr — 1 — 9

near Tuolumne Meadows in Yosemite National Park

This hike is one of the easiest in the Yosemite high country, and since it starts out beautiful and stays that way, you can hike it as long or as short as you like. The total trail length is eight miles one-way, paralleling the Lyell Fork of the Tuolumne River on the Pacific Crest Trail/John Muir Trail. But most people just head out for two or three miles, carrying their fishing rods, and then turn back. To reach the Lyell Fork, you must first cross the Dana Fork on a footbridge less than 0.5 mile from the parking lot. Then after 0.5 mile, you cross the Lyell Fork on a second footbridge, and head left along the river's south side. A third bridge takes you across Rafferty Creek and into Lyell Canyon. If you like looking at gorgeous meadows and a meandering river, this is your hike. Small trout are plentiful. A bonus is that backpacking sites are located three to four miles out on the trail, so if you get a wilderness permit, you can linger for a few days in paradise.

User Groups: Hikers and horses. No dogs or mountain bikes. No wheelchair facilities.

Permits: No permits are required. There is a $20 entrance fee per vehicle at Yosemite National Park, good for seven days.

Maps: A Tuolumne Meadows or Yosemite National Park map is available from Tom Harrison Maps. For a topographic map, ask the USGS for Vogelsang Peak.

Directions: From Merced, drive 70 miles northeast on Highway 140 to Yosemite National Park. Follow the signs toward Yosemite Valley, entering through the Arch Rock entrance station. Continue 4.5 miles to the left turnoff for Highway 120, looping back out of the valley on Big Oak Flat Road. In 9.3 miles at Crane Flat, turn right on Tioga Pass Road and drive 39.5 miles to the Tuolumne Lodge and Wilderness Permits turnoff, on the right. Turn right and drive 0.4 mile toward Tuolumne Lodge; park in the lot on the left signed for Dog Lake and John Muir Trail. The John Muir Trail begins across the road from the parking lot. Additional parking is available in the Wilderness Permit parking lot, at the turnoff from Tioga Pass Road.

Contact: Yosemite National Park, P.O. Box 577, Yosemite, CA 95389, 209/372-0200, www.nps.gov/yose.

34 YOUNG LAKES LOOP

14.6 mi / 1.0 or 2.0 days — 3 — 10

near Tuolumne Meadows in Yosemite National Park

Starting from the Lembert Dome parking lot at 8,600 feet in elevation, the Young Lakes Loop is a classic Yosemite trip that works equally well as a short backpacking trip or a long day hike. The destination is a series of lakes set in a deep and wide glacial cirque—the kind of awesome scenery that sticks in your mind months later, when you're sitting at a desk somewhere staring at your computer screen. The trip starts with a walk down the wide dirt road that leads to Soda Spring. Pick up the trail near Parson's Lodge that leads to

Glen Aulin, and follow it through lodgepole pines for 1.8 miles until you see the right turnoff for Young Lakes. Follow Young Lakes Trail for 3.5 more miles, climbing steadily. At 5.5 miles out, you'll see the return leg of your loop leading off to the right (signed for Dog Lake). You'll continue straight for another 1.5 miles to Lower Young Lake and a stunning view of Ragged Peak, Mount Conness, and White Mountain. Two more lakes are accessible within a mile to the east. If you have the energy, don't miss the third, upper lake, the most visually stunning of them all, perched in a high meadow at 10,218 feet in elevation. When you're ready to head home, retrace your steps to the junction, and take the eastern (left) fork, returning via Dog Lake and Lembert Dome. Be forewarned: If you loop back this way, it won't be an all-downhill cruise, but the scenery makes the additional climbing worthwhile. If you're exhausted from your trip to the lakes, skip the loop and return the way you came—it's downhill all the way.

User Groups: Hikers and horses. No dogs or mountain bikes. No wheelchair facilities.

Permits: There is a $20 entrance fee per vehicle at Yosemite National Park, good for seven days. Free wilderness permits are required for overnight stays. They are available on a first-come, first-served basis up to one day in advance at the Yosemite Wilderness kiosk near your chosen trailhead or farther in advance by mail, phone, or online for a $5 reservation fee per person.

Maps: A Yosemite National Park map is available from Tom Harrison Maps. For topographic maps, ask the USGS for Tioga Pass and Falls Ridge.

Directions: From Merced, drive 70 miles northeast on Highway 140 to Yosemite National Park. Follow the signs toward Yosemite Valley, entering through the Arch Rock entrance station. Continue 4.5 miles to the left turnoff for Highway 120, looping back out of the valley on Big Oak Flat Road. In 9.3 miles at Crane Flat, turn right on Tioga Pass Road and drive 39 miles to the Lembert Dome/Soda Spring/Dog Lake/Glen Aulin trailhead parking, on the left. Begin hiking on the western edge of the parking lot, where there is a gated dirt road signed for Soda Spring.

Contact: Yosemite National Park, P.O. Box 577, Yosemite, CA 95389, 209/372-0200 or 209/372-0740 (permit reservations), www.nps.gov/yose or www.nps.gov/yose/wilderness (permit reservations).

35 WATERWHEEL FALLS

16.0 mi / 1.0 or 2.0 days 3 10

near Tuolumne Meadows in Yosemite National Park

BEST

This hike could be called the Epic Waterfall Trip. If you hike the entire route, you'll see so many waterfalls and so much water along the way that you'll have enough memories to get you through a 10-year drought. Arrange for a wilderness permit in advance, or reserve a stay at the Glen Aulin High Sierra Camp, so that you can divide the 16 miles over two or more days. If you're in good enough shape, you can do the trip in one day, because the trail is nearly level for the first four miles (a 400-foot elevation loss), then descends more steeply over the next four miles (a 1,500-foot elevation loss). Unfortunately, all the climbing must be done on the way home, so you must reserve your energy and have plenty of food and water (or at least a purifying device so you can filter water from the river).

Follow the trail notes for Glen Aulin and Tuolumne Falls (see next listing) for the first four miles of trail; then continue downstream past Glen Aulin Camp, alternating between stretches of stunning flower- and aspen-lined meadows and stark granite slabs. Waterwheel Falls is only three miles from the camp, and two other major cascades, California and LeConte, are along the way. To see all three falls, make sure you take each spur trail you see that leads to the river; none of the waterfalls is apparent from the main trail. Other hikers will stop you on the trail to ask if you know where the waterfalls are. Whereas all three falls are long whitewater cascades, Waterwheel is considered Yosemite's most unusual-looking waterfall because it has sections of churning water that dip into deep holes in the granite, then shoot out with such velocity that they double back on themselves. When the river level is high, they actually appear to circle around like waterwheels.

User Groups: Hikers and horses. No dogs or mountain bikes. No wheelchair facilities.

Permits: There is a $20 entrance fee per vehicle at Yosemite National Park, good for seven days. Free wilderness permits are required for overnight stays. They are available on a first-come, first-served basis up to one day in advance at the Yosemite Wilderness kiosk near your chosen trailhead or farther in advance by mail, phone, or online for a $5 reservation fee per person.

Maps: A Tuolumne Meadows or Yosemite National Park map is available from Tom Harrison Maps. For topographic maps, ask the USGS for Tioga Pass and Falls Ridge.

Directions: From Merced, drive 70 miles northeast on Highway 140 to Yosemite National Park. Follow the signs toward Yosemite Valley, entering through the Arch Rock entrance station. Continue 4.5 miles to the left turnoff for Highway 120, looping back out of the valley on Big Oak Flat Road. In 9.3 miles at Crane Flat, turn right on Tioga Pass Road and drive 39 miles to the Lembert Dome/Soda Spring/Dog Lake/Glen Aulin trailhead parking, on the left. Begin hiking on the western edge of the parking lot, where there is a gated dirt road signed for Soda Spring.

Contact: Yosemite National Park, P.O. Box 577, Yosemite, CA 95389, 209/372-0200 or 209/372-0740 (permit reservations), www.nps.gov/yose or www.nps.gov/yose/wilderness (permit reservations).

36 GLEN AULIN AND TUOLUMNE FALLS

9.0 mi / 5.0 hr 2 9

near Tuolumne Meadows in Yosemite National Park

BEST

Those who aren't up for the Epic Waterfall Trip to Waterwheel Falls (see previous listing) can take this trip instead and maybe even sneak in a good meal at the Glen Aulin High Sierra Camp. To stay in the camp, you must reserve a spot far in advance, but you can often purchase a hot meal just by showing up. Tuolumne Falls drop right by the High Sierra Camp, and reaching the waterfall requires only a 4.5-mile walk with a 400-foot elevation loss. The return climb is easy, with most of the ascent being in the first mile as you head up and over the various cascades of Tuolumne Falls on granite stairs. Follow the dirt road from the Lembert Dome parking lot toward Soda Spring. When you near Parson's Lodge, veer right on the signed trail to Glen Aulin. You'll walk through lodgepole pine forest, then move closer to the Tuolumne River and get incredible views of Cathedral and Unicorn Peaks, as well as Fairview Dome. After three miles, you'll cross the Tuolumne on a footbridge, and in another 0.25 mile, you'll reach the first stunning drop of Tuolumne Falls, a 100-foot, churning freefall. Keep descending past more cascades to the base of the falls, where another footbridge leads back across the river and to Glen Aulin. Pick a spot downstream beside a river pool or near the bridge at the base of the waterfall, have a seat, and ponder the exquisite beauty of this place.

User Groups: Hikers and horses. No dogs or mountain bikes. No wheelchair facilities.

Permits: No permits are required. There is a $20 entrance fee per vehicle at Yosemite National Park, good for seven days.

Maps: A Tuolumne Meadows or Yosemite National Park map is available from Tom Harrison Maps. For topographic maps, ask the USGS for Tioga Pass and Falls Ridge.

Directions: From Merced, drive 70 miles northeast on Highway 140 to Yosemite National Park. Follow the signs toward Yosemite Valley, entering through the Arch Rock entrance station. Continue 4.5 miles to the left turnoff for Highway 120, looping back out of the valley on Big Oak Flat Road. In 9.3 miles at Crane Flat, turn right on Tioga Pass Road and drive 39 miles to the Lembert Dome/Soda Spring/Dog Lake/Glen Aulin trailhead parking, on the left. Begin hiking on the western edge of the parking lot, where there is a gated dirt road signed for Soda Spring.

Contact: Yosemite National Park, P.O. Box 577, Yosemite, CA 95389, 209/372-0200, www.nps.gov/yose.

37 LEMBERT DOME

2.8 mi / 1.5 hr 3 10

near Tuolumne Meadows in Yosemite National Park

Lembert Dome is a *roche moutonnée* (a French geologic term that means it looks something like a sheep). We never see the resemblance, but we did feel like a couple of mountain goats when we climbed Lembert Dome, elevation 9,450 feet. From the parking area at the base, you can see rock climbers practicing their stuff on the steep side of the dome, but luckily the hiker's trail heads around to the more-sloped back side. You can walk right up the granite—no ropes necessary. The Dog Lake and Lembert Dome Trail winds its way steeply around to the dome's north side (see next listing); from there, pick any route along the granite that looks manageable. When you reach the top of the dome, you know that you've accomplished something. The view from its highest point—of Tuolumne Meadows and surrounding peaks and domes—is more than worth the effort.

User Groups: Hikers only. No dogs, horses, or mountain bikes. No wheelchair facilities.

Permits: No permits are required. There is a $20 entrance fee per vehicle at Yosemite National Park, good for seven days.

Maps: A Tuolumne Meadows or Yosemite National Park map is available from Tom Harrison Maps. For a topographic map, ask the USGS for Tioga Pass.

Directions: From Merced, drive 70 miles northeast on Highway 140 to Yosemite National Park. Follow the signs toward Yosemite Valley, entering through the Arch Rock entrance station. Continue 4.5 miles to the left turnoff for Highway 120, looping back out of the valley on Big Oak Flat Road. In 9.3 miles at Crane Flat, turn right on Tioga Pass Road and drive 39 miles to the Lembert Dome/Soda Spring/Dog Lake/Glen Aulin trailhead parking, on the left. Begin hiking on the trail near the restrooms.

Contact: Yosemite National Park, P.O. Box 577, Yosemite, CA 95389, 209/372-0200, www.nps.gov/yose.

38 DOG LAKE

3.4 mi / 2.0 hr 2 8

near Tuolumne Meadows in Yosemite National Park

Dog Lake is an easy-to-reach destination from Tuolumne Meadows, a perfect place for a family to spend an afternoon in the high country. The hike begins near the base of Lembert Dome, then heads through a gorgeous meadow that offers views of snowy Cathedral and Unicorn Peaks. The trail traverses a granite slab, then splits off from the path to Lembert Dome and starts to climb quite steeply through a lodgepole pine and fir forest. When you reach an intersection with Young Lakes Trail, you're only 0.25 mile from Dog Lake. The lake is a delight, although with its grassy shoreline, it is often plagued with mosquitoes (don't forget the bug spray). Set at 9,170 feet in elevation, it is wide, shallow, and deep blue. The colorful peaks to the east are

Mount Dana and Mount Gibbs. You can hike around Dog Lake's perimeter if you please, take a swim in late summer, or just sit by the peaceful shoreline and relax.

User Groups: Hikers and horses. No dogs or mountain bikes. No wheelchair facilities.

Permits: No permits are required. There is a $20 entrance fee per vehicle at Yosemite National Park, good for seven days.

Maps: A Tuolumne Meadows or Yosemite National Park map is available from Tom Harrison Maps. For a topographic map, ask the USGS for Tioga Pass.

Directions: From Merced, drive 70 miles northeast on Highway 140 to Yosemite National Park. Follow the signs toward Yosemite Valley, entering through the Arch Rock entrance station. Continue 4.5 miles to the left turnoff for Highway 120, looping back out of the valley on Big Oak Flat Road. In 9.3 miles at Crane Flat, turn right on Tioga Pass Road and drive 39 miles to the Lembert Dome/Soda Spring/Dog Lake/Glen Aulin trailhead parking, on the left. Begin hiking on the trail near the restrooms.

Contact: Yosemite National Park, P.O. Box 577, Yosemite, CA 95389, 209/372-0200, www.nps.gov/yose.

39 TUOLUMNE MEADOWS TO SONORA PASS (PCT)

77.0 mi one-way / 8.0 days 5 10

from Tuolumne Meadows on Highway 120 north to Sonora Pass on Highway 108

This is a spectacular week-plus backpack trip that follows a section of the Pacific Crest Trail (PCT). The beauty of this region's deep canyons, glacial-cut peaks, verdant meadows, and abundant wildlife make it a hiker's paradise.

From Tuolumne Meadows, the trail starts out deceptively easy as it follows the Tuolumne River toward the Grand Canyon of the Tuolumne River. It heads gently downhill to Glen Aulin, where you get a great view of Tuolumne Falls. When you cross the bridge at the base of the falls and head up-canyon, you'll leave the day hikers behind. In the next three days, you'll go up one canyon and down the next, one after another, with breathtaking views and long, demanding climbs. Highlights include Matterhorn Canyon (many deer, trout, and views), Benson Lake (the largest white-sand beach in the Sierra Nevada), Dorothy Lake (panoramic views to the north), and many pristine, high-country meadows. The incredible clouds of mosquitoes at the Wilmer Lake area during early summer can be a major annoyance.

When you leave Yosemite and enter Humboldt-Toiyabe National Forest, the landscape changes quickly from glacial-cut granite to volcanic rock. The trail drops past several pretty lakes and into a river drainage, and at points can be difficult to follow. In a few areas, you may be surprised to meet up with grazing cows, especially from midsummer onward. You'll make a long, slow, climb up toward Leavitt Pass, set just below 10,800-foot Leavitt Peak. This landscape is entirely above tree line, in gray, stark country. At Leavitt Pass, the wind whistles by at high speed almost year-round. The final drop down to Sonora Pass is a one-hour descent that seems to wind all over the mountain. When you reach Highway 108, cross the road and walk about 100 yards west to a large day-use parking area. That's where your car shuttle should be waiting for you.

User Groups: Hikers and horses. No dogs or mountain bikes. No wheelchair facilities.

Permits: A wilderness permit is required for traveling through various wilderness and special-use areas the trail traverses. Contact either the Wilderness Office of the National Park Service or the Stanislaus National Forest for a permit that is good for the length of your trip. There is a $20 entrance fee per vehicle at Yosemite National Park, good for seven days.

Maps: For topographic maps, ask the USGS for Pickel Meadow, Tower Peak, Piute Mountain, Matterhorn Peak, Dunderberg Peak,

Vogelsang Peak, Tioga Pass, Falls Ridge, Buckeye Ridge, and Sonora Pass.

Directions: From Merced, drive 70 miles northeast on Highway 140 to Yosemite National Park. Follow the signs toward Yosemite Valley, entering through the Arch Rock entrance station. Continue 4.5 miles to the left turnoff for Highway 120, looping back out of the valley on Big Oak Flat Road. In 9.3 miles at Crane Flat, turn right on Tioga Pass Road and drive 39 miles to the Lembert Dome/Soda Spring/Dog Lake/Glen Aulin trailhead parking, on the left. Begin hiking on the western edge of the parking lot, where there is a gated dirt road signed for Soda Spring.

Contact: Yosemite National Park, P.O. Box 577, Yosemite, CA 95389, 209/372-0200, www.nps.gov/yose; Stanislaus National Forest, Calaveras Ranger Station, P.O. Box 500, Hathaway Pines, CA 95233, 209/795-1381, www.fs.fed.us/r5/stanislaus.

40 TUOLUMNE MEADOWS TO YOSEMITE VALLEY (JMT)

22.0 mi one-way / 2.0 days 5 10

from Tuolumne Meadows Campground in Yosemite

The first glimpses of Yosemite Valley will seem like a privileged view into heaven after having hiked the entire John Muir Trail (JMT) from Mount Whitney. For hikers making only this 22-mile section, the rewards can seem just as profound. The trip starts at Tuolumne Meadows, where backpackers can buy a good cheap breakfast, obtain wilderness permits, and camp in a special area set aside for JMT hikers. When you take your first steps away from Tuolumne Meadows, resist the urge to rush to the finish line in order to close out a historic expedition. Instead, relax and enjoy the downhill glide, always remembering that you are in sacred land. Compared to the rest of the JMT, this leg will come with far less strain, starting with a 3.1-mile tromp past Cathedral Lakes and requiring a 0.5-mile walk on a signed cutoff trail. If you can time it right, this area can make a great layover camp, with deep, emerald-green water and Cathedral Peak in the background. Beyond Cathedral Lakes, the trail makes a relatively short 500-foot climb over Cathedral Pass, skirts Tresidder Peak, and then descends through pristine Long Meadow. After passing Sunrise Trail Camp, a decent layover, the trail picks up little Sunrise Creek and follows it all the way down to Little Yosemite Valley, a popular trail camp. From Cathedral Lakes, it's 14.5 miles to the junction of Half Dome Trail, and another 2.2 miles to Little Yosemite.

For JMT hikers, making the climb to the top of Half Dome is a must, even though it often means putting up with a parade of people and even delays waiting for the line to move at the climbing cable. The Half Dome climb starts with a steep hike for the first mile, followed by steep switchbacks across granite on good trail to the foot of Half Dome's back wall. Here you'll find climbing cables to aid your final 300-foot ascent, and as you go, you'll discover breathtaking views of Tenaya Canyon. This is considered one of the world's glamour hikes, and while it turns hiking into an act of faith, we have seen eight-year-olds and 70-year-olds make the cable climb. By the way, if you take on Half Dome, be certain to have two canteens of water per person. Adding the Half Dome side trip to the rest of the JMT leg will add a round-trip of 5.2 miles to your hike. Because of its proximity to Half Dome, the Little Yosemite Valley Trail Camp is often crowded. From here, though, it's an easy five-mile hike downhill to Yosemite Valley. Again, try not to speed through to the end, even though it's an easy tromp downhill all the way. The magic is in the moment.

From Little Yosemite, the JMT is routed along the Merced River. In a mile, you'll reach Liberty Cap, and shortly later, Nevada Fall. Then down, down you go, with the trail often turning to giant granite steps, down past Emerald Pool and then to Vernal Fall, another spectacular waterfall. Since Vernal Fall is just 1.7 miles from the end of the trail, you'll start meeting lots of day hikers coming from the other direction, many gasping for breath as they make the uphill climb out of Yosemite Valley. Many will ask how far you've hiked; some may even want to take your photograph. It may feel a bit inane, but, hey, enjoy it. After all, you just finished John Muir Trail, the greatest hiking trail in the world.

User Groups: Hikers and horses. No dogs or mountain bikes. No wheelchair facilities.

Permits: A wilderness permit is required for traveling through various wilderness and special-use areas that the trail traverses. Contact the Wilderness Office of the National Park Service for a permit that is good for the length of your trip. There is a $20 entrance fee per vehicle at Yosemite National Park, good for seven days.

Maps: A John Muir Trail Map Pack is available from Tom Harrison Maps. For topographic maps, ask the USGS for Vogelsang Peak, Half Dome, Yosemite Falls, and Tenaya Peak.

Directions: From Merced, drive 70 miles northeast on Highway 140 to Yosemite National Park. Follow the signs toward Yosemite Valley, entering through the Arch Rock entrance station. Continue 4.5 miles to the left turnoff for Highway 120, looping back out of the valley on Big Oak Flat Road. In 9.3 miles at Crane Flat, turn right on Tioga Pass Road and drive 39.5 miles to the Tuolumne Lodge and Wilderness Permits turnoff, on the right. Turn right and drive 0.4 mile toward Tuolumne Lodge; park in the lot on the left signed for Dog Lake and John Muir Trail. The John Muir Trail begins across the road from the parking lot. Additional parking is available in the Wilderness Permit parking lot, at the turnoff from Tioga Road.

Contact: Yosemite National Park, P.O. Box 577, Yosemite, CA 95389, 209/372-0200 or 209/372-0740 (permit reservations), www.nps.gov/yose or www.nps.gov/yose/wilderness (permit reservations).

41 MONO PASS

8.4 mi / 4.5 hr 2 9

near Tioga Pass in Yosemite National Park

With an elevation gain of only 900 feet spread out over four miles, you'll hardly even notice you're climbing on the route to Mono Pass. That's if you're acclimated, of course, because you start out at 9,700 feet, where the air is mighty thin. The Mono Pass Trail begins in a mix of lodgepole pines and grassy meadows, then crosses the Dana Fork of the Tuolumne River, which is an easy boulder-hop by midsummer. (Earlier in the season you may need to find a log to cross.) The trail soon meets up with Parker Pass Creek and parallels it for most of the trip. As you proceed, you'll gain great views of Mount Gibbs, Mount Dana, and the Kuna Crest. At a trail junction at 2.0 miles, bear left and start to climb more noticeably. When you reach the Mono Pass sign at 3.8 miles, take the right spur trail (unsigned). It leads 0.3 mile to a cluster of four 19th-century mining cabins, which have been beautifully restored. It's fascinating to explore the small cabins and surrounding mine ruins and consider the hard life of those who lived and worked here. Then, heading back to the main trail, continue another 0.5 mile beyond the sign marking Mono Pass for the best views of the trip. From a granite promontory above a water-filled tarn, you can see far down Bloody Canyon to Mono Lake and the surrounding desert.

User Groups: Hikers and horses. No dogs or mountain bikes. No wheelchair facilities.

Permits: No permits are required. There is a $20 entrance fee per vehicle at Yosemite National Park, good for seven days.

Maps: A Yosemite High Country map is available from Tom Harrison Maps. For a topographic map, ask the USGS for Tioga Pass.

Directions: From Merced, drive 70 miles northeast on Highway 140 to Yosemite National Park. Follow the signs toward Yosemite Valley, entering through the Arch Rock entrance station. Continue 4.5 miles to the left turnoff for Highway 120, looping back out of the valley on Big Oak Flat Road. In 9.3 miles at Crane Flat, turn right on Tioga Pass Road and drive 44.5 miles to the Mono Pass trailhead on the right, 1.5 miles west of Tioga Pass.

Contact: Yosemite National Park, P.O. Box 577, Yosemite, CA 95389, 209/372-0200, www.nps.gov/yose.

42 SPILLWAY & HELEN LAKES

9.0 mi / 5.0 hr 3 9

near Tioga Pass in Yosemite National Park

Another option on the Mono Pass Trail (see trail notes for previous hike) is to take the right fork at 2.0 miles and head for Spillway Lake, a wide, shallow lake that is only 1.6 miles from this junction, and then large Helen Lake, which is reached by some easy cross-country travel. It seems like a completely different trip than the aforementioned hike to Mono Pass. The highlights here are two high alpine lakes that epitomize the beauty of the Yosemite high country. Backpackers rarely travel to these lakes, so day hikers are likely to have more solitude here. The views of the Kuna Crest and the high alpine meadow surrounding the upper reaches of Parker Pass Creek will take your breath away. A maintained trail travels to Spillway Lake, and from its southeast edge you simply follow Helen Lake's outlet creek uphill to the shores of Helen Lake. Helen Lake is set at 11,000 feet in elevation, and it's as lovely as any high mountain lake can be. Total elevation gain to see both lakes is only 1,300 feet.

User Groups: Hikers only. No dogs, horses, or mountain bikes. No wheelchair facilities.

Permits: No permits are required. There is a $20 entrance fee per vehicle at Yosemite National Park, good for seven days.

Maps: A Yosemite High Country map is available from Tom Harrison Maps. For a topographic map, ask the USGS for Tioga Pass.

Directions: From Merced, drive 70 miles northeast on Highway 140 to Yosemite National Park. Follow the signs toward Yosemite Valley, entering through the Arch Rock entrance station. Continue 4.5 miles to the left turnoff for Highway 120, looping back out of the valley on Big Oak Flat Road. In 9.3 miles at Crane Flat, turn right on Tioga Pass Road and drive 44.5 miles to the Mono Pass trailhead on the right, 1.5 miles west of Tioga Pass.

Contact: Yosemite National Park, P.O. Box 577, Yosemite, CA 95389, 209/372-0200, www.nps.gov/yose.

43 MIDDLE AND UPPER GAYLOR LAKES

4.0 mi / 2.5 hr 3 9

near Tioga Pass in Yosemite National Park

Middle and Upper Gaylor Lakes are deservedly popular destinations, because of the short distance required to reach them and their great opportunities for trout fishing. Oh yeah, and then there is the amazing high-alpine scenery. Starting near Tioga Pass (at nearly 10,000 feet), the trail climbs a steep ridge and then drops down to Middle Gaylor Lake. Although it's only one mile of ascent, it's a high-elevation butt-kicker that causes many to beg for mercy. From the middle lake, you can follow the creek gently uphill to the east for another mile to reach smaller Upper Gaylor Lake. Be sure to take the trail around its north side and uphill for a few hundred yards to the site of the Great Sierra Mine and the remains of an old stone cabin. The Great Sierra Mine turned out to be not so great—no silver ore was ever refined, and the mine was eventually abandoned. The hauntingly beautiful glacial scenery is what remains. Total elevation gain on the hike to Upper Gaylor Lake is about 1,000 feet, and it's worth every step. If you want to see more of this sublime lake basin, the twin Granite Lakes lie about 0.75 mile northwest of Middle

Gaylor Lake. Although there is no formal trail, it's an easy cross-country ramble to see the Granite Lakes as well, which are tucked in below a massive granite cirque.

User Groups: Hikers only. No dogs, horses, or mountain bikes. No wheelchair facilities.

Permits: No permits are required. There is a $20 entrance fee per vehicle at Yosemite National Park, good for seven days.

Maps: A Yosemite High Country map is available from Tom Harrison Maps. For a topographic map, ask the USGS for Tioga Pass.

Directions: From Merced, drive miles northeast on Highway 140 to Yosemite National Park. Follow the signs toward Yosemite Valley, entering through the Arch Rock entrance station. Continue 4.5 miles to the left turnoff for Highway 120, looping back out of the valley on Big Oak Flat Road. In 9.3 miles at Crane Flat, turn right on Tioga Pass Road and drive 46 miles to the parking lot just west of the Tioga Pass entrance station, on the north side of Tioga Pass Road.

Contact: Yosemite National Park, P.O. Box 577, Yosemite, CA 95389, 209/372-0200, www.nps.gov/yose.

44 MOUNT DANA

6.0 mi / 4.0 hr 4 9

near Tioga Pass in Yosemite National Park

BEST

Mount Dana is a grueling hike. Yet many hikers make the trip every summer, perhaps as some sort of rite of passage to affirm that the long winter has truly ended in the high country. The path to the 13,053-foot summit requires a 3,100-foot elevation gain condensed into a mere three miles. To make matters more difficult, there is no maintained trail, only a series of informal "use" trails created by generations of hearty Yosemite hikers who have traveled the route. To join their ranks, leave your car at the Gaylor Lakes trailhead by the Tioga Pass entrance station, then cross the road and hike southeast on the unsigned but obvious trail that begins just a few feet from the park entrance kiosk. The path starts with a pleasant ramble through Dana Meadows, then enters a dense lodgepole pine forest. Soon the grade becomes more intense, but this first stretch of climbing is highlighted by a spectacular wildflower show that usually peaks in late July. Lupine, larkspur, Indian paintbrush, senecia—they're all here, in all their glory. The climbing gets tougher on the second mile of the hike, but stick with it and soon you've climbed above 11,000 feet, and now you're above tree line. The path keeps ascending to the 11,600-foot mark, where a giant trail cairn marks a large, rock-covered plateau. This is a good place to rest and do a check on your physical and mental state. Although the summit may look close from here, you still have a long, hard way to go. Two fairly obvious paths head uphill from this point; if you're feeling comfortable with the altitude, pick either one and continue onward, zigzagging your way up the shale-covered slope. In the final mile you must gain 1,500 feet, and to say it is slow going would be a major understatement. There's no shade, often a fierce wind, plenty of loose rock underfoot, and the breathtakingly thin air of high altitude. With what may seem like your last breath, you finally reach the summit, where you are witness to one of the finest views in the Sierra. Your field of vision encompasses Mono Lake, Ellery and Saddlebag Lakes, Glacier Canyon, Tuolumne Meadows, Lembert Dome, and an untold wealth of high peaks. Bring a map and identify all you can survey, or forget the map and just take in the majesty of it all.

A few tips for making the ascent safely: First, wait until mid-July or later to make the trip, as Mount Dana can be snow-covered long into the summer. Second, get an early start in the morning so you have no chance of encountering afternoon thunderstorms. Third, carry (and drink) as much water as you can. Fourth, wear good sunglasses and sun protection at this high elevation. And lastly, pace yourself to give your body a chance to adjust to the 13,000-foot altitude.

User Groups: Hikers only. No dogs, horses, or mountain bikes. No wheelchair facilities.
Permits: No permits are required. There is a $20 entrance fee per vehicle at Yosemite National Park, good for seven days.
Maps: A Yosemite High Country map is available from Tom Harrison Maps. For a topographic map, ask the USGS for Tioga Pass.
Directions: From Merced, drive miles northeast on Highway 140 to Yosemite National Park. Follow the signs toward Yosemite Valley, entering through the Arch Rock entrance station. Continue 4.5 miles to the left turnoff for Highway 120, looping back out of the valley on Big Oak Flat Road. In 9.3 miles at Crane Flat, turn right on Tioga Pass Road and drive 46 miles to the parking lot just west of the Tioga Pass entrance station, on the north side of Tioga Pass Road. The trail begins on the south side of Tioga Pass Road; begin hiking on the unsigned trail across from the park entrance kiosk.
Contact: Yosemite National Park, P.O. Box 577, Yosemite, CA 95389, 209/372-0200, www.nps.gov/yose.

45 BENNETTVILLE

2.6 mi / 2.0 hr — 2 — 10

in Inyo National Forest just east of Tioga Pass

This first-class high-country hike is suitable for even the most novice hikers, and is sure to spark your imagination. The remote high-country region of Bennettville was the site of a 19th-century silver mining community. Although the town thrived only from 1882 to 1884, it was the primary reason for the construction of the Tioga Pass Road from the west. The original road, called the Great Sierra Wagon Road, was built by the Great Sierra Consolidated Silver Company in anticipation of the riches they would make from the mines at Bennettville and nearby. Ultimately, no valuable minerals were ever extracted, and the company went broke in record time. A mostly level trail leads to the two buildings that remain from Bennettville's heyday: the assay office and barn/bunkhouse. An open mine tunnel lined with railcar tracks can also be seen, as well as some rusting mining equipment. Much of the machinery and supplies for this mine was hauled here from the May Lundy Mine over Dore Pass. Men and animals carried several tons of equipment on their backs and on sleds, sometimes through driving snowstorms in the middle of winter at this 10,000-foot elevation.

You can extend this hike by following the trail alongside Mine Creek 0.5 mile uphill from the mine buildings to small Shell Lake, followed by three more shallow lakes in the next mile or so: Mine, Fantail, and finally Spuller. More mine sites can be seen along the way. The high-country landscape here is a mix of open meadows, delicate high-alpine wildflowers, and wind-sculpted whitebark pines. The scenery is as good as you'll find anywhere, and you'll want to return to this area again and again.

User Groups: Hikers, horses, dogs, and mountain bikes. No wheelchair facilities.
Permits: No permits are required. Parking and access are free.
Maps: A Yosemite High Country map is available from Tom Harrison Maps. An Inyo National Forest map is available from the U.S. Forest Service. For a topographic map, ask the USGS for Tioga Pass.
Directions: From Merced, drive 70 miles northeast on Highway 140 to Yosemite National Park. Follow the signs toward Yosemite Valley, entering through the Arch Rock entrance station. Continue 4.5 miles to the left turnoff for Highway 120, looping back out of the valley on Big Oak Flat Road. In 9.3 miles at Crane Flat, turn right on Tioga Pass Road and drive 48 miles (you'll exit the park) to the Saddlebag Lake turnoff, on the left, two miles east of Tioga Pass. Turn left, and then left again immediately, to enter Junction Campground. The trail begins at the campground entrance.

Contact: Inyo National Forest, Mono Basin Scenic Area Visitors Center, P.O. Box 429, Lee Vining, CA 93541, 760/647-3044, www.fs.fed.us/r5/inyo.

46 GARDISKY LAKE

2.0 mi / 2.0 hr 3 8

in Inyo National Forest just east of Tioga Pass

How can a two-mile round-trip hike be rated a 3 for difficulty? It can because it goes straight up, gaining 700 feet in just one mile, with not nearly enough switchbacks. Although the trail distance is short, the trailhead is set at 9,800 feet, which means you need to be well acclimated to pant your way through that steep of a grade. The trip offers many rewards, though, including many fewer people than at nearby Saddlebag Lake and a stellar high-alpine setting. Once you huff and puff your way to the ridgetop, you have a nearly level 0.25-mile stroll through a fragile alpine meadow to reach the lake, a shallow body of water, surrounded by high-alpine meadows. That 11,513-foot mountain you see as you climb (ahead and to your right) is Tioga Peak; from the southwest edge of Gardisky Lake it's a short but steep tromp to its windy summit (this will add a couple extra miles and 1,000 feet of extra elevation gain to your day). White Mountain and Mount Conness are also prominent, both over 12,000 feet.

User Groups: Hikers, horses, dogs, and mountain bikes. No wheelchair facilities.

Permits: No permits are required. Parking and access are free.

Maps: A Yosemite High Country map is available from Tom Harrison Maps. An Inyo National Forest map is available from the U.S. Forest Service. For a topographic map, ask the USGS for Tioga Pass.

Directions: From Merced, drive 70 miles northeast on Highway 140 to Yosemite National Park. Follow the signs toward Yosemite Valley, entering through the Arch Rock entrance station. Continue 4.5 miles to the left turnoff for Highway 120, looping back out of the valley on Big Oak Flat Road. In 9.3 miles at Crane Flat, turn right on Tioga Pass Road and drive 48 miles (you'll exit the park) to the Saddlebag Lake turnoff, on the left, two miles east of Tioga Pass. Turn left and go 1.3 miles to the trailhead parking area, on the west side of the road before you reach Saddlebag Lake. The trail begins across the road.

Contact: Inyo National Forest, Mono Basin Scenic Area Visitors Center, P.O. Box 429, Lee Vining, CA 93541, 760/647-3044, www.fs.fed.us/r5/inyo.

47 SLATE CREEK TRAIL TO GREEN TREBLE LAKE

4.5 mi / 2.0 hr 2 9

in Inyo National Forest just east of Tioga Pass

One of the most beautiful and serene campgrounds in the High Sierra, Sawmill Walk-In Camp is accessed by a quarter-mile walk from its parking area. A wide trail continues through and past the campsites into Hall Research Natural Area, a specially protected region of Inyo National Forest that is open to day hikers only (no backpacking). The trail leads one mile to Timberline Station, an old research station built in 1929. From here you can cross Slate Creek and hike another mile to Green Treble Lake at the headwaters of Slate Creek. Where two forks of the creek join, about 0.5 mile beyond Timberline Station, follow the south fork (left) another 0.5 mile to Green Treble Lake. This is a remarkably level hike at 10,000-plus feet in elevation—pristine high country that is only accessible a few months each year. You know you are in a special place when you are here.

User Groups: Hikers, horses, dogs, and mountain bikes. No wheelchair facilities.

Permits: No permits are required. Parking and access are free.

Maps: A Yosemite High Country map is available from Tom Harrison Maps. An Inyo National Forest map is available from the U.S. Forest Service. For a topographic map, ask the USGS for Tioga Pass.

Directions: From Merced, drive 70 miles northeast on Highway 140 to Yosemite National Park. Follow the signs toward Yosemite Valley, entering through the Arch Rock entrance station. Continue 4.5 miles to the left turnoff for Highway 120, looping back out of the valley on Big Oak Flat Road. In 9.3 miles at Crane Flat, turn right on Tioga Pass Road and drive 48 miles (you'll exit the park) to the Saddlebag Lake turnoff, on the left, two miles east of Tioga Pass. Turn left and drive 1.5 miles north on Saddlebag Lake Road to Sawmill Campground's parking area on the left.

Contact: Inyo National Forest, Mono Basin Scenic Area Visitors Center, P.O. Box 429, Lee Vining, CA 93541, 760/647-3044, www.fs.fed.us/r5/inyo.

48 SADDLEBAG LAKE LOOP

3.6-8.4 mi / 2.0-4.0 hr 2 9

in Inyo National Forest just east of Tioga Pass

Starting from the resort buildings at the south end of 10,087-foot Saddlebag Lake, you can design a wonderfully scenic hiking trip into the 20 Lakes Basin of any length that suits your time and energy. A benefit of hiking here is that you can cut off some miles by taking the boat taxi across the lake, rather than hiking along its lakeshore. A one-way ride on the boat taxi will cut 1.5 miles off your mileage; a round-trip cuts off three miles. Unfortunately, this high-country region is so beautiful, so easy to access, and so close to Yosemite that on summer weekends, it can be as crowded as the most popular trails in the park. A great time to hike here is a few weeks after Labor Day, when the vacation crowds have dispersed.

To hike alongside Saddlebag Lake instead of riding in the boat taxi, follow the trail on either the lake's east or west side. The east side trail is more scenic; the west side trail is shorter. If you just want to make a short 3.6-mile loop, hike out on one trail and back on the other, but be sure to take the short left spur at Saddlebag's northwest edge to Greenstone Lake, which is backed by photogenic North Peak. If you want to hike farther, you can continue past Greenstone Lake to Wasco Lake and then on to deep, stark Steelhead Lake (three miles out if you start on the west side trail). Several more lakes lie beyond, including Shamrock, Helen, and Odell. If you hike the entire loop and visit all six lakes that lie immediately beyond Saddlebag, you'll have an 8.4-mile day (or a 5.4-mile day, if you take the boat taxi round-trip). No matter how far you go, you'll be awed by the incredible high-country scenery—a blend of blue sky, granite, water, and hardy whitebark pines.

User Groups: Hikers and dogs. No horses or mountain bikes. No wheelchair facilities.

Permits: No permits are required. Parking and access are free.

Maps: A Yosemite High Country map is available from Tom Harrison Maps. An Inyo National Forest map is available from the U.S. Forest Service. For a topographic map, ask the USGS for Tioga Pass.

Directions: From Merced, drive 70 miles northeast on Highway 140 to Yosemite National Park. Follow the signs toward Yosemite Valley, entering through the Arch Rock entrance station. Continue 4.5 miles to the left turnoff for Highway 120, looping back out of the valley on Big Oak Flat Road. In 9.3 miles at Crane Flat, turn right on Tioga Pass Road and drive 48 miles (you'll exit the park) to the Saddlebag Lake turnoff, on the left, two miles east of Tioga Pass. Turn left and drive another 2.7 miles to the trailhead parking area.

Contact: Inyo National Forest, Mono Basin Scenic Area Visitors Center, P.O. Box 429, Lee Vining, CA 93541, 760/647-3044, www.fs.fed.us/r5/inyo.

49 GIBBS LAKE

5.4 mi / 2.5 hr or 2.0 days 3 9

west of Lee Vining on the northern boundary of the Ansel Adams Wilderness

The 2.7-mile hike from Upper Horse Meadow to Gibbs Lake is a great day hike that sees surprisingly few people. Since the trailhead isn't located at a lake or some other attractive setting, nobody gets here by accident. The trail starts at Upper Horse Meadow (elevation 8,000 feet), and climbs up Gibbs Canyon to Gibbs Lake, at 9,530 feet. That's about a 1,500-foot climb, but unfortunately the first stretch goes straight uphill on an old dirt road with nary a switchback. Once you get through that grunt of an ascent, the rest of the route is on a much mellower grade as it travels alongside Gibbs Creek. The trail ends at Gibbs Lake, a lovely glacial cirque that is backed by bare granite and fronted by conifers. Are you feeling ambitious? If you study the lake's back wall for a few minutes, it will soon become obvious that there is another, higher lake in this drainage. If you are sure-footed and have plenty of energy, you can pick out your route and go take a look at that lake. Although Gibbs Lake is pretty, the higher Kidney Lake (10,388 feet) is a stunner. It will take you about 40 minutes of challenging cross-country scrambling to get from Gibbs to Kidney; you'll gain almost 900 feet in less than a mile. Just pick your route carefully and go slow. Kidney Lake is indeed kidney-shaped, and it is flanked by the Dana Plateau on one side and Mount Gibbs (12,773 feet) on the other.

Special Note: While not required, high-clearance vehicles are a good idea on Forest Road 1N16.

User Groups: Hikers, horses, and dogs. No mountain bikes beyond the wilderness boundary. No wheelchair facilities.

Permits: A free wilderness permit is required for overnight stays and is available from the Mono Basin Scenic Area Visitors Center. Quotas are in effect from May 1 to November 1; for this period, permits are available in advance for a $5 reservation fee per person.

Maps: Mono Lake and Mammoth High Country maps are available from Tom Harrison Maps. An Inyo National Forest or Ansel Adams Wilderness map is available from the U.S. Forest Service. For a topographic map, ask the USGS for Lee Vining.

Directions: From Lee Vining, drive 1.3 miles south on U.S. 395 and turn west on unsigned Forest Road 1N16 (look for the sign indicating Horse Meadow). Drive 3.4 miles past Upper Horse Meadow to the trailhead at the end of the road. A high-clearance vehicle is recommended.

Contact: Inyo National Forest, Mono Basin Scenic Area Visitors Center, P.O. Box 429, Lee Vining, CA 93541, 760/647-3044, www.fs.fed.us/r5/inyo.

50 MONO LAKE SOUTH TUFA TRAIL

1.0 mi / 0.5 hr 1 9

at the southern end of Mono Lake in Mono Lake Tufa State Reserve

BEST

The strange and remarkable tufa towers at Mono Lake create one of the most extraordinary landscapes in California. The terrain resembles a moonscape, but a strangely beautiful one. The area is extremely popular with photographers, especially at sunset. This short loop trail is the best way to get a good look at the tufa formations, which are formed when calcium-rich underwater springs are released from the lake bottom and then combine with Mono Lake's saline water, forming calcium carbonate. The trail leads through sagebrush plains to the southern shore of the lake, where the tufas rest like old, untouched earth castles. Some of them poke out of the lake surface; others are high and dry on land. Mono Lake itself is vast (covering 60 square miles) and is estimated to be more than 700,000 years old, making it one of the oldest lakes in North America. The lake's basin has become one of the world's most prolific stopover points for gulls, grebes, plovers, and phalaropes during their annual southbound flights. That's because the alkaline properties of the water create prime habitat for brine shrimp (an ideal food for these birds), and the lake's two large islands provide isolation from predators. Eighty-five percent of the California gull population was born at Mono Lake.

User Groups: Hikers, horses, dogs, and wheelchairs. No mountain bikes.

Permits: No permits are required. A $3 entrance fee is charged per adult. Youth ages 17 and under are free.

Maps: A Mono Lake map is available from Tom Harrison Maps. For topographic maps, ask the USGS for Lee Vining and Mono Mills.

Directions: From Lee Vining, drive five miles south on U.S. 395 and turn east on Highway 120 (signed for Mono Lake South Tufa). Drive 4.7 miles, then turn left and drive one mile on a dirt road to the parking area.

Contact: Mono Lake Tufa State Reserve, 760/647-6331, www.parks.ca.gov; Inyo National Forest, Mono Basin Scenic Area Visitors Center, P.O. Box 429, Lee Vining, CA 93541, 760/647-3044, www.fs.fed.us/r5/inyo.

51 BLOODY CANYON TRAIL

8.2 mi / 5.0 hr 4 9

southwest of Lee Vining at the northeastern boundary of the Ansel Adams Wilderness

Lower Sardine Lake is a jewel cradled in a high glacial cirque at 9,888 feet, the kind of lake that makes the Ansel Adams Wilderness one of the most treasured places in the world. Beyond the first easy mile, this hike is tough and steep. Much of the trail is a historic Native American trading route, used by the Indians of the Mono Basin to visit the Indians of the Yosemite high country. The first mile to Walker Lake is an easy downhill cruise, dropping 600 feet in elevation. Walker Lake is a popular destination for anglers and has a small private resort on its eastern shore. From the aspen-lined western edge of the lake, you head up Bloody Canyon, climbing nearly 2,000 feet in about three miles. The hike parallels Walker Creek, requiring two stream crossings on the way up to Lower Sardine Lake. For anyone who is either out of shape or not acclimated to the altitude, the climb can be rough going. As you near Lower Sardine Lake, the sight of a beautiful waterfall (the lake's outlet stream) will help to spur you on. When you reach the lake at elevation 9,888 feet, you'll find it is surrounded by rocky cliffs on three sides and provides great views of the Mono Basin to the east. Backpackers can continue hiking up and over Mono Pass and into Yosemite National Park's backcountry, but to do so, they face still more of a climb. Remember that if you are entering the national park, dogs are not allowed.

User Groups: Hikers, horses, and dogs. No mountain bikes beyond the wilderness boundary. No wheelchair facilities.

Permits: A free wilderness permit is required for overnight stays and is available from the Mono Basin Scenic Area Visitors Center. Quotas are in effect from May 1 to November 1; for this period, permits are available in advance for a $5 reservation fee per person.

Maps: Yosemite High Country and Mammoth High Country maps are available from Tom Harrison Maps. An Inyo National Forest or Ansel Adams Wilderness map is available from the U.S. Forest Service. For topographic maps, ask the USGS for Mount Dana and Koip Peak.

Directions: From Lee Vining, drive five miles south on U.S. 395 to the north end of the June Lake Loop (Highway 158). Turn right and drive 1.3 miles on Highway 158, then turn right on a dirt road signed for Parker and Walker Lakes. Drive 0.5 mile to a junction, turn right, then drive 0.3 mile and turn right again, following the signs for Walker Lake. Drive 0.5 mile and turn left on Forest Road 1S23. Drive 2.7 miles to the Walker Lake trailhead.

Contact: Inyo National Forest, Mono Basin Scenic Area Visitors Center, P.O. Box 429, Lee Vining, CA 93541, 760/647-3044, www.fs.fed.us/r5/inyo.

52 PARKER LAKE TRAIL

3.8 mi / 2.0 hr 2 8

in the Ansel Adams Wilderness west of Grant Lake

BEST

This short trail has a whole lot going for it. The beauty of Parker Lake and towering Parker Peak just might knock your boots off—or at least your socks. Although the nearby June Lake Loop gets a lot of vacation traffic, this trailhead is obscure enough that most visitors pass it by. And get this: The 1.9-mile-long trail has an elevation gain of only a little more than 300 feet. Beginning at an elevation of 8,000 feet above Parker Creek, the trail follows the creek upstream on a fairly mellow grade before arriving at Parker Lake, at 8,318 feet. As you ascend, the landscape transitions from sagebrush plains into a mixed forest alongside Parker Creek, complete with quaking aspens and mammoth-sized Jeffrey pines. Look behind you once in a while, and you'll catch great views of Mono Lake. In short order, you will suddenly emerge from the forest onto the lake's shore. Parker Lake is a deep blue beauty backed by 12,861-foot Parker Peak—a great place to have a picnic or just sit and enjoy the scenery. The only downer on this trip is that many of the largest aspen trees have had their trunks carved with initials by idiots. Let's hope they didn't know any better. Please teach your children never, ever to carve into trees.

User Groups: Hikers, dogs, and horses. No mountain bikes. No wheelchair facilities.

Permits: A free wilderness permit is required for overnight stays and is available from the Mono Basin Scenic Area Visitors Center. Quotas are in effect from May 1 to November 1; for this period, permits are available in advance for a $5 reservation fee per person.

Maps: A Mammoth High Country map is available from Tom Harrison Maps. An Inyo National Forest or Ansel Adams Wilderness map is available from the U.S. Forest Service. For topographic maps, ask the USGS for Mount Dana and Koip Peak.

Directions: From Lee Vining, drive five miles south on U.S. 395 to the north end of the June Lake Loop (Highway 158). Turn right and drive 1.3 miles on Highway 158, then turn right on a dirt road signed for Parker and Walker Lakes. Drive 2.4 miles to the Parker Lake trailhead, at the end of the road.

Contact: Inyo National Forest, Mono Basin Scenic Area Visitors Center, P.O. Box 429, Lee Vining, CA 93541, 760/647-3044, www.fs.fed.us/r5/inyo.

53 RUSH CREEK TRAIL

19.2 mi / 3.0 days 4 10

on the eastern boundary of the Ansel Adams Wilderness west of June Lake

Some places will never change, and people are drawn to them because they provide a sense of permanence that can't be found anywhere else. That is how it is at the Rush Creek headwaters. Created from drops of melting snow near the Sierra crest (at 10,500 feet), this stream runs downhill for miles, rolling into the forest like a swirling, emerald-green fountain. Even a short visit requires a long drive to the trailhead, followed by a demanding backpacking trek. In the process, hikers contend with a 10-mile climb out, ice-cold stream crossings, and the possibility of afternoon thunderstorms, in which lightning bolts and thunderclaps rattle off the canyon rims.

The trailhead lies near the pack station at Silver Lake (elevation 7,215 feet). After departing Silver Lake, follow the trail as it climbs above the June Lake Loop and soon starts to parallel Lower Rush Creek. You'll cross over an old tramway system that was used for the hydroelectric projects found in this watershed. Near the dam at Agnew Lake, you reach a trail junction, 2.2 miles from your start. The left fork heads up to Agnew Pass, but continue straight and in one more mile you arrive at beautiful Gem Lake (9,058 feet) and then Waugh Lake (9,442 feet), at the seven-mile point. Many visitors never venture farther than these lakes, simply stopping to camp, swim, or fish. But upstream of Waugh Lake is where you find the Rush Creek headwaters, along with the flawless symmetry of the untouched high country. Getting there requires a total climb of 3,300 feet over the course of 9.6 miles, but it is one of the prettiest streams anywhere and is well worth the effort.

Note that because this trail begins near the Silver Lake pack station, it is heavily used by horses. On some days, the amount of horse "evidence" on this trail can be a real downer, especially in the first few miles.

User Groups: Hikers, dogs, and horses. No mountain bikes. No wheelchair facilities.

Permits: A free wilderness permit is required for overnight stays and is available from the Mono Basin Scenic Area Visitors Center. Quotas are in effect from May 1 to November 1; for this period, permits are available in advance for a $5 reservation fee per person.

Maps: A Mammoth High Country map is available from Tom Harrison Maps. An Inyo National Forest or Ansel Adams Wilderness map is available from the U.S. Forest Service. For topographic maps, ask the USGS for June Lake and Koip Peak.

Directions: From Lee Vining, drive about 11 miles south on U.S. 395 to June Lake Junction. Turn right on Highway 158/June Lake Road and drive 7.2 miles to the Rush Creek trailhead, between Silver Lake Resort and the pack station.

Contact: Inyo National Forest, Mono Basin Scenic Area Visitors Center, P.O. Box 429, Lee Vining, CA 93541, 760/647-3044, www.fs.fed.us/r5/inyo.

54 YOST LAKE

4.8–9.4 mi / 2.5 hr–1.0 day 3 7

in Inyo National Forest near June Lake

Yost Lake is a small glacial lake hidden at 9,000 feet on the June Mountain slopes. Many people visit the June Lake area for years without even knowing Yost exists. But it is up here, tucked away and accessible only to those willing to hike. From the trailhead (7,800 feet) at June Lake, Yost Meadows Trail rises very steeply in the first mile, climbing 800 feet—a real butt-kicker for many. That discourages many from going farther—after all, it is 4.7 miles to the lake. But after that first grunt of a climb, the trail gets much easier, contouring across the mountain slopes. It rises gradually to the headwaters of Yost Creek and then drops into the small basin that guards the lake.

A shorter option is to begin at the Yost Creek/Fern Lake trailhead, making it a much shorter, 4.8-mile round-trip. It is just as pretty, but it has a more difficult grade and can be slippery for those not wearing heavy, firm-gripping hiking boots. The trailhead is located three miles west of the town of June Lake, on the west (left) side of June Lake Road, past the ski resort.

User Groups: Hikers, dogs, horses, and mountain bikes. No wheelchair facilities.

Permits: No permits are required. Parking and access are free.

Maps: A Mammoth High Country map is available from Tom Harrison Maps. An Inyo National Forest or Ansel Adams Wilderness map is available from the U.S. Forest Service. For topographic maps, ask the USGS for June Lake and Mammoth Mountain.

Directions: From Lee Vining, drive about 11 miles south on U.S. 395 to June Lake Junction. Go right on Highway 158/June Lake Road and drive two miles to the town of June Lake. The trailhead is on the west (left), across the road from the fire station.

Contact: Inyo National Forest, Mono Basin Scenic Area Visitors Center, P.O. Box 429, Lee Vining, CA 93541, 760/647-3044, www.fs.fed.us/r5/inyo.

55 INYO CRATERS

0.5 mi / 0.5 hr 2 8

in Inyo National Forest north of Mammoth Lakes

A geologic phenomenon, the Inyo Craters make a great destination for an easy day hike in the Mammoth Lakes area. They are part of a chain of craters and other volcanic formations that reaches from Mammoth Lake to Mono Lake. The craters—evidence of Mammoth's fiery past—are the remains of a volcanic explosion of steam that occurred a mere 600 years ago. At that time, the mountain was a smoldering volcano. Melted snow found its way inside, and when the cold water hit hot magma—kaboom! The hike is a short, gentle uphill, but the elevation sucks the air out of many visitors who have just arrived in Mammoth. The trail leads through a lovely open forest of red fir and Jeffrey pine. In each of the two Inyo Craters lies a tiny pond that fills with melted snow each spring, then dries up during summer.

User Groups: Hikers, horses, and dogs. No mountain bikes. No wheelchair facilities.

Permits: No permits are required. Parking and access are free.

Maps: A Mammoth High Country map is available from Tom Harrison Maps. An Inyo National Forest map is available from the U.S. Forest Service. For a topographic map, ask the USGS for Mammoth Mountain.

Directions: From the Mammoth Lakes junction on U.S. 395, turn west on Highway 203 and drive four miles through the town of Mammoth Lakes to the junction of Minaret Road/Highway 203 and Lake Mary Road. Turn right on Minaret Road and drive one mile. At the sign for Mammoth Lakes Scenic Loop, turn right and drive 2.7 miles. Turn left at the sign for Inyo Craters (the road turns to dirt) and drive 1.3 more miles to the Inyo Craters parking lot.

Contact: Inyo National Forest, Mammoth Ranger Station, P.O. Box 148, Mammoth Lakes, CA 93546, 760/924-5500, www.fs.fed.us/r5/inyo.

56 BARRETT AND TJ LAKES

1.0 mi / 0.5 hr 1 8

at Lake George in Mammoth Lakes

Campers at Lake George, and Mammoth visitors who just want a short and easy day hike, will be pleased to find that this no-sweat trail provides access to hidden Barrett and TJ Lakes. The trail starts on the northeast shore of Lake George (which in itself is a gorgeous spot), follows the lakeshore for about 100 yards, then climbs alongside a small stream to little Barrett Lake. The tiny lake is framed by Red Mountain in the background. Hey, this was so easy, you might as well continue another 0.25 mile to TJ Lake, the more scenic of the two lakes. The distinctive granite fin of Crystal Crag (10,377 feet) towers above TJ Lake's basin, adding drama to the scene. In addition to the pretty but popular lakes, this trail shows off some lovely mountain meadows, gilded with colorful penstemen, shooting stars, and paintbrush in midsummer.

User Groups: Hikers and horses. No mountain bikes. No wheelchair facilities.

Permits: No permits are required. Parking and access are free.

Maps: A Mammoth High Country map is available from Tom Harrison Maps. An Inyo National Forest map is available from the U.S. Forest Service. For a topographic map, ask the USGS for Crystal Crag.

Directions: From the Mammoth Lakes junction on U.S. 395, turn west on Highway 203 and drive four miles through the town of Mammoth Lakes to the junction of Minaret Road/Highway 203 and Lake Mary Road. Continue straight on Lake Mary Road and drive four miles to a junction for Lake George. Turn left here, drive 0.3 mile, then turn right and drive another 0.4 mile to Lake George. The trailhead is located near the campground.

Contact: Inyo National Forest, Mammoth Ranger Station, P.O. Box 148, Mammoth Lakes, CA 93546, 760/924-5500, www.fs.fed.us/r5/inyo.

57 CRYSTAL LAKE

3.8 mi / 2.0 hr 2 9

at Lake George in Mammoth Lakes

If you think Lake George is gorgeous, wait until you see Crystal Lake, located southwest of Lake George in a bowl scoured by glaciers and tucked into a hollow below 10,377-foot Crystal Crag. The trail to reach it has a 700-foot elevation gain and is pleasantly shaded by a hearty hemlock, pine, and fir forest. The path begins near the cabins at Woods Lodge but rises quickly above them. Many hikers huff and puff as they climb this ridge, but the view of the Mammoth Lakes Basin makes it all worthwhile. This high ridge gives you a bird's-eye look at the basin's four major lakes: George, Mary, Mamie, and Twin. At a junction at one mile, go left and descend to Crystal Lake. The lake is a true jewel, highlighted by permanent snowfields that line its granite backdrop. You aren't likely to find much solitude here, since the lake is so easy to reach, but the scenery more than makes up for it.

If you want to turn this into a longer hike, you can take the other trail at the fork and head for Mammoth Crest, at 10,400 feet, two miles farther. The trail gains another 700 feet as it leaves the forest and enters a stark, volcanic landscape peppered with whitebark pines. The expansive view from the high point on the crest includes the Mammoth Lakes Basin, the San Joaquin River, the Minarets and the Ritter Range, and Mammoth Mountain. If this hike hasn't taken your breath away, the vista will.

User Groups: Hikers, horses, and dogs. Mountain bikes are not advised. No wheelchair facilities.

Permits: No permits are required. Parking and access are free.

Maps: A Mammoth High Country map is available from Tom Harrison Maps. An Inyo National Forest map is available from the U.S. Forest Service. For a topographic map, ask the USGS for Crystal Crag.

Directions: From the Mammoth Lakes junction on U.S. 395, turn west on Highway 203 and drive four miles through the town of Mammoth Lakes to the junction of Minaret Road/Highway 203 and Lake Mary Road. Continue straight on Lake Mary Road and drive four miles to a junction for Lake George. Turn left, drive 0.3 mile, then turn right and drive another 0.4 mile to Lake George. The trailhead is on the right, near some cabins.

Contact: Inyo National Forest, Mammoth Ranger Station, P.O. Box 148, Mammoth Lakes, CA 93546, 760/924-5500, www.fs.fed.us/r5/inyo.

58 EMERALD LAKE AND SKY MEADOWS

4.0 mi / 2.0 hr 2 9

at Lake Mary in Mammoth Lakes

This is one of the Eastern Sierra's premier wildflower trails, and it's easy enough for children to hike. The trail starts just south of Lake Mary, at the end of the Coldwater Campground road. The hike is short and direct, climbing straight to Emerald Lake on an easy grade. Picnickers are often found seated among the rocks by the water's edge, although by midsummer, the tiny lake dwindles to something that more closely resembles a pond. No matter, the lake is not the star of the show here—the flowers are. The trail skirts the east shore of Emerald Lake and continues along its inlet stream. Three brief climbs lead you past Gentian Meadow to the southeast edge of Sky Meadows, which is filled with wildflowers throughout the summer. Beyond the meadows, permanent snow fields decorate the granite cliffs of Mammoth Crest. Among the wide variety of flower species to be seen and admired, one standout is the tall orange tiger lilies, a flower that is showy enough to be in a florist's shop.

User Groups: Hikers, dogs, and horses. No mountain bikes allowed past the wilderness boundary. No wheelchair facilities.

Permits: No day permits are required. Parking and access are free.

Maps: A Mammoth High Country map is available from Tom Harrison Maps. An Inyo National Forest map is available from the U.S. Forest Service. For a topographic map, ask the USGS for Crystal Crag.

Directions: From the Mammoth Lakes junction on U.S. 395, turn west on Highway 203 and drive four miles through the town of Mammoth Lakes to the junction of Minaret Road/Highway 203 and Lake Mary Road. Continue straight on Lake Mary Road and drive 3.5 miles to a fork just before Lake Mary; turn left and drive 0.6 mile to the Coldwater Campground turnoff, on the left. Turn left and drive 0.5 mile through the camp to the trailhead, at the first parking lot.

Contact: Inyo National Forest, Mammoth Ranger Station, P.O. Box 148, Mammoth Lakes, CA 93546, 760/924-5500, www.fs.fed.us/r5/inyo.

59 DUCK LAKE

10.0 mi / 6.0 hr or 2.0 days 3 9

in the John Muir Wilderness near Mammoth Lakes

How far you hike on Duck Pass Trail is up to you, but if it were up to us, we'd hike at least as far as five miles to Duck Lake, elevation 10,450 feet. Sure, lots of people stop at the other lakes this trail passes along the way—Arrowhead Lake at 1.3 miles out, Skelton Lake at two miles, or Barney Lake at three miles—and these make fine destinations. But you might as well see them all and then keep climbing through Duck Pass to much larger Duck Lake, at five miles. The pass is a 1,600-foot climb from the trailhead at Coldwater Campground. Just beyond the pass, the trail drops 300 feet to reach Duck Lake, one of the largest natural lakes in the Eastern Sierra. Most of the climbing is in the stretch from Barney Lake to the pass, as the trail switchbacks up a talus-covered slope. Day hikers can make their way from Duck Lake on a faint path to Pika Lake, which is visible in the distance about a half-mile away. Backpackers can continue on to Purple Lake (at 7.5 miles) and Lake Virginia (at nine miles). The only downer on this trail is the presence of horses and pack mules, which can make the trail quite dusty by late summer. There are usually tons of people on the trail, too, but with this kind of scenery, everybody is in a good mood.

User Groups: Hikers, dogs, and horses. No mountain bikes allowed past the wilderness boundary. No wheelchair facilities.

Permits: A free wilderness permit is required for overnight stays and is available from the Mammoth Ranger Station. Quotas are in effect from May 1 to November 1; for this period, permits are available in advance for a $5 reservation fee per person.

Maps: A Mammoth High Country map is available from Tom Harrison Maps. An Inyo National Forest or John Muir Wilderness map is available from the U.S. Forest Service. For a topographic map, ask the USGS for Crystal Crag.

Directions: From the Mammoth Lakes junction on U.S. 395, turn west on Highway 203 and drive four miles, through the town of Mammoth Lakes, to the junction of Minaret Road/Highway 203 and Lake Mary Road. Continue straight on Lake Mary Road and drive 3.5 miles to a fork just before Lake Mary; turn left and drive 0.6 mile to the Coldwater Campground turnoff, on the left. Turn left and drive 0.8 mile through the camp to the Duck Pass trailhead at the farthest parking lot.

Contact: Inyo National Forest, Mammoth Ranger Station, P.O. Box 148, Mammoth Lakes, CA 93546, 760/924-5500, www.fs.fed.us/r5/inyo.

60 VALENTINE LAKE TRAIL

11.2 mi / 6.0 hr or 2.0 days 3 9

in the John Muir Wilderness south of Mammoth Lakes

The Mammoth Lakes area is one of the Eastern Sierra's star attractions, yet nearby Valentine Lake is perhaps overlooked because the trailhead (at 7,600 feet) is not found at one of the lakes in the Mammoth Lakes Basin. Or perhaps it's because the climb required to get there is so steep. Regardless of the reason, a morning's hike—rising some 1,900 feet over 5.6 miles, but with most of the climb compressed into two miles—gets you to the lake, which sits at 9,698 feet.

Some say the lake is shaped like a teardrop, but we think it looks more like a drop of sweat. The hike starts out with a very steep climb (including 0.5 mile of sandy switchbacks in a dry pine forest) and doesn't level out for the first two miles. You'll pass a side trail to the Sherwin Lakes at 2.9 miles (a fine destination for those who have had enough, or those who just want to catch fish). Continue uphill, much more gently now, finally meeting up with Valentine Lake's outlet stream. Valentine Lake has rocky cliffs ringing its edges, making it difficult to explore its shoreline. Pick a spot and toss in a line; the lake has plentiful brook trout.

User Groups: Hikers, dogs, and horses. No mountain bikes. No wheelchair facilities.

Permits: A free wilderness permit is required for overnight stays and is available from the Mammoth Ranger Station. Quotas are in effect from May 1 to November 1; for this period, permits are available in advance for a $5 reservation fee per person.

Maps: A Mammoth High Country map is available from Tom Harrison Maps. An Inyo National Forest or John Muir Wilderness map is available from the U.S. Forest Service. For a topographic map, ask the USGS for Crystal Crag.

Directions: From the Mammoth Lakes junction on U.S. 395, turn west on Highway 203 and drive 2.6 miles to Old Mammoth Road. Turn left and drive 0.8 mile to Sherwin Creek Road. Turn left and drive 2.9 miles to the signed trailhead on the right for Valentine Lake (past the Sherwin Creek Campground and YMCA camp.)

Contact: Inyo National Forest, Mammoth Ranger Station, P.O. Box 148, Mammoth Lakes, CA 93546, 760/924-5500, www.fs.fed.us/r5/inyo.

61 RED CONES LOOP

6.7 mi / 4.0 hr 3 7

at Horseshoe Lake in Mammoth Lakes

Horseshoe Lake, elevation 8,900 feet, lies at the end of the Mammoth Lakes road and has an excellent trailhead that makes for a great day hike. Don't be put off by the dead trees and the barren look of the place. A relatively small area by the lake has been affected by carbon-dioxide gas venting up through the soil—the result of seismic activity. You get away from this strange-looking forest quickly. Set out from the northwest side of the lake, ascend the slope, and take the left fork for McLeod Lake. In just under two miles, you'll reach the start of the loop. Go right to reach Crater Meadow, a beautiful little spot set just below Red Cones, and then circle around to Upper Crater Meadow. Either meadow is a fine destination for a picnic lunch in peace. The contrast is striking: Just a short distance below, there are typically many people at Twin Lakes, Lake Mary, Lake Mamie, and Lake George, yet you are separated from them by Mammoth Pass. You will be surprised at how relatively few people take this loop hike, and glad that you made the choice to do so.

User Groups: Hikers, dogs, and horses. No mountain bikes. No wheelchair facilities.

Permits: No permits are required. Parking and access are free.

Maps: A Mammoth High Country map is

available from Tom Harrison Maps. An Inyo National Forest map is available from the U.S. Forest Service. For a topographic map, ask the USGS for Crystal Crag.

Directions: From the Mammoth Lakes junction on U.S. 395, turn west on Highway 203 and drive four miles through the town of Mammoth Lakes to the junction of Minaret Road/Highway 203 and Lake Mary Road. Continue straight on Lake Mary Road and drive 4.8 miles to the road's end, at Horseshoe Lake. The trailhead is on the northwest side of the lake, signed for Mammoth Pass.

Contact: Inyo National Forest, Mammoth Ranger Station, P.O. Box 148, Mammoth Lakes, CA 93546, 760/924-5500, www.fs.fed.us/r5/inyo.

62 DEVILS POSTPILE AND RAINBOW FALLS

2.0-5.0 mi / 1.0-2.0 hr 2 10

in Devils Postpile National Monument west of Mammoth Lakes

BEST

The first time you lay eyes on 101-foot Rainbow Falls, the tall, wide, and forceful waterfall comes as an awesome surprise. Most first-time visitors see it before or after a trip to the Devils Postpile, a fascinating collection of volcanic rock columns and rubble left from a lava flow nearly 100,000 years ago. It's like nothing you've seen anywhere else. You can hike to Rainbow Falls two ways, either from the ranger station at Devils Postpile National Monument or from the Rainbow Falls trailhead, near Reds Meadow Resort. Either way, this is one of the best short hikes in California.

Your best bet is to start at the ranger station, then pass by the Devils Postpile lava columns in only 0.5 mile. Stop and gape at this geologic wonder, and perhaps take the short but steep side trip to the top of the columns, then continue downhill to Rainbow Falls, at 2.5 miles. (If you start at the trailhead by Reds Meadow, your trip to Rainbow Falls is only one mile, but you'll miss out on the Postpile.)

In order to see the rainbow that gives the waterfall its name, you must show up in late morning or at midday. The rainbow is the result of a prism effect from sun's rays refracting through the falling water. Two overlook areas across from the waterfall's brink give you an excellent view, but you can hike down a series of stairs to the falls' base for an even better vantage point. If you're inspired, you can travel another 0.5 mile on the trail to find a smaller waterfall on the San Joaquin River, called Lower Falls.

User Groups: Hikers and horses. No mountain bikes. Dogs must be leashed in the national monument. No wheelchair facilities.

Permits: Each person entering the Devils Postpile/Reds Meadow area must purchase an access pass. (See *Access Note,* below.) The fee is $7 per adult and $4 for children ages 3 to 15. Children age two and under are free. Passes may be purchased at the Mammoth Mountain shuttle bus terminal or at Minaret Station.

Maps: A Devils Postpile map is available from Tom Harrison Maps. An Inyo National Forest map is available from the U.S. Forest Service. For a topographic map, ask the USGS for Mammoth Mountain.

Directions: From the Mammoth Lakes junction on U.S. 395, turn west on Highway 203 and drive four miles through the town of Mammoth Lakes to Minaret Road (still Highway 203). Turn right and drive 4.5 miles to the shuttle bus terminal (adjacent to the Mammoth Mountain Ski Area). Purchase an access pass and board a shuttle bus here. Disembark at the Devils Postpile Ranger Station or Rainbow Falls trailhead, which is just before Reds Meadow Resort.

Access Note: Visitors arriving between 7 A.M. and 7 P.M. are required to ride a shuttle bus (free with purchase of an access pass) from Mammoth Mountain Ski Area. If you are camping in the Devils Postpile area, you are permitted to drive your own car instead of taking the shuttle, but each passenger in the car must purchase an access pass (the maximum fee charged is $20 per car).

Contact: Inyo National Forest, Mammoth Ranger Station, P.O. Box 148, Mammoth Lakes, CA 93546, 760/924-5500, www.fs.fed.us/r5/inyo; Devils Postpile National Monument, P.O. Box 3999, Mammoth Lakes, CA 93546, 760/934-2289 (summer only), www.nps.gov/depo.

63 MINARET LAKE

16.0 mi / 2.0 days 3 9

in the Ansel Adams Wilderness west of Mammoth Lakes

Minaret Lake is a real prize, set just below the awesome glacial-carved Ritter Range, at 9,793 feet. Reaching it requires an eight-mile hike with a 1,800-foot elevation gain, and every step is completely worth it. From the trailhead at Devils Postpile Ranger Station, you hike south to access a bridge across the San Joaquin River, then head northward two miles on John Muir Trail. (You can also start from Upper Soda Spring Campground and hike south on the Pacific Crest Trail, then turn north on the John Muir Trail. The distance is about the same.) After passing tiny Johnston Lake, you reach the junction with Minaret Lake Trail. Turn left and follow Minaret Creek. The trail rises with the creek and in the last mile climbs steeply above tree line before skirting the Minaret Lake outlet and tracing the line of the north shore. The granite peaks that form the lake's backdrop are Clyde and Ken Minaret. Good campsites are found near Minaret Lake's rocky shore. If you want to do some exploring, Cecile Lake (at 10,239 feet) can be reached via a cross-country route to the northwest of the lake.

User Groups: Hikers, dogs, and horses. Dogs must be leashed in national monument. No mountain bikes. No wheelchair facilities.

Permits: Each person entering the Devils Postpile/Reds Meadow area must purchase an access pass. (See *Access Note,* below.) The fee is $7 per adult and $4 for children ages 3 to 15. Children age two and under are free. Passes may be purchased at the Mammoth Mountain shuttle bus terminal or at Minaret Station.

A free wilderness permit is required for overnight stays and is available from the Mammoth Ranger Station. Quotas are in effect from May 1 to November 1; for this period, permits are available in advance for a $5 reservation fee per person.

Maps: A Devils Postpile map is available from Tom Harrison Maps. An Inyo National Forest or Ansel Adams Wilderness map is available from the U.S. Forest Service. For topographic maps, ask the USGS for Mammoth Mountain and Mount Ritter.

Directions: From the Mammoth Lakes junction on U.S. 395, turn west on Highway 203 and drive four miles through the town of Mammoth Lakes to Minaret Road (still Highway 203). Turn right and drive 4.5 miles to the shuttle bus terminal (adjacent to the Mammoth Mountain Ski Area). Purchase an access pass and board a shuttle bus here. Disembark at the Devils Postpile Ranger Station.

Access Note: Visitors arriving between 7 A.M. and 7 P.M. are required to ride a shuttle bus (free with purchase of an access pass) from Mammoth Mountain Ski Area. If you are camping in the Devils Postpile area, you are permitted to drive your own car instead of taking the shuttle, but each passenger in the car must purchase an access pass (the maximum fee charged is $20 per car).

Contact: Inyo National Forest, Mammoth Ranger Station, P.O. Box 148, Mammoth Lakes, CA 93546, 760/924-5500, www.fs.fed.us/r5/inyo; Devils Postpile National Monument, P.O. Box 3999, Mammoth Lakes, CA 93546, 760/934-2289 (summer only), www.nps.gov/depo.

64 FERN LAKE LOOP

10.0-16.0 mi / 1.0-2.0 days 3 9

in the Ansel Adams Wilderness west of Mammoth Lakes

Fern Lake can be the destination on an ambitious day hike from Devils Postpile, or the start of a great 15-mile backpacking loop. Either way, this is an excellent hike that has become very popular. Starting from the ranger station at Devils Postpile, you head south to access the bridge across the San Joaquin River, then follow the King Creek Trail. About two miles in, you face a crossing of King Creek that can be tricky early in the summer. Exercise some caution. Then climb through the pine forest to reach a junction, at 4.9 miles. Follow the spur to Fern Lake, elevation 8,800 feet, where many good campsites are found. The lake is set in a small rock bowl at tree line, below Iron Mountain, in the Minarets. Day hikers will often while away a few hours here and then retrace their steps for a 10-mile round-trip.

Those continuing onward will find the trail pokes in and out of sparse forest for the next two miles to Becks Cabin. From here, a one-mile side trip leads to Superior Lake (7.5 miles from your start, and at 9,400 feet), another excellent spot for an overnight. A faint path leads 0.7 mile from Superior Lake to the two Beck Lakes (at 9,800 feet), which are surrounded by high granite ridges. A visit to Beck Lakes—set in a glacial-formed pocket below the Minarets and amid celestial mountain scenery—is highly recommended. When you return to the loop at Becks Cabin, you have a 4.8-mile descent to reach John Muir Trail, where you turn right and head back to the bridge and the ranger station.

User Groups: Hikers, dogs, and horses. Dogs must be leashed in national monument. No mountain bikes. No wheelchair facilities.

Permits: Each person entering the Devils Postpile/Reds Meadow area must purchase an access pass. (See *Access Note,* below.) The fee is $7 per adult and $4 for children ages 3 to 15. Children age two and under are free. Passes may be purchased at the Mammoth Mountain shuttle bus terminal or at Minaret Station.

A free wilderness permit is required for overnight stays and is available from the Mammoth Ranger Station. Quotas are in effect from May 1 to November 1; for this period, permits are available in advance for a $5 reservation fee per person.

Maps: A Devils Postpile map is available from Tom Harrison Maps. An Inyo National Forest or Ansel Adams Wilderness map is available from the U.S. Forest Service. For topographic maps, ask the USGS for Mammoth Mountain and Mount Ritter.

Directions: From the Mammoth Lakes junction on U.S. 395, turn west on Highway 203 and drive four miles through the town of Mammoth Lakes to Minaret Road (still Highway 203). Turn right and drive 4.5 miles to the shuttle bus terminal (adjacent to the Mammoth Mountain Ski Area). Purchase an access pass and board a shuttle bus here. Disembark at the Devils Postpile Ranger Station.

Access Note: Visitors arriving between 7 A.M. and 7 P.M. are required to ride a shuttle bus (free with purchase of an access pass) from Mammoth Mountain Ski Area. If you are camping in the Devils Postpile area, you are permitted to drive your own car instead of taking the shuttle, but each passenger in the car must purchase an access pass (the maximum fee charged is $20 per car).

Contact: Inyo National Forest, Mammoth Ranger Station, P.O. Box 148, Mammoth Lakes, CA 93546, 760/924-5500, www.fs.fed.us/r5/inyo; Devils Postpile National Monument, P.O. Box 3999, Mammoth Lakes, CA 93546, 760/934-2289 (summer only), www.nps.gov/depo.

65 SHADOW LAKE

7.6 mi / 4.0 hr or 2.0 days 3 9

in the Ansel Adams Wilderness west of Mammoth Lakes

Shadow Lake is one of the most popular destinations in the Devils Postpile region simply because of its sheer beauty. The only unpleasant part of this hike is making your way through the busy trailhead parking lots at Agnew Meadows. Once that's accomplished and you're on the trail, all is bliss, as long as you're in good condition and ready for a sustained climb. (Campers at Agnew Meadows can cut a half mile off this trip each way by starting from the trail at camp, not from the trailhead parking lot.) The route starts out quite mellow as it wanders through the wildflowers at Agnew Meadows. It then follows the River Trail along the middle fork of the San Joaquin River. Just beyond shallow Olaine Lake (at two miles) lies a junction, where you go left for Shadow Lake. Cross a bridge and prepare to climb. A long series of steep, shadeless switchbacks ensues as you climb alongside a narrow creek gorge. Fortunately the view looking down the San Joaquin River Canyon becomes ever more grand as you rise upward. At last you reach the waterfall on Shadow Lake's outlet stream and then climb the final stretch to the lake. Its backdrop is like something you've seen on a million Sierra postcards, with the Minarets and Mounts Ritter and Banner towering above the lake. Day hikers have the best deal here; they can just pick a spot along the 8,737-foot lakeshore and drink in the view. Camping is not permitted at Shadow Lake, so backpackers must continue on to smaller Rosalie Lake (much more climbing over the next two miles). Ediza Lake is also a popular overnight option, 2.5 miles from Shadow Lake.

User Groups: Hikers, dogs, and horses. No mountain bikes. No wheelchair facilities.

Permits: Each person entering the Devils Postpile/Reds Meadow area must purchase an access pass. (See *Access Note,* below.) The fee is $7 per adult and $4 for children ages 3 to 15. Children age two and under are free. Passes may be purchased at the Mammoth Mountain shuttle bus terminal or at Minaret Station.

A free wilderness permit is required for overnight stays and is available from the Mammoth Ranger Station. Quotas are in effect from May 1 to November 1; for this period, permits are available in advance for a $5 reservation fee per person.

Maps: A Devils Postpile map is available from Tom Harrison Maps. An Inyo National Forest or Ansel Adams Wilderness map is available from the U.S. Forest Service. For topographic maps, ask the USGS for Crystal Crag and Cattle Mountain.

Directions: From the Mammoth Lakes junction on U.S. 395, turn west on Highway 203 and drive four miles through the town of Mammoth Lakes to Minaret Road (still Highway 203). Turn right and drive 4.5 miles to the shuttle bus terminal (adjacent to the Mammoth Mountain Ski Area). Purchase an access pass and board a shuttle bus here. Disembark at the Agnew Meadows Campground. Walk through the trailhead parking lots to the Shadow Lake trailhead.

Access Note: Visitors arriving between 7 A.M. and 7 P.M. are required to ride a shuttle bus (free with purchase of an access pass) from Mammoth Mountain Ski Area. If you are camping in the Devils Postpile area, you are permitted to drive your own car instead of taking the shuttle, but each passenger in the car must purchase an access pass (the maximum fee charged is $20 per car).

Contact: Inyo National Forest, Mammoth Ranger Station, P.O. Box 148, Mammoth Lakes, CA 93546, 760/924-5500, www.fs.fed.us/r5/inyo; Devils Postpile National Monument, P.O. Box 3999, Mammoth Lakes, CA 93546, 760/934-2289 (summer only), www.nps.gov/depo.

HIKING

66 AGNEW MEADOWS TO TUOLUMNE MEADOWS (JMT/PCT)

28.0 mi one-way / 3.0 days 5 10

from the Agnew Meadows trailhead north to the trailhead parking area at Tuolumne Meadows on Highway 120

This section of the JMT/PCT features breathtaking views of the Minarets, many glacial-cut lakes, and the wondrous descent into Yosemite. The PCT starts here by leaving Reds Meadows, an excellent place to arrange a food drop and a chance to eat your first cheeseburger in weeks. The trail heads out into the most beautiful section of Inyo National Forest and the Ansel Adams Wilderness. All in a row, the PCT passes Rosalie, Shadow, Garnet, and Thousand Island Lakes. If they look like Ansel Adams' pictures in real life, it's because they are. The background setting of Banner and Ritter Peaks is among the most spectacular anywhere. From Thousand Island Lake, the PCT makes a fair climb over Island Pass (10,200 feet), then drops down into the headwaters of Rush Creek, where emerald green flows swirl over boulders, pouring like a wilderness fountain. From here, it's a decent, steady ascent back above tree line to Donohue Pass (11,056 feet), the southern wilderness border of Yosemite National Park. It was here, while munching a trail lunch, that we saw a huge landslide on the westward canyon wall. A massive amount of rock material fell in just a few seconds—an unforgettable show of natural forces. The trail becomes quite blocky at Donohue Pass, and you rock hop your way down to the headwaters of Lyell Fork, a pretzel-like stream that meanders through the meadows. It pours all the way to Tuolumne Meadows, and following it, the trail is nearly flat for more than four miles. At Tuolumne Meadows you can resupply—and get another cheeseburger.

To continue north on the JMT, see the *Tuolumne Meadows to Yosemite Valley (JMT)* hike in this chapter. If you are walking this trail in reverse, see the *Lake Thomas Edison to Agnew Meadows (JMT/PCT)* hike in *Moon California Camping.*

User Groups: Hikers and horses. No dogs or mountain bikes. No wheelchair facilities.

Permits: A wilderness permit is required for traveling through various wilderness and special-use areas the trail traverses. Contact either the Inyo National Forest or Yosemite National Park for a permit that is good for the length of your trip.

Maps: A John Muir Trail Map Pack is available from Tom Harrison Maps. An Inyo National Forest map is available from the U.S. Forest Service. For topographic maps, ask the USGS for Vogelsang Peak, Mount Ritter, Koip Peak, and Mammoth Mountain.

Directions: From Lee Vining, drive 26 miles south on Highway 395 to Mammoth Junction. Turn west on Highway 203/Minaret Summit Road to the town of Mammoth Lakes and drive 14 miles to the Agnew Meadows Campground and the trailhead parking area.

Contact: Yosemite National Park, P.O. Box 577, Yosemite, CA 95389, 209/372-0200, www.nps.gov/yose; Inyo National Forest, Mono Basin Scenic Area Visitors Center, P.O. Box 429, Lee Vining, CA 93541, 760/647-3044, www.fs.fed.us/r5/inyo.

67 HITE COVE TRAIL

9.0 mi / 5.0 hr 2 10

on the South Fork Merced River in Sierra National Forest

BEST

Considered by many to be the premier Sierra spring wildflower trail, Hite Cove Trail offers hikers a look at 60 flower varieties, including goldfields, lupine, poppies, brodaiea, monkeyflower, shooting stars, fiesta flowers, fairy lanterns, baby blue eyes, and Indian pinks. To see them, visit from late February to early May, before the show is over. Conveniently, this is usually the only time of the year when the trail is open, because the first 0.75 mile of trail is on private property, and access is restricted during fire season.

You start hiking on a paved driveway, but the asphalt only lasts for a few yards, then the trail transitions to a narrow single track that hugs the side of the steep canyon wall, high above the South Fork Merced River. Even if you aren't terribly interested in wildflowers, the river and canyon views are tremendous. About one mile out is an obvious rock outcrop, a few feet off the trail, where you can sit and enjoy the rushing river below. Another 0.5 mile farther, the trail drops down right alongside the river, and where the current mellows out, there are many tempting swimming holes. Those wishing to turn this hike into an overnight trip can camp at Hite Cove, the site of the 1879 Hite Cove Hotel. A campfire permit is required for overnight stays. From there, you can continue hiking to Devils Gulch, 2.5 miles farther. To do so, however, requires crossing the South Fork Merced River at Hite Cove, a difficult feat early in the year.

Special Note: Call the Bass Lake Ranger Station or visit the Sierra National Forest website to make sure this trail is open before planning your trip. Access to the trail is restricted during fire season.

User Groups: Hikers, dogs, and horses. No mountain bikes. No wheelchair facilities.

Permits: No permits are required. Parking and access are free.

Maps: A Sierra National Forest map is available from the U.S. Forest Service. For a topographic map, ask the USGS for El Portal.

Directions: From Mariposa, drive 22 miles east on Highway 140 to Savage's Trading Post. The parking area is on the north side of the road, but the trail begins on the south side, near Savage's Trading Post.

Contact: Sierra National Forest, Bass Lake Ranger Station, 57003 Road 225, North Fork, CA 93643, 559/877-2218, www.fs.fed.us/r5/sierra.

68 UPPER YOSEMITE FALL

7.4 mi / 5.0 hr 4 10

in Yosemite Valley

BEST

At 2,425 feet, Yosemite Falls is the highest waterfall in North America. That's why hundreds of park visitors hike this strenuous trail every day in the spring and summer. There's no feeling quite like standing at the waterfall's brink and realizing you've conquered a landmark of this magnitude.

Still, if you tucker out on this demanding climb to Upper Yosemite Fall, just remember that you always have a fallback position: you can hike only 1.2 miles one-way to the Columbia Point overlook, which is reached via more than 100 switchbacks and a total gain of 1,200 feet, then call it a day. The view of Yosemite Valley from Columbia Point is a stunner, and plenty of people who planned on hiking to Upper Yosemite Fall turn around here and still leave satisfied.

Those who push on are also rewarded. After a level section and then a short, surprising descent, you get your first full-impact view of horsetail-shaped Upper Yosemite Fall. In the spring and early summer months, this view will blow you away. The trail then switchbacks upward, more steeply now, through a canyon to the west of the fall, which allows passage to the top of the north rim of Yosemite Valley. At this point, you've gained 2,700 feet and hiked 3.5 miles; it's only another 0.2 mile to the brink of Upper Yosemite Fall. (Make sure you take the spur trail signed as Overlook.) From the metal fence above the fall's lip, you gain an incredible perspective on the waterfall's drop and the valley floor far below.

If this trip hasn't provided you with enough exertion, continue another 0.75 mile, crossing the bridge above the falls, to Yosemite Point at 6,936 feet in elevation, where you get a stunning view of the south rim of the Valley, Half Dome, and North Dome, and a look at the top of Lost Arrow Spire, a single shaft of granite jutting into the sky.

User Groups: Hikers only. No dogs, horses, or mountain bikes. No wheelchair facilities.
Permits: No permits are required. There is a $20 entrance fee per vehicle at Yosemite National Park, good for seven days.
Maps: A Half Dome or Yosemite National Park map is available from Tom Harrison Maps. For a topographic map, ask the USGS for Yosemite Falls.
Directions: From Merced, drive 70 miles northeast on Highway 140 to Yosemite National Park. Follow the signs toward Yosemite Valley, entering through the Arch Rock entrance station. Continue on Highway 140/El Portal Road, which becomes Southside Drive, for 10.5 miles. Just beyond the Yosemite Chapel, bear left at the fork and head toward Yosemite Village and the visitors center, then turn left and drive west on Northside Drive 0.75 mile to the Yosemite Lodge parking lot. Park in the lot (do not park in the spaces marked Permit Parking Only), then walk to Camp 4, which is across Northside Drive and 0.25 mile west of Yosemite Lodge. You may not park in the Camp 4 lot unless you are camping there. If you are riding the free Yosemite Valley shuttle bus, disembark at Camp 4 or Yosemite Lodge.
Contact: Yosemite National Park, P.O. Box 577, Yosemite, CA 95389, 209/372-0200, www.nps.gov/yose.

69 EAGLE PEAK

13.5 mi / 1.0 or 2.0 days 4 10

in Yosemite Valley

If you seek more of a challenge than the day hike to Upper Yosemite Fall, the trail to Eagle Peak delivers the stunning destinations of the shorter trip (Columbia Point and Upper Yosemite Fall) plus an additional three miles one-way to a lookout atop of the highest rock of the Three Brothers formation. Here, the vista is sublime. All of Yosemite Valley comes into view from the top of Eagle Peak, including an interesting perspective on North Dome, Clouds Rest, and Half Dome. On rare, extremely clear days you can also see the mountains and foothills of the Coast Range, 100 miles to the west.

Follow the trail notes for the hike to Upper Yosemite Fall (see previous listing), then after taking the spur trail to the fall's brink, backtrack 0.25 mile to the trail junction for Eagle Peak Trail. Follow Eagle Peak Trail northwest for 1.5 miles, enjoying plentiful shade from Jeffrey pines and white firs, then hike south for one mile through Eagle Peak Meadows (prepare to get your feet wet here unless it is very late in summer). At a trail junction with El Capitan Trail, bear left for a 0.6-mile ascent to your final destination—the summit of Eagle Peak, elevation 7,779 feet. After completing this trip, you'll never view the Three Brothers from the valley floor the same way again.
User Groups: Hikers only. No dogs, horses, or mountain bikes. No wheelchair facilities.
Permits: There is a $20 entrance fee per vehicle at Yosemite National Park, good for seven days. Free wilderness permits are required for overnight stays. They are available on a first-come, first-served basis up to one day in advance at the Yosemite Wilderness kiosk near your chosen trailhead or farther in advance by mail, phone, or online for a $5 reservation fee per person.
Maps: A Half Dome or Yosemite National Park map is available from Tom Harrison Maps. For a topographic map, ask the USGS for Yosemite Falls.
Directions: From Merced, drive 70 miles northeast on Highway 140 to Yosemite National Park. Follow the signs toward Yosemite Valley and enter through the Arch Rock entrance station. Continue on Highway 140/El Portal Road, which becomes Southside Drive, for 10.5 miles. Just beyond the Yosemite Chapel, bear left at the fork and head toward Yosemite Village and the visitors center, then turn left and drive west on Northside Drive 0.75 mile to the Yosemite Lodge parking lot. Park in the lot (do not park in the spaces marked Permit Parking Only), then walk to Camp 4, which is across

Northside Drive and 0.25 mile west of Yosemite Lodge. You may not park in the Camp 4 lot unless you are camping there. If you are riding the free Yosemite Valley shuttle bus, disembark at Camp 4 or Yosemite Lodge.

Contact: Yosemite National Park, P.O. Box 577, Yosemite, CA 95389, 209/372-0200 or 209/372-0740 (permit reservations), www.nps.gov/yose or www.nps.gov/yose/wilderness (permit reservations).

70 LOWER YOSEMITE FALL

0.5 mi / 0.5 hr — 1, 9

in Yosemite Valley

BEST

It's so short you can hardly call it a hike, and the route is perpetually crawling with people. Still, the trail to Lower Yosemite Fall is an absolute must for visitors to Yosemite Valley. When the falls are roaring with snowmelt in the spring and early summer, they never disappoint even the most seasoned hiker.

The Lower Yosemite Fall Trail received a major facelift in 2004. The old parking lot was removed, the trail was extended so that it now makes a pleasant loop, and new, modern restrooms and facilities were added. The only problem is that now that the parking lot is gone, many visitors can't figure out where to leave their car and start the hike. Your best bet is to ride the shuttle bus from other points in the Valley, which deposits you at the "new" Yosemite Fall Trailhead, which is an attractive log structure right alongside Northside Drive. You can also park your car alongside the road near the shuttle bus stop or in the Yosemite Lodge parking lot, but good luck finding a space in the summer months. Either way, once you get started, the trail is simple enough to follow. Within about 10 minutes of walking, you are standing at the footbridge below the falls, and in the spring you can get soaking wet from the incredible mist and spray. By late summer, on the other hand, the fall often dries up completely. Be sure to walk the entire loop instead of just heading out-and-back to the falls; there is much to see along the way. And most important of all: if you really want to see the waterfall at its most magnificent, plan your trip for sometime between April and June, during peak snowmelt. Seasoned waterfall lovers should also plan to visit on full moon nights in spring, when if conditions are just right, they are treated to the appearance of a "moonbow" surrounding the lower fall.

User Groups: Hikers and wheelchairs. No dogs, horses, or mountain bikes.

Permits: No permits are required. There is a $20 entrance fee per vehicle at Yosemite National Park, good for seven days.

Maps: A Half Dome or Yosemite National Park map is available from Tom Harrison Maps. For a topographic map, ask the USGS for Half Dome.

Directions: From Merced, drive 70 miles northeast on Highway 140 to Yosemite National Park. Follow the signs to Yosemite Valley, entering through the Arch Rock entrance station. Continue on Highway 140/El Portal Road, which becomes Southside Drive, for 10.5 miles. Just beyond the Yosemite Chapel, bear left at the fork and head toward Yosemite Village and the visitors center, then turn left and drive west on Northside Drive 0.75 mile to the Yosemite Lodge parking lot. Park in the lot (do not park in the spaces marked Permit Parking Only). The trail begins across Northside Drive from Yosemite Lodge. You can also park on either side of Northside Drive near the Lower Yosemite Fall bus shuttle stop and walk from there.

Contact: Yosemite National Park, P.O. Box 577, Yosemite, CA 95389, 209/372-0200, www.nps.gov/yose.

71 MIST TRAIL TO TOP OF VERNAL FALL

3.0 mi / 2.0 hr — 2, 10

in Yosemite Valley

This is a hike that every visitor to the Valley should take, even if it's the only trail they walk all year. Despite how crowded the trail inevitably is, this is a world-class hike to one of the most photographed waterfalls in the world. Make your trip more enjoyable by starting as early in the morning as possible, before the hordes are out in full force.

Start by taking the free Yosemite shuttle bus to the trailhead at Happy Isles. (Or you can add on an extra mile each way by hiking from the day-use parking area in Curry Village to Happy Isles.) The partially paved route is a moderate 500-foot climb to the Vernal Fall footbridge, then a very steep tromp up the seemingly endless granite staircase to the top of the fall. Although many people hike only to the footbridge, 0.8 mile from Happy Isles, it's definitely worth the extra effort to push on another 0.5 mile to reach the top of Vernal Fall.

Doing so means ascending another 500 feet on the Mist Trail's famous granite stairway, which frames the edge of Vernal Fall. You will come so close to the plunging spray that you may feel as if you are part of it. Sometimes you are—during peak snowmelt in spring, hikers are frequently drenched in spray and mist. Remember to bring a rain poncho if you don't like getting wet.

When you reach the 317-foot-high fall's brink, you can stand at the railing and watch the dizzying flow of rushing whitewater as it tumbles downward. This is a trip you have to do at least once in your life.

User Groups: Hikers only. No dogs, horses, or mountain bikes. No wheelchair facilities.

Permits: No permits are required. There is a $20 entrance fee per vehicle at Yosemite National Park, good for seven days.

Maps: A Half Dome or Yosemite National Park map is available from Tom Harrison Maps. For a topographic map, ask the USGS for Half Dome.

Directions: From Merced, drive 70 miles northeast on Highway 140 to Yosemite National Park. Follow the signs toward Yosemite Valley, entering through the Arch Rock entrance station. Continue on Highway 140/El Portal Road, which becomes Southside Drive, for 11.6 miles to the day-use parking lot at Curry Village. Then ride the free Yosemite Valley shuttle bus to Happy Isles. In winter, when the shuttle does not run, you must hike from the day-use parking lot in Curry Village, adding two miles to your round-trip. The Mist Trail may be closed in winter; call to check on weather conditions.

Contact: Yosemite National Park, P.O. Box 577, Yosemite, CA 95389, 209/372-0200, www.nps.gov/yose.

72 MIST AND JOHN MUIR LOOP TO NEVADA FALL

6.8 mi / 4.0 hr 3 10

in Yosemite Valley

BEST

You can hike either the John Muir Trail or Mist Trail to reach Yosemite's classic Nevada Fall, but the best choice is to make a loop out of it by hiking up on the Mist Trail, then down partway or all the way on the John Muir Trail. Both trails join above and below Nevada Fall, so you have some options. By hiking uphill rather than downhill on the Mist Trail's treacherous granite staircase, you can look around at the gorgeous scenery every time you stop to catch your breath. The John Muir Trail is somewhat less scenic, especially in its lower reaches, so save it for the way back downhill.

Start at Happy Isles and follow the signed trail to the footbridge over the Merced River, below Vernal Fall. After crossing the bridge, stay close along the river's edge on the Mist Trail for 1.2 miles to the top of Vernal Fall. If it's springtime, make sure you bring your rain gear for this stretch, or you will be drenched in spray. After a brief rest at the waterfall overlook, continue along the river's edge, passing a gorgeous stretch of stream known as the Emerald Pool, still following the Mist Trail. In 0.5 mile, the path crosses the river again, then climbs another mile to the brink of Nevada Fall. Total elevation gain to the top of the 594-foot falls is 2,600 feet, a healthy ascent. But when you get to walk this close to two world-class waterfalls, who's complaining? For your return trip, cross the footbridge above Nevada Fall and follow John Muir Trail to loop back. As you descend, check out the great view of Nevada Fall with Liberty Cap in the background. This is one of the most memorable scenes in Yosemite Valley.

Note that you can cut back over to the Mist Trail at Clark Point, just above Vernal Fall, if you so desire. That way, you get a second chance to see Vernal Fall and hike the Mist Trail's granite staircase. But let your knees decide—plenty of hikers don't want to face those stairs a second time, especially in the downhill direction.

User Groups: Hikers only. No dogs or mountain bikes. Horses are allowed only on John Muir Trail. No wheelchair facilities.

Permits: No permits are required. There is a $20 entrance fee per vehicle at Yosemite National Park, good for seven days.

Maps: A Half Dome or Yosemite National Park map is available from Tom Harrison Maps. For a topographic map, ask the USGS for Half Dome.

Directions: From Merced, drive 70 miles northeast on Highway 140 to Yosemite National Park. Follow the signs toward Yosemite Valley, entering through the Arch Rock entrance station. Continue on Highway 140/El Portal Road, which becomes Southside Drive, for 11.6 miles to the day-use parking lot at Curry Village. Then ride the free Yosemite Valley shuttle bus to Happy Isles, stop No. 16. In winter, when the shuttle does not run, you must hike from the day-use parking lot in Curry Village, adding two miles to your round-trip. Trails may be closed in winter; call to check on weather conditions.

Contact: Yosemite National Park, P.O. Box 577, Yosemite, CA 95389, 209/372-0200, www.nps.gov/yose.

73 MIRROR LAKE LOOP

4.6 mi / 2.0 hr 1 7

in Yosemite Valley

Thousands of Yosemite visitors walk to Mirror Lake every day in summer, but the vast majority of them miss the best part of this hike. The first thing you need to know: Mirror Lake is not really a lake; it's a large, shallow pool in Tenaya Creek. The pool is undergoing the process of sedimentation (filling with sand and gravel from Tenaya Creek), so every year it shrinks a little more. Many visitors walk up and down this canyon, shake their heads, and ask each other "Where's Mirror Lake?" If you know what you are looking for, the shallow pool is interesting to see, especially when its still waters produce a lovely reflective image of the granite domes above. But if you leave Mirror Lake behind and head back a mile or more into Tenaya Canyon, you will get the most out of this hike, and perhaps find the kind of quiet nature experience that most visitors seek in Yosemite.

Start by riding the free shuttle from Curry Village parking lot to Mirror Lake Junction. (Or walk there, if you wish, adding 1.5 miles round-trip to your hike.) From the bus stop, walk 0.5 mile on pavement to Mirror Lake and check out the interpretive signs at its edges. Then follow the foot trail up Tenaya Creek for 1.5 miles, passing the left turnoff for Snow Creek Trail. When you reach a footbridge across Tenaya Creek, cross it and loop back on the other side. Views of Half Dome, Mount Watkins, and neighboring granite walls are spectacular, and the forested creek canyon presents an intimate amphitheater in which to view them. Find a boulder somewhere, have a seat, and take in the show. This loop trail is nearly level the whole way, and once you go beyond Mirror Lake and into the lower Tenaya Creek Canyon, you are likely to find a little solitude.

User Groups: Hikers only. No dogs, horses, or mountain bikes. No wheelchair facilities.

Permits: No permits are required. There is a $20 entrance fee per vehicle at Yosemite National Park, good for seven days.
Maps: A Half Dome or Yosemite National Park map is available from Tom Harrison Maps. For a topographic map, ask the USGS for Half Dome.
Directions: From Merced, drive 70 miles northeast on Highway 140 to Yosemite National Park. Follow the signs toward Yosemite Valley, entering through the Arch Rock entrance station. Continue on Highway 140/El Portal Road, which becomes Southside Drive, for 11.6 miles to the day-use parking lot at Curry Village. Then ride the free Yosemite Valley shuttle bus to Mirror Lake Junction.
Contact: Yosemite National Park, P.O. Box 577, Yosemite, CA 95389, 209/372-0200, www.nps.gov/yose.

74 HALF DOME

17.0 mi / 1.0 or 2.0 days 5 9

in Yosemite Valley

BEST

No argument about it, Half Dome is one of those once-in-your-life-you-gotta-do-it hikes. Just be sure you know what you're in for before you set out on this epic trail. You're in for 17 miles round-trip, a 4,800-foot elevation gain, and an unbelievable amount of company. During the summer about 500 people a day make the trek to Half Dome's summit. The vast majority do it as a day hike, not a backpacking trip (although that is an option if you can get a permit). All day hikers should be sure to bring a load of water and food with them. You'll be handing it out to others who are not so well prepared, as well as gulping it down yourself.

Follow either the John Muir Trail or the Mist Trail from Happy Isles to the top of Nevada Fall (the Mist Trail is 0.6 mile shorter), then go left and enter Little Yosemite Valley, where backpackers make camp. At 6.2 miles the John Muir Trail splits off from the Half Dome Trail and you head left for Half Dome. Just under two miles later you approach Half Dome's shoulder, which is a massive hump that is informally called Sub Dome. A granite stairway, consisting of about 600 mostly handmade steps, leads you up the dauntingly steep face of Sub Dome. Then the trail descends a bit, and you reach the steel cables that run 200 yards up the back of Half Dome. This is when many start praying a lot and wishing there weren't so many other hikers on the cables at the same time. Do some soul-searching before you begin the cable ascent—turning around is not an option once you're halfway up. Pick up a pair of old work gloves from the pile at the base of the cable route; you'll need them to protect your hands as you pull yourself up the cables. It takes two hands and two feet to haul yourself up 440 feet of nearly vertical granite. Unless you somehow managed to get here before the rest of the Half Dome hopefuls, the going will be slow as you wait for the masses ahead to make the ascent. When you reach the top, the views are so incredible that you forget all about your tired arms and feet. There's plenty of room for everyone on top of Half Dome; its vast, mostly flat surface covers about 13 acres.

To make the trip easier, camp at Little Yosemite Valley, 4.7 miles in (wilderness permit required), and save the final ascent for the next day. Don't plan on sleeping much, though. Little Yosemite Valley is one zoo of a backpacking camp.

User Groups: Hikers only. No dogs, horses, or mountain bikes. No wheelchair facilities.
Permits: There is a $20 entrance fee per vehicle at Yosemite National Park, good for seven days. Free wilderness permits are required for overnight stays. They are available on a first-come, first-served basis up to one day in advance at the Yosemite Wilderness kiosk near your chosen trailhead or farther in advance by mail, phone, or online for a $5 reservation fee per person.
Maps: A Half Dome or Yosemite National Park map is available from Tom Harrison Maps. For a topographic map, ask the USGS for Half Dome.

Directions: From Merced, drive 70 miles northeast on Highway 140 to Yosemite National Park. Follow the signs toward Yosemite Valley, entering through the Arch Rock entrance station. Continue on Highway 140/El Portal Road, which becomes Southside Drive, for 11.6 miles to the day-use parking lot at Curry Village. Then ride the free Yosemite Valley shuttle bus to Happy Isles.

Contact: Yosemite National Park, P.O. Box 577, Yosemite, CA 95389, 209/372-0200 or 209/372-0740 (permit reservations), www.nps.gov/yose or www.nps.gov/yose/wilderness (permit reservations).

75 INSPIRATION AND STANFORD POINTS

7.6 mi / 4.0 hr — 3 / 9

in Yosemite Valley near the Wawona Tunnel

Many consider the view from Inspiration Point at the entrance to the Wawona Tunnel to be one of the finest scenes in Yosemite—a wide panorama of Yosemite Valley, El Capitan, Half Dome, and Bridalveil Fall. If you like this view, you might want to see more of it by taking this hike from the trailhead at the vista point parking lot. The Pohono Trail leads uphill on a moderately steep grade until at 1.3 miles it reaches the "old" Inspiration Point. This is where the road to Yosemite Valley went through in the days before the Wawona Tunnel, and the view is now largely obscured by trees. Keep climbing, however, because with another 1,000 feet of elevation gain, you will cross Meadow Brook and reach the left cutoff trail for Stanford Point. You're 3.8 miles from the trailhead and you've climbed 2,200 feet, but your reward is an eagle's-eye view of the valley floor, 3,000 feet below, and a vista to the east of Half Dome and all its granite cousins. This stretch of the Pohono Trail is a dependable workout and the trail is never crowded with hikers.

User Groups: Hikers only. No dogs, horses, or mountain bikes. No wheelchair facilities.

Permits: No permits are required. There is a $20 entrance fee per vehicle at Yosemite National Park, good for seven days.

Maps: A Yosemite National Park map is available from Tom Harrison Maps. For a topographic map, ask the USGS for El Capitan.

Directions: From Merced, drive 70 miles northeast on Highway 140 to Yosemite National Park. Follow the signs to Yosemite Valley, entering through the Arch Rock entrance station. Continue 6.3 miles on Highway 140/El Portal Road, which becomes Southside Drive, and turn right at the fork for Highway 41/Wawona/Fresno. Continue 1.5 miles to the parking lots on either side of the road just before you enter the Wawona Tunnel. The trailhead is at the parking lot on the left (south) side of the road.

Contact: Yosemite National Park, P.O. Box 577, Yosemite, CA 95389, 209/372-0200, www.nps.gov/yose.

76 BRIDALVEIL FALL

0.5 mi / 0.5 hr — 1 / 9

in Yosemite Valley

BEST

Bridalveil Fall is right up there with Lower Yosemite Fall as a must-do walk for visitors (including nonhikers) to Yosemite Valley. Like that other famous waterfall walk, the path to Bridalveil Fall is paved with people. But the best thing about this waterfall is that unlike other falls in Yosemite Valley, Bridalveil runs year-round. It never dries up and disappoints visitors. The walk to its overlook is short and nearly level; the trail delivers you to a small viewing area about 70 yards from the fall. You can look straight up and see Bridalveil Creek plunging 620 feet off the edge of the south canyon wall. In high wind the fall billows and sways; if you are lucky you might see rainbows dancing in its mist. Another bonus is that your position at the Bridalveil overlook is such that if you do an about-face, you have an excellent view of Ribbon Fall flowing off the northern

Yosemite Valley rim. Ribbon Fall is the highest single drop in the park at 1,612 feet, but it only flows in the earliest months of spring.

User Groups: Hikers and wheelchairs. No dogs, horses, or mountain bikes.

Permits: No permits are required. There is a $20 entrance fee per vehicle at Yosemite National Park, good for seven days.

Maps: A Yosemite National Park map is available from Tom Harrison Maps. For a topographic map, ask the USGS for El Capitan.

Directions: From Merced, drive 70 miles northeast on Highway 140 to Yosemite National Park. Follow the signs toward Yosemite Valley, entering through the Arch Rock entrance station. Continue for 6.3 miles on Highway 140/El Portal Road, which becomes Southside Drive, and turn right at the fork for Highway 41/Wawona/Fresno. Turn left almost immediately into the Bridalveil Fall parking lot. The trail begins at the far end of the parking lot. If you are driving into Yosemite Valley on Highway 41 from the south, watch for the Bridalveil Fall turnoff on your right about one mile after you exit the Wawona Tunnel.

Contact: Yosemite National Park, P.O. Box 577, Yosemite, CA 95389, 209/372-0200, www.nps.gov/yose.

77 FOUR-MILE TRAIL

9.6 mi / 6.0 hr 3 8

in Yosemite Valley

Many years ago, we hiked this trail on our first-ever visit to Yosemite and were shocked when we got to the top and found a giant parking lot and refreshment stand located there. What, you mean we could have driven to the high point on this trail? It's true, but your arrival at dramatic Glacier Point is somehow made all the more meaningful if you get there the hard way, which means hiking Four-Mile Trail all the way up from the valley floor, gaining 3,220 feet in 4.8 miles (not 4.0 miles, as the name implies). The trail is partially shaded and makes for a terrific day hike with an early morning start. Then you can have a leisurely brunch or lunch from your bird's-eye perch on Glacier Point. Don't like what you brought in your daypack? No problem. A snack shop sells hot dogs and the like all summer. From Glacier Point, you have unobstructed views of just about every major landmark in Yosemite Valley—most notably Half Dome, Basket Dome, Yosemite Falls, Vernal and Nevada Falls, and the valley floor far, far below you.

User Groups: Hikers only. No dogs, horses, or mountain bikes. No wheelchair facilities.

Permits: No permits are required. There is a $20 entrance fee per vehicle at Yosemite National Park, good for seven days.

Maps: A Half Dome or Yosemite National Park map is available from Tom Harrison Maps. For a topographic map, ask the USGS for Half Dome.

Directions: From Merced, drive 70 miles northeast on Highway 140 to Yosemite National Park. Follow the signs to Yosemite Valley, entering through the Arch Rock entrance station. Continue on Highway 140/El Portal Road, which becomes Southside Drive, for 9.5 miles. The trailhead is located next to mile marker V18 on the right side of Southside Drive. Park in the pullouts along the road.

Contact: Yosemite National Park, P.O. Box 577, Yosemite, CA 95389, 209/372-0200, www.nps.gov/yose.

78 McGURK MEADOW AND DEWEY POINT

2.0–7.0 mi / 1.0–4.0 hr 2 8

off Glacier Point Road in Yosemite National Park

BEST

Some trails seem to capture the essence of Yosemite, and the McGurk Meadow Trail is one of those. The trailhead is the first one you reach as you wind along Glacier Point Road to spectacular Glacier Point. It's worth a stop to take the short walk through a fir and pine forest to pristine McGurk Meadow, a mile-long meadow crossed by a footbridge over a small feeder creek. A quarter-mile before the meadow the trail passes an old pioneer cabin, still standing in half-decent repair.

You can turn around at the meadow for a short and easy trip, or you can follow the trail until it connects to the Pohono Trail, which traverses Yosemite's south rim. An ideal destination is Dewey Point, a spectacular promontory with an unforgettable view of Yosemite Valley, located just off the Pohono Trail. That option turns this hike into a seven-mile round-trip.

User Groups: Hikers only. No dogs, horses, or mountain bikes. No wheelchair facilities.

Permits: No permits are required. There is a $20 entrance fee per vehicle at Yosemite National Park, good for seven days.

Maps: A Yosemite National Park map is available from Tom Harrison Maps. For a topographic map, ask the USGS for El Capitan.

Directions: From Merced, drive 70 miles northeast on Highway 140 to Yosemite National Park. Follow the signs toward Yosemite Valley, entering through the Arch Rock entrance station. Continue 6.3 miles on Highway 140/El Portal Road, which becomes Southside Drive, and turn right at the fork for Highway 41/Wawona/Fresno. Continue for 9.2 miles, turn left on Glacier Point Road, and drive 7.5 miles to the McGurk Meadow trailhead, on the left. Park in the pullout about 75 yards farther up the road.

Contact: Yosemite National Park, P.O. Box 577, Yosemite, CA 95389, 209/372-0200, www.nps.gov/yose.

79 BRIDALVEIL CREEK

3.2 mi / 1.5 hr 1 7

off Glacier Point Road in Yosemite National Park

Perhaps the best time to take this hike to Bridalveil Creek is immediately after visiting Bridalveil Fall. After a short walk from Glacier Point Road through a forested area, you wind up at the edge of Bridalveil Creek, a babbling brook that seems far too tame to produce the giant waterfall downstream. To make the trip, follow Ostrander Lake Trail from Glacier Point Road for 1.4 miles. This stretch is almost completely level and is framed by colorful bunches of lupine in midsummer. When the trail splits, take the right fork toward Bridalveil Creek. The stream is so tame here that there is no bridge to cross—it's an easy rock hop by midsummer, although it can be a dangerous crossing in late spring. Pick a spot along its banks, and spend some time counting the wildflowers or the small, darting trout. If you are camping at Bridalveil Creek Campground or just heading up the road to visit Glacier Point, this easy walk is a pleasant leg-stretcher that will take you away from the crowds that throng so many of Yosemite's famous destinations.

User Groups: Hikers only. No dogs, horses, or mountain bikes. No wheelchair facilities.

Permits: No permits are required. There is a $20 entrance fee per vehicle at Yosemite National Park, good for seven days.

Maps: A Yosemite National Park map is available from Tom Harrison Maps. For a topographic map, ask the USGS for Half Dome.

Directions: From Merced, drive 70 miles northeast on Highway 140 to Yosemite National Park. Follow the signs toward Yosemite Valley, entering through the Arch Rock entrance station. Continue for 6.3 miles on Highway 140/El Portal Road, which becomes Southside Drive, and turn right at the fork for Highway 41/Wawona/Fresno. Continue for 9.2 miles, turn left on Glacier Point Road, and drive another 8.9 miles to the Ostrander Lake trailhead, on the right.

Contact: Yosemite National Park, P.O. Box 577, Yosemite, CA 95389, 209/372-0200, www.nps.gov/yose.

80 OSTRANDER LAKE

12.5 mi / 1.0 or 2.0 days 2 8

off Glacier Point Road in Yosemite National Park

While many people take short day hikes from Glacier Point Road, a longer 12.5-mile trip to Ostrander Lake may better suit your taste. The trail is surprisingly easy, considering the long miles, and the first half is quite level. You can hike out and back in a day, or get a wilderness permit and camp near the lake's shores. The wide blue lake, set at 8,580 feet, is a popular destination for cross-country skiers in the winter, as is evidenced by the stone Ostrander Ski Hut and the ski markers tacked high up on trees along the route. Although the trail (really an old road) begins in a regenerated forest fire area, it traverses a typical high-country landscape of firs, pines, and, as you ascend, granite. You have to gain 1,600 feet along the way, most of it in the final three miles to the lake. The culmination of the climb occurs at nearly six miles out, as you reach the trail's highest point, a saddle on top of 8,700-foot Horizon Ridge. Here you are rewarded with excellent views of Half Dome, North Dome, Basket Dome, and Liberty Cap. This is a fine place to catch your breath. From here, the lake is less than 0.5 mile farther. On summer days, bring your swimsuit and a book, and plan to spend a few hours on Ostrander's sand- and boulder-lined shoreline.

User Groups: Hikers only. No dogs, horses, or mountain bikes. No wheelchair facilities.

Permits: There is a $20 entrance fee per vehicle at Yosemite National Park, good for seven days. Free wilderness permits are required for overnight stays. They are available on a first-come, first-served basis up to one day in advance at the Yosemite Wilderness kiosk near your chosen trailhead or farther in advance by mail, phone, or online for a $5 reservation fee per person.

Maps: A Yosemite National Park map is available from Tom Harrison Maps. For topographic maps, ask the USGS for Half Dome and Mariposa Grove.

Directions: From Merced, drive 70 miles northeast on Highway 140 to Yosemite National Park. Follow the signs toward Yosemite Valley, entering through the Arch Rock entrance station. Continue for 6.3 miles on Highway 140/El Portal Road, which becomes Southside Drive, and turn right at the fork for Highway 41/Wawona/Fresno. Continue for 9.2 miles, turn left on Glacier Point Road, and drive 8.9 miles to the Ostrander Lake trailhead, on the right.

Contact: Yosemite National Park, P.O. Box 577, Yosemite, CA 95389, 209/372-0200 or 209/372-0740 (permit reservations), www.nps.gov/yose or www.nps.gov/yose/wilderness (permit reservations).

81 SENTINEL DOME

2.2 mi / 1.0 hr 1 9

off Glacier Point Road in Yosemite National Park

BEST

It's hard to believe you can get so much for so little, but on Sentinel Dome Trail, you can. The granite dome is located about a mile before Glacier Point on Glacier Point Road, and its elevation is 1,000 feet higher than the point's. Views from the dome's summit extend a full 360 degrees. A short and nearly level walk leads you to the base of the dome, and a 100-yard climb up its smooth granite backside brings you to its summit. There you are greeted by stunning vistas in all directions, including an unusual perspective on Upper and Lower Yosemite Falls. This is one of the best places in Yosemite to watch the sun set. To make a longer excursion, you can easily combine this hike with the hike to Taft Point and the Fissures (see next listing), which starts from the same trailhead but heads in the opposite direction.

User Groups: Hikers only. No dogs, horses, or mountain bikes. No wheelchair facilities.

Permits: No permits are required. There is a $20 entrance fee per vehicle at Yosemite National Park, good for seven days.

Maps: A Half Dome or Yosemite National Park map is available from Tom Harrison Maps. For a topographic map, ask the USGS for Half Dome.
Directions: From Merced, drive 70 miles northeast on Highway 140 to Yosemite National Park. Follow the signs to Yosemite Valley, entering through the Arch Rock entrance station. Continue 6.3 miles on Highway 140/El Portal Road, which becomes Southside Drive, and turn right at the fork for Highway 41/Wawona/Fresno. Continue for 9.2 miles, turn left on Glacier Point Road, and drive 13.2 miles to the Taft Point/Sentinel Dome trailhead parking lot, on the left side of the road.
Contact: Yosemite National Park, P.O. Box 577, Yosemite, CA 95389, 209/372-0200, www.nps.gov/yose.

82 TAFT POINT AND THE FISSURES

2.2 mi / 1.0 hr 1 8

off Glacier Point Road in Yosemite National Park

It's not so much the sweeping vista from Taft Point that you remember (although certainly you could say that the views of Yosemite's north rim and the valley floor are stunning). What you remember is the incredible sense of awe that you feel, perhaps mixed with a little fear and a lot of respect, as you peer down into the fissures in Taft Point's granite—huge cracks in the rock that plunge hundreds of feet down toward the valley. One of the fissures has a couple of large boulders captured in its jaws; they're stuck there, waiting for the next big earthquake or ice age to set them free. Be sure to walk to the metal railing along the edge of Taft Point's cliff, where you can hold on tight and peer down at the valley far, far below. If you have kids with you or anyone who is afraid of heights, be sure to keep a tight handhold on them.

User Groups: Hikers only. No dogs, horses, or mountain bikes. No wheelchair facilities.
Permits: No permits are required. There is a $20 entrance fee per vehicle at Yosemite National Park, good for seven days.
Maps: A Half Dome or Yosemite National Park map is available from Tom Harrison Maps. For a topographic map, ask the USGS for Half Dome.
Directions: From Merced, drive 70 miles northeast on Highway 140 to Yosemite National Park. Follow the signs to Yosemite Valley, entering through the Arch Rock entrance station. Continue for 6.3 miles on Highway 140/El Portal Road, which becomes Southside Drive, and turn right at the fork for Highway 41/Wawona/Fresno. Continue for 9.2 miles, turn left on Glacier Point Road, and drive 13.2 miles to the Taft Point/Sentinel Dome trailhead parking lot, on the left side of the road.
Contact: Yosemite National Park, P.O. Box 577, Yosemite, CA 95389, 209/372-0200, www.nps.gov/yose.

83 POHONO TRAIL

13.0 mi one-way / 7.0 hr 3 10

off Glacier Point Road in Yosemite National Park

If you can arrange a shuttle trip, Pohono Trail from Glacier Point downhill to its end at Wawona Tunnel is worth every step of its 13 miles. The two ends of the trail have the best drive-to viewpoints in all of Yosemite, and in between, you are treated to dozens of other scenic spots (including Sentinel Dome, at 1.5 miles, and Taft Point, at 3.8 miles), as well as four bird's-eye lookouts over the valley floor: Inspiration, Stanford, Dewey, and Crocker Points. Starting at Glacier Point and ending at Wawona Tunnel, you'll cover a 2,800-foot descent, but there are some "ups" along the way, too—like at the very beginning (from Glacier Point to Sentinel Dome), and between

HIKING

Bridalveil Creek and Dewey Point. The trail stays on or near Yosemite Valley's southern rim the entire way except for one major detour into the woods to access the bridge crossing of Bridalveil Creek. Remember to bring along a good map, because many of the trail's best offerings are just off the main path. If you don't take the short spur routes to reach them, you'll miss out on some spectacular scenery.

The view of Yosemite Falls from Pohono Trail in front of Sentinel Dome is the best in all of Yosemite. For the best overall vista along the trail, it's a toss-up between Glacier Point, Taft Point, and Dewey Point.

User Groups: Hikers only. No dogs, horses, or mountain bikes. No wheelchair facilities.

Permits: There is a $20 entrance fee per vehicle at Yosemite National Park, good for seven days. Free wilderness permits are required for overnight stays. They are available on a first-come, first-served basis up to one day in advance at the Yosemite Wilderness kiosk near your chosen trailhead, or farther in advance by mail, phone, or online for a $5 reservation fee per person.

Maps: A Yosemite National Park map is available from Tom Harrison Maps. For topographic maps, ask the USGS for Half Dome and El Capitan.

Directions: From Merced, drive 70 miles northeast on Highway 140 to Yosemite National Park. Follow the signs to Yosemite Valley, entering through the Arch Rock entrance station. Continue for 6.3 miles on Highway 140/El Portal Road, which becomes Southside Drive, and turn right at the fork for Highway 41/Wawona/Fresno. Continue for 9.2 miles, turn left on Glacier Point Road, and drive 15.7 miles to Glacier Point. Park and walk toward the main viewing area across from the café and gift shop. Look for the Pohono Trail sign about 150 feet southeast of the café building, on your right.

Contact: Yosemite National Park, P.O. Box 577, Yosemite, CA 95389, 209/372-0200 or 209/372-0740 (permit reservations), www.nps.gov/yose or www.nps.gov/yose/wilderness (permit reservations).

84 PANORAMA TRAIL

8.5 mi one-way / 5.0 hr 3 10

off Glacier Point Road in Yosemite National Park

BEST

The Panorama Trail follows a spectacular route from Glacier Point to Yosemite Valley, heading downhill most of the way, but you must have a shuttle car waiting at the end or it's one heck of a long climb back up. A great option is to take the Yosemite Lodge tour bus for one leg of the trip; call 209/372-1240 to reserve a seat (fee required).

The aptly named Panorama Trail begins at Glacier Point, elevation 7,214 feet. You switchback downhill, accompanied by ever-changing perspectives on Half Dome, Basket Dome, North Dome, Liberty Cap, and, in the distance, Vernal and Nevada Falls. You will gape a lot. After passing Illilouette Fall and ascending a bit for the first time on the trip, continue eastward to the Panorama Trail's end near the top of Nevada Fall. Turn right to reach the top of the fall and have a rest at the overlook, then continue downhill on the Mist Trail on the north side of the river. After a view-filled descent along the north side of Nevada Fall, you'll cross the river in 1.4 miles and walk alongside lovely Emerald Pool on your way to the top of Vernal Fall. Enjoy the show here, then tromp down the granite staircase on the busy trail back to Happy Isles. From there you can take the free valley shuttle bus back to your car, parked somewhere in Yosemite Valley.

Note that the route has a 3,200-foot elevation loss over its course, but there is also a 760-foot climb after you cross Illilouette Creek. Also be forewarned that while the starting miles of the trip are quite tranquil, the final two miles by Vernal Fall are usually a parade of people.

User Groups: Hikers only. No dogs, horses, or mountain bikes. No wheelchair facilities.

Permits: No permits are required. There is a $20 entrance fee per vehicle at Yosemite National Park, good for seven days.

Maps: A Half Dome or Yosemite National Park map is available from Tom Harrison Maps. For a topographic map, ask the USGS for Half Dome.

Directions: From Merced, drive 70 miles northeast on Highway 140 to Yosemite National Park. Follow the signs to Yosemite Valley, entering through the Arch Rock entrance station. Continue for 6.3 miles on Highway 140/El Portal Road, which becomes Southside Drive, and turn right at the fork for Highway 41/Wawona/Fresno. Continue for 9.2 miles, turn left on Glacier Point Road, and drive 15.7 miles to Glacier Point. Park and walk toward the main viewing area, across from the café and gift shop. Look for the Panorama Trail sign about 150 feet southeast of the café building, on your right.

Contact: Yosemite National Park, P.O. Box 577, Yosemite, CA 95389, 209/372-0200, www.nps.gov/yose; Yosemite Lodge Tour Buses, 209/372-1240.

85 ILLILOUETTE FALL

4.0 mi / 2.5 hr 2 10

off Glacier Point Road in Yosemite National Park

Those who can't afford the time or make the car shuttle arrangements necessary to hike the entire Panorama Trail should at least take this incredible out-and-back trip on the top portion of the route. Glacier Point is your starting point, and the bridge above Illilouette Fall becomes your destination, but what happens in between is sheer magic. Some say that hiking Panorama Trail is like staring at a life-size Yosemite postcard, but we say it's more like being in the postcard. As you walk, you feel as if you've become one with the magnificent panorama of Half Dome, Basket Dome, North Dome, Liberty Cap, and far-off Vernal and Nevada Falls. The trail is downhill all the way to Illilouette Fall in two miles, which means you have a 1,200-foot elevation gain on the return trip. The path is extremely well graded, so even children can make the climb. After viewing the waterfall from a trailside overlook, walk another 0.25 mile and stand on the bridge that is perched just above the 370-foot drop. For obvious reasons, don't think about swimming here.

User Groups: Hikers only. No dogs, horses, or mountain bikes. No wheelchair facilities.

Permits: No permits are required. There is a $20 entrance fee per vehicle at Yosemite National Park, good for seven days.

Maps: A Half Dome or Yosemite National Park map is available from Tom Harrison Maps. For a topographic map, ask the USGS for Half Dome.

Directions: From Merced, drive 70 miles northeast on Highway 140 to Yosemite National Park. Follow the signs to Yosemite Valley, entering through the Arch Rock entrance station. Continue for 6.3 miles on Highway 140/El Portal Road, which becomes Southside Drive, and turn right at the fork for Highway 41/Wawona/Fresno. Continue for 9.2 miles, turn left on Glacier Point Road, and drive 15.7 miles to Glacier Point. Park and walk toward the main viewing area, across from the café and gift shop. Look for the Panorama Trail sign on your right, about 150 feet southeast of the café building.

Contact: Yosemite National Park, P.O. Box 577, Yosemite, CA 95389, 209/372-0200, www.nps.gov/yose.

86 ALDER CREEK FALLS

8.2 mi / 5.0 hr 3 9

off Highway 41 near Wawona in Yosemite National Park

Maybe the best thing about Alder Creek Falls is that with all the world-famous waterfalls in Yosemite, this one just plain gets overlooked. Or maybe the best thing is the fun hike to reach it, starting with the challenge of locating the hidden trailhead along Highway 41.

HIKING

After you accomplish this feat, you begin with a one-mile beeline hike straight uphill through the forest, which will surely get your heart pumping. At the top of the ridge and a trail junction, turn left and hike through the trees for two more miles, still heading uphill but now more gently. Three miles from the trailhead, the route suddenly goes level as it joins an old railroad grade, and then it's a one-mile easy stroll to the spot where Alder Creek takes the plunge off a granite lip. The waterfall is about 250 feet tall, and the best view of it is from the trail, about 100 yards away from it. If you choose to keep hiking beyond the falls, you'll find many fine picnic spots among meadows filled with wildflowers.

User Groups: Hikers and horses. No dogs or mountain bikes. No wheelchair facilities.

Permits: There is a $20 entrance fee per vehicle at Yosemite National Park, good for seven days. Free wilderness permits are required for overnight stays. They are available on a first-come, first-served basis up to one day in advance at the Yosemite Wilderness kiosk near your chosen trailhead, or farther in advance by mail, phone, or online for a $5 reservation fee per person.

Maps: A Yosemite National Park map is available from Tom Harrison Maps. For a topographic map, ask the USGS for Wawona.

Directions: From Merced, drive 55 miles northeast on Highway 140 to Yosemite National Park. Follow the signs to Yosemite Valley, entering through the Arch Rock entrance station. Continue for 6.3 miles on Highway 140/El Portal Road, which becomes Southside Drive, and turn right at the fork for Highway 41/Wawona/Fresno. Drive south on Highway 41 for 21 miles to a hairpin turn in the road (if you are coming from the south, it is exactly 4.2 miles north of Chilnualna Falls Road in Wawona). Park in the large dirt pullout on the west side of the road; the trailhead is on the east side of Highway 41. There is no marker except for a Yosemite Wilderness sign.

Contact: Yosemite National Park, P.O. Box 577, Yosemite, CA 95389, 209/372-0200 or 209/372-0740 (permit reservations), www.nps.gov/yose or www.nps.gov/yose/wilderness (permit reservations).

87 WAWONA MEADOW LOOP

3.2 mi / 1.25 hr 1 7

off Highway 41 near Wawona in Yosemite National Park

Sometimes you just want to take a stroll in the park, and the Wawona Meadow Loop is exactly that. Many hikers ignore this trail because of its proximity to the Wawona Golf Course, but they are missing out on an easy, pleasant meander. On this level trail (a former stage road), you can see terrific wildflowers in early summer and enjoy the good company of butterflies as you take a lazy stroll. From the signed trailhead across the road from the Wawona Hotel, hike to your left on the dirt road, following the split rail fence. At the end of the meadow the old road crosses the stream and returns to the hotel on the north side of the golf course. If you wish, you can even bring your dog or ride your bike on this trail. If you're staying at the Wawona Hotel, you can hike from there, crossing the Wawona Road on your way out and back.

User Groups: Hikers, dogs, and mountain bikes. No horses. No wheelchair facilities.

Permits: No permits are required. There is a $20 entrance fee per vehicle at Yosemite National Park, good for seven days.

Maps: A Yosemite National Park map is available from Tom Harrison Maps. For a topographic map, ask the USGS for Wawona.

Directions: From Merced, drive 70 miles northeast on Highway 140 to Yosemite National Park. Follow the signs toward Yosemite Valley, entering through the Arch Rock entrance station. Continue for 6.3 miles on Highway 140/El Portal Road, which becomes Southside Drive, and turn right at the fork for Highway 41/Wawona/Fresno. Drive 27 miles to the trailhead, which is just south of the golf course and across the road from the Wawona Hotel.

Contact: Yosemite National Park, P.O. Box 577, Yosemite, CA 95389, 209/372-0200, www.nps.gov/yose.

88 CHILNUALNA FALL

8.2 mi / 5.0 hr 3 9

off Highway 41 near Wawona in Yosemite National Park

Are you ready to climb? It's good to be mentally prepared for this hike, which includes a steady four-mile uphill, gaining 2,400 feet to reach the top of Chilnualna Falls. Pick a nice, cool day because this trail is in the lower-elevation part of Yosemite. Your nose will be continually assaulted with the intoxicating smell of bear clover, which together with manzanita and oaks makes up the majority of the vegetation along the route. Halfway up you get a great view of Wawona Dome (elevation 6,897 feet) from a granite overlook. This is a great place to take a break and stretch your hamstrings. Shortly thereafter you glimpse a section of Chilnualna Falls high up on a cliff wall, still far ahead. The trail leads above the brink of the fall's lower drop to a series of higher cascades. Keep hiking until you reach the uppermost cascade, which consists of five pool-and-drop tiers just 100 yards off the granite-lined trail. You'll want to spread out a picnic here before you begin the long descent back to the trailhead.

User Groups: Hikers and horses. No dogs or mountain bikes. No wheelchair facilities.

Permits: There is a $20 entrance fee per vehicle at Yosemite National Park, good for seven days. Free wilderness permits are required for overnight stays. They are available on a first-come, first-served basis up to one day in advance at the Yosemite Wilderness kiosk near your chosen trailhead, or farther in advance by mail, phone, or online for a $5 reservation fee per person.

Maps: A Yosemite National Park map is available from Tom Harrison Maps. For topographic maps, ask the USGS for Wawona and Mariposa Grove.

Directions: From Merced, drive 55 miles northeast on Highway 140 to Yosemite National Park. Follow the signs to Yosemite Valley, entering through the Arch Rock entrance station. Continue for 6.3 miles on Highway 140/El Portal Road, which becomes Southside Drive, and turn right at the fork for Highway 41/Wawona/Fresno. Drive south on Highway 41 for 25 miles to Wawona, and turn left on Chilnualna Falls Road. Drive 1.7 miles east and park in the lot on the right side of the road. Walk back to Chilnualna Falls Road and pick up the single-track trail across the pavement.

Contact: Yosemite National Park, P.O. Box 577, Yosemite, CA 95389, 209/372-0200 or 209/372-0740 (permit reservations), www.nps.gov/yose or www.nps.gov/yose/wilderness (permit reservations).

89 MARIPOSA GROVE

2.0–6.4 mi / 1.0–3.0 hr 2 8

off Highway 41 near Wawona in Yosemite National Park

The Mariposa Grove is the largest of the three groves of giant sequoias in Yosemite National Park. That's why in summer the parking lot fills up and people wait in line in their cars to see the hundreds of big trees here (and on the busiest days, you will be required to ride a shuttle bus to the trailhead). The star tree in the Mariposa Grove is the Grizzly Giant, with a circumference of more than 100 feet. At approximately 2,700 years old, it's one of the oldest known giant sequoias. If you want to see only the most famous trees in the grove, including the Grizzly Giant, take the well-signed two-mile hike through the lower grove and turn around at the signs pointing to the upper grove. If you hike the entire lower and upper grove, you will cover 6.4 miles of trail. One surprise to first-time visitors is the motorized open-air trams that run through the grove, which are ideal for people who don't want to hike. Some visitors choose to ride the tram to the top of the grove, then hike back downhill for a one-way trip of about three miles. For the best chance of avoiding the summer crowds, time your visit for early in the morning or just before sunset.

User Groups: Hikers only. No dogs, horses, or mountain bikes. No wheelchair facilities.

Permits: No permits are required. There is a $20 entrance fee per vehicle at Yosemite National Park, good for seven days.

Maps: A brochure and trail map are available at the trailhead. A Yosemite National Park map is available from Tom Harrison Maps. For a topographic map, ask the USGS for Mariposa Grove.

Directions: From Merced, drive 70 miles northeast on Highway 140 to Yosemite National Park. Follow the signs toward Yosemite Valley, entering through the Arch Rock entrance station. Continue for 6.3 miles on Highway 140/El Portal Road, which becomes Southside Drive, and turn right at the fork for Highway 41/Wawona/Fresno. Drive 32 miles to the well-signed Mariposa Grove access road by Yosemite's south entrance. Turn east and drive two miles to the parking lot. During the busy summer months, park your car at the Wawona Store and ride the free shuttle bus into the Mariposa Grove. During the winter, the two-mile-long road into the grove is usually closed due to snow and ice, but you can still walk or snowshoe in.

If you enter the park on Highway 41 from the south, the Mariposa Grove is on the right, just after you drive through the park entrance station.

Contact: Yosemite National Park, P.O. Box 577, Yosemite, CA 95389, 209/372-0200, www.nps.gov/yose.

90 LEWIS CREEK TRAIL

4.0 mi / 2.0 hr — 1 — 8

off Highway 41 north of Oakhurst

Three separate trailheads access Lewis Creek Trail, but unless you want to hike its entire 3.7-mile one-way distance, the best place to start is at the trail's midpoint, just off Highway 41. From this roadside trailhead, you can take a 10-minute walk south to Corlieu Falls and/or walk 1.8 miles north to see Red Rock Falls. Neither waterfall is a showstopper, although both are pretty. Instead, the highlight of the trip is the hike itself, a gorgeous walk along flower-lined Lewis Creek, following the route of the historic Madera Sugar Pine lumber flume. Sugar Pine Lumber Company used the flume (an artificial river in a huge wooden trough) to float lumber over 50 miles to the town of Madera. You'll pass many anglers along the hike; Lewis Creek is stocked with catchable trout. Fishing is best below Corlieu Falls. In addition, the white western azaleas along the stream bloom in profusion in early summer, shaded by a thick canopy of dogwoods, oaks, ponderosa pines, and incense cedars.

User Groups: Hikers and dogs. No horses or mountain bikes. No wheelchair facilities.

Permits: No permits are required. Parking and access are free.

Maps: A Sierra National Forest map is available from the U.S. Forest Service. For a topographic map, ask the USGS for Ahwahnee.

Directions: From Oakhurst, drive north on Highway 41 for eight miles to the signed trailhead for Lewis Creek Trail, on the east side of the highway. The trailhead is four miles south of Westfall Picnic Area.

Contact: Sierra National Forest, Bass Lake Ranger Station, 57003 Road 225, North Fork, CA 93643, 559/877-2218, www.fs.fed.us/r5/sierra.

91 SHADOW OF THE GIANTS

1.2 mi / 0.5 hr 1 9

off Highway 41 south of Yosemite National Park and north of Oakhurst in Sierra National Forest

BEST

Shadow of the Giants is a National Recreation Trail that is located within the Nelder Grove of Giant Sequoias. For the sheer numbers of sequoias and the blissful peace and quiet, it beats the heck out of the sequoia groves a few miles north, in Yosemite National Park. On a Saturday afternoon in June, it's not impossible to walk the one-mile interpretive trail all by yourself. The self-guided signs along the trail are interesting and informative, and the babble of Nelder Creek is a perfect accompaniment to the huge, majestic trees. In addition to the sequoias, the forest is filled with western azaleas, dogwoods, incense cedars, wild rose, sugar pines, and white firs. What's the best thing we learned on the trail? The bark of mature sequoias is so soft that squirrels use it to line their nests. The trail makes an easy loop and is set at 5,000 feet in elevation. The best sequoias are at the far end of the loop, so make sure you walk all the way.

User Groups: Hikers and dogs. No horses or mountain bikes. No wheelchair facilities.

Permits: No permits are required. Parking and access are free.

Maps: A Sierra National Forest map is available from the U.S. Forest Service. For a topographic map, ask the USGS for Bass Lake.

Directions: From Oakhurst, drive north on Highway 41 for five miles to Sky Ranch Road/Road 632. Turn east on Sky Ranch Road and drive six miles to the turnoff for Nelder Grove. Turn left, drive 1.5 miles, and take the left fork, signed for Shadow of the Giants. Drive 0.5 mile to the trailhead.

Contact: Sierra National Forest, Bass Lake Ranger Station, 57003 Road 225, North Fork, CA 93643, 559/877-2218, www.fs.fed.us/r5/sierra.

92 FRESNO DOME

2.0 mi / 1.0 hr 2 10

off Highway 41 south of Yosemite National Park and north of Oakhurst

It's best to plan one hour of time for this trip, but you might want to leave room for more, because once you reach the top of Fresno Dome, you won't want to leave. The trailhead elevation is 8,000 feet, and the trail is beautiful right from the start. It traverses a verdant meadow filled with corn lilies, quaking aspens, and lavender shooting stars. The first 0.5 mile is completely flat; in the second 0.5 mile, you climb up the sloped back side of Fresno Dome. After a moderate ascent (manageable by almost anybody), you're rewarded with 360-degree views, mostly of conifer-filled valleys. You can just make out a corner of Bass Lake, the town of Oakhurst, and the far-off snowy peaks of the John Muir Wilderness. From up on top of Fresno Dome, it all looks like heaven.

User Groups: Hikers and dogs. No horses or mountain bikes. No wheelchair facilities.

Permits: No permits are required. Parking and access are free.

Maps: A Sierra National Forest map is available from the U.S. Forest Service. For a topographic map, ask the USGS for Bass Lake.

Directions: From Oakhurst, drive north on Highway 41 for five miles to Sky Ranch Road/Road 632. Turn east on Sky Ranch Road, drive approximately 12 miles, and bear left at the sign for Fresno Dome Campground. Drive 4.8 miles to the trailhead (two miles past the camp).

Contact: Sierra National Forest, Bass Lake Ranger Station, 57003 Road 225, North Fork, CA 93643, 559/877-2218, www.fs.fed.us/r5/sierra.

HIKING

93 THE NICHE AND CORA LAKES

8.6 mi / 4.0 hr–2.0 days 2 8

in the Ansel Adams Wilderness southeast of Yosemite National Park

Reaching the trailhead for The Niche and Cora Lakes requires a long drive on the Sierra Vista National Scenic Byway, the showpiece road of the North Fork area. If you have the time for it, it's a great trip. The best approach is to drive out and spend the night at Granite Creek Campground or nearby Clover Meadow Campground, then start hiking the next day. The trip starts with a 3.1-mile gentle ascent through red firs and lodgepole pines to The Niche (at 8,000 feet), where you enter the Ansel Adams Wilderness boundary. Bear left and follow the signs to Cora Lakes, at 4.3 miles. Only one of the Cora Lakes is of substantial size; that's the lower lake, the first one you come to, on the left. The lake is partly forested and has dependable trout fishing. Because the total ascent to Cora Lakes is only 1,200 feet, you may have some energy left to burn. Backpackers should consider adding on a jaunt to Joe Crane Lake, another four miles to the north. The lake has a long and lovely sandy beach, good fishing, and even better swimming than at Cora Lakes.

User Groups: Hikers, dogs, and horses. No mountain bikes. No wheelchair facilities.

Permits: A free wilderness permit is required for overnight stays and is available from the Bass Lake Ranger Station. Quotas are in effect year-round; permits can be reserved in advance for a $5 reservation fee per person.

Maps: A Sierra National Forest or Ansel Adams Wilderness map is available from the U.S. Forest Service. For a topographic map, ask the USGS for Timber Knob.

Directions: From the town of North Fork south of Bass Lake, drive southeast on Road 225 to Minarets Road. Turn left (north) on Minarets Road/Road 81 and follow it for approximately 50 winding miles to the Clover Meadow Ranger Station/Granite Creek turnoff, on the right. Drive 4.5 miles to the Isberg trailhead, just beyond Granite Creek Campground.

Contact: Sierra National Forest, Bass Lake Ranger Station, 57003 Road 225, North Fork, CA 93643, 559/877-2218, www.fs.fed.us/r5/sierra.

94 JACKASS LAKES

7.2 mi / 4.0 hr or 2.0 days 2 8

in the Ansel Adams Wilderness southeast of Yosemite National Park

Campers in the Clover Meadow and Upper Chiquito campground areas have this pleasant day hike to look forward to. The trailhead is an easy reach (right off of Beasore Road), and in about two hours of hiking, you can be cooling your toes in the crystal-blue waters of Lower Jackass Lake. The trail climbs immediately from the road, then enters the Ansel Adams Wilderness boundary in one mile. This first mile can be hot and steep, but it's over with quickly. At the boundary, the grade mellows out, and you reach a junction just before the lakes, at 3.4 miles. The right fork goes to Lower Jackass Lake (the largest of three choices) in 0.2 mile, and the left fork goes to the tiny upper lake. A third lake lies in the basin above the upper lake. Many people just bear right at the junction and visit Lower Jackass Lake, which at 8,600 feet is backed by granite cliffs and offers good swimming and fishing prospects. No, this isn't the most beautiful lake in the Sierra, but if you just want to visit a pretty spot without a whole lot of effort, this trip fits the bill.

User Groups: Hikers, dogs, and horses. No mountain bikes. No wheelchair facilities.

Permits: A free wilderness permit is required for overnight stays and is available from the Bass Lake Ranger Station. Quotas are in effect year-round; permits can be reserved in advance for a $5 reservation fee per person.

Maps: A Sierra National Forest or Ansel Adams Wilderness map is available from the U.S. Forest Service. For a topographic map, ask the USGS for Timber Knob.
Directions: From Oakhurst, drive north on Highway 41 for four miles, then turn right on Road 222 toward Bass Lake. In four miles, bear left on Road 274. Drive two miles and turn left on Beasore Road (gravel). Drive 29 miles to a turnoff for the Norris Trailhead. Bear left and drive two miles to the trailhead parking area.
Contact: Sierra National Forest, Bass Lake Ranger Station, 57003 Road 225, North Fork, CA 93643, 559/877-2218, www.fs.fed.us/r5/sierra.

95 CONVICT CANYON TO LAKE DOROTHY

15.0 mi / 2.0 days 3 10

in the John Muir Wilderness south of Mammoth Lakes

BEST

Framed by a back wall of bare granite peaks, Convict Lake is a mountain shrine, and the trail that leads from here into the backcountry wilderness makes hikers feel as if they're ascending into heaven. But this is no easy trip. Not only is there a 2,700-foot climb, but a tricky and sometimes dangerous stream crossing is involved. The trail starts near Convict Lake (at 7,621 feet), skirts along the lake's north shore, and then leads up through a canyon alongside Convict Creek. At 2.8 miles, you have to ford the creek, which usually requires getting wet and can be dangerous in the early summer because of high snowmelt. The trail meets the creek in the middle of a small waterfall. Many attempts to bridge this crossing have failed, as the bridge always gets washed out by high flows in early summer.

If you can get past that crossing, you follow the trail up to a series of large, untouched lakes: Mildred Lake at 4.9 miles, Lake Dorothy at 6.2 miles (10,275 feet), Lake Genevieve at 7.2 miles (10,000 feet), and beyond them, Bighorn, Edith, and Cloverleaf Lakes. Take your pick. Lake Dorothy is by far the largest of the lot. You can spend days exploring this high-mountain paradise.

Special Note: The crossing of Convict Creek is considered to be one of the most treacherous in the Sierra Nevada. This trail should only be hiked late in the season, when the stream flow has dropped. Check with the Mammoth Ranger Station for current conditions before planning a trip.
User Groups: Hikers, dogs, and horses. No mountain bikes. No wheelchair facilities.
Permits: A free wilderness permit is required for overnight stays and is available from the Mammoth Ranger Station. Quotas are in effect from May 1 to November 1; for this period, permits are available in advance for a $5 reservation fee per person.
Maps: A Mammoth High Country map is available from Tom Harrison Maps. An Inyo National Forest or John Muir Wilderness map is available from the U.S. Forest Service. For a topographic map, ask the USGS for Bloody Mountain.
Directions: From U.S. 395 at the Mammoth Lakes junction, drive south for six miles to Convict Lake Road. Turn west and drive 1.8 miles to a spur road on the right as you near the lake. Turn right and drive 0.25 mile to the parking area for the trailhead.
Contact: Inyo National Forest, Mammoth Ranger Station, P.O. Box 148, Mammoth Lakes, CA 93546, 760/924-5500, www.fs.fed.us/r5/inyo.

96 McGEE CREEK TO STEELHEAD LAKE

11.4 mi / 6.0 hr or 2.0 days 3 9

in the John Muir Wilderness

BEST

Unlike many trails leading into the John Muir Wilderness, the McGee Creek Trail has the benefit of starting out with a mostly level stretch. It follows the remains of an old mining road, giving your legs and lungs the opportunity to warm up before you start to climb. In the first two miles, you pass plains of sage and rabbit brush, heading toward a colorful and dramatic mountain backdrop: Mount Baldwin on the right, Mount Crocker on the left, and Red and White Mountain straight ahead—all at over 12,000 feet in elevation. To your left, along McGee Creek, grows a lush garden of aspens and cottonwoods. Pass Horsetail Falls on the right at two miles out. Soon the trail enters a lodgepole pine forest and the climb steepens, and at 4.5 miles, you reach a junction with Steelhead Lake Trail heading left (east). Switchbacks carry you to a short spur to tiny Grass Lake, then to much larger Steelhead Lake (10,350 feet). The total climb is 2,300 feet over 5.7 miles, but most of the work is in the last 1.2 miles.

User Groups: Hikers, dogs, and horses. No mountain bikes. No wheelchair facilities.

Permits: A free wilderness permit is required for overnight stays and is available from the Bishop/White Mountain Ranger Station. Quotas are in effect from May 1 to November 1; for this period, permits are available in advance for a $5 reservation fee per person.

Maps: A Mammoth High Country map is available from Tom Harrison Maps. An Inyo National Forest or John Muir Wilderness map is available from the U.S. Forest Service. For a topographic map, ask the USGS for Convict Lake.

Directions: From U.S. 395 at the Mammoth Lakes junction, drive south eight miles to the McGee Creek Road turnoff on the right (30 miles north of Bishop). Drive three miles southwest on McGee Creek Road (past the pack station) to the trailhead.

Contact: Inyo National Forest, White Mountain Ranger District, 798 N. Main Street, Bishop, CA 93514, 760/873-2500, www.fs.fed.us/r5/inyo.

97 MONO PASS

7.4 mi / 4.0 hr 4 10

in the John Muir Wilderness

Since wilderness permits are hard to come by for this trail, your best bet is a day hike up to scenic, austere Mono Pass, where William Brewer and his party crossed the Sierra in 1864. Trailhead elevation is 10,300 feet, and the pass is at 12,600 feet, so get ready to climb in thin air (gasp). Also, expect it to be cold and windy at the pass, no matter how warm it is at the trailhead. Start your trip by following the trail alongside Rock Creek, with a wall of mammoth mountain peaks surrounding you. A half mile in, leave most of the crowds behind as you bear right for Mono Pass, switchbacking uphill. As you climb, you gain a view of Little Lakes Valley below, as well as continual eyefuls of classic Sierra scenery—clear blue sky, jagged mountain backdrops, and plenty of rock. Pass the side trail to Ruby Lake at two miles out (save this 0.25-mile spur for your return trip). Continue on the rocky, treeless trail until at last you reach the summit, where you get a full panoramic view, which is probably hardly different from when Brewer saw it more than a century ago. That peak just to the east of you is Mount Starr, elevation 12,835 feet. To the south, the 13,000-foot-plus peaks reign: Mount Abbot and Mount Mills. Mono Rock and the Mono Recesses lie to the west, and the blue lakes of the Pioneer Basin are to the north.

User Groups: Hikers, dogs, and horses. No mountain bikes. No wheelchair facilities.

Permits: No permits are required. Parking and access are free.

Maps: A Mono Divide High Country map is available from Tom Harrison Maps. A John Muir Wilderness map is available from the U.S. Forest Service. For topographic maps, ask the USGS for Mount Morgan and Mount Abbot.

Directions: From U.S. 395 at the Mammoth Lakes junction, drive south 15 miles to Tom's

Place and the Rock Creek Road turnoff, on the right (24 miles north of Bishop). Follow Rock Creek Road southwest for 10.5 miles to its end, at the Mosquito Flat parking area.

Contact: Inyo National Forest, White Mountain Ranger District, 798 N. Main Street, Bishop, CA 93514, 760/873-2500, www.fs.fed.us/r5/inyo.

98 LITTLE LAKES VALLEY

3.0-9.0 mi / 2.0-5.0 hr 2 10

in the John Muir Wilderness

If the mileage shown above reflects some indecision, that's because the Little Lakes Valley makes it hard to decide which lake to visit or how far to hike. It's best to decide as you go, depending on how busy the trail is and how your energy is holding up. The Little Lakes Valley is a spectacularly beautiful, glacially carved area that is littered with lakes both large and small, and is surrounded by 13,000-foot peaks. What makes it even more special is that its trailhead is at 10,300 feet, so your car does most of the climbing, instead of your feet. For this reason, the trail is extremely popular, especially with beginning backpackers, day hikers, and dog walkers.

The trail leads past Mack Lake and shallow Marsh Lake to Heart Lake, 1.5 miles in. Box Lake is 0.25 mile farther, and then another 0.25 mile farther is the still larger Long Lake, both popular destinations right along the trail. Those with more stamina can continue to Chickenfoot Lake, at 3.0 miles out, or the Gem Lakes, at 3.5 miles. Most people consider the Gem Lakes to be the most gorgeous of the lot, but frankly, it's pretty hard to choose. Those who are willing and able continue upward through 11,100-foot Morgan Pass and descend a couple hundred feet to Upper and Lower Morgan Lakes, at 4 and 4.5 miles out, respectively. There are enough hiking options along this one trail to keep most lake-lovers busy for a week.

User Groups: Hikers, dogs, and horses. No mountain bikes. No wheelchair facilities.

Permits: A free wilderness permit is required for overnight stays and is available from the Bishop/White Mountain Ranger Station. Quotas are in effect from May 1 to November 1; for this period, permits are available in advance for a $5 reservation fee per person.

Maps: A Mono Divide High Country map is available from Tom Harrison Maps. A John Muir Wilderness map is available from the U.S. Forest Service. For topographic maps, ask the USGS for Mount Morgan and Mount Abbot.

Directions: From U.S. 395 at the Mammoth Lakes junction, drive south 15 miles to Tom's Place and the Rock Creek Road turnoff, on the right (24 miles north of Bishop). Follow Rock Creek Road southwest for 10.5 miles to its end, at the Mosquito Flat parking area.

Contact: Inyo National Forest, White Mountain Ranger District, 798 N. Main Street, Bishop, CA 93514, 760/873-2500, www.fs.fed.us/r5/inyo.

99 TAMARACK LAKES

9.4 mi / 6.0 hr or 2.0 days 3 10

in the John Muir Wilderness

This fantastic Eastern Sierra hike offers a great deal of variety in terrain, a couple of gorgeous lakes with good fishing prospects, and the chance of seeing bighorn sheep. Perhaps best of all, this trail sees a lot less foot traffic than the other pathways in the popular Rock Creek area. The trailhead elevation at Rock Creek Lake is 9,700 feet, so the first stretch of this trail can be a bit breathtaking as you climb steadily for a mile on a brushy slope. Soon the trail levels out and follows an old dirt road for awhile, which connects to a mountain-biking route in Sand Canyon. The terrain you are walking through is dry and sandy, with only a few pines to create some sparse shade, and it gives little indication of the dramatic high-country scenery that lies ahead. You'll pass a turnoff for Francis Lake on the right (0.7 mile distant), and shortly thereafter, Kenneth Lake on the left (0.1 mile distant). Kenneth Lake is really just a muddy pond, but its surrounding meadow is filled with blooming gentian in late summer. Stay on the path to Tamarack Lakes, and you'll find that the climbing you will face will result in a dramatic change of landscape. The trail ascends over a series of glacial moraines, and you soon find yourself in a high-alpine area, where bighorn sheep are sometimes seen grazing on the fragile grasses. You'll pass the left turnoff for Dorothy Lake (there are good fishing prospects for brook trout here, as well as good camping spots), but stay right, and in another mile, you will begin to follow the outlet stream from the Tamarack Lakes. Now the real work begins, as you must gain 800 more feet to climb into the high basin where the Tamarack Lakes lie. The trail ends at a small tarn just before the largest Tamarack Lake. Just beyond the big Tamarack Lake is Buck Lake, which most people assume is just another of the Tamarack Lakes. The lakes are set in a steeply sloped rocky bowl and have that barren, austere look that is common to lakes above 11,000 feet. You won't find much in the way of flat, soft spots to put your tent, but the scenery more than makes up for it. The largest Tamarack Lake has good fishing for golden trout. The total elevation gain on this hike is 2,000 feet, and it is worth every bit of it.

User Groups: Hikers, dogs, and horses. No mountain bikes. No wheelchair facilities.

Permits: A free wilderness permit is required for overnight stays and is available from the Bishop/White Mountain Ranger Station. Quotas are in effect from May 1 to November 1; for this period, permits are available in advance for a $5 reservation fee per person.

Maps: A Mono Divide High Country map is available from Tom Harrison Maps. A John Muir Wilderness map is available from the U.S. Forest Service. For a topographic map, ask the USGS for Mount Morgan.

Directions: From U.S. 395 at the Mammoth Lakes junction, drive south 15 miles to Tom's Place and the Rock Creek Road turnoff, on the right (24 miles north of Bishop). Follow Rock Creek Road southwest for 8.5 miles to the left turnoff for Rock Creek Lakes campground. Turn left and drive 0.4 mile to the trailhead.

Contact: Inyo National Forest, White Mountain Ranger District, 798 N. Main Street, Bishop, CA 93514, 760/873-2500, www.fs.fed.us/r5/inyo.

100 RUBY LAKE

4.5 mi / 2.5 hr 2 10

in the John Muir Wilderness

For both day hikers and backpackers, the Little Lakes Valley is the premier destination from the Rock Creek Canyon trailhead. The only problem is the crowds, especially on the weekends, which can turn a supposedly peaceful wilderness experience into a large group encounter. A visit to Ruby Lake is a possible solution, because it's off the main trail that leads into the Little Lakes Valley, situated instead on the right fork that leads to Mono Pass. Since most trail users on this fork are backpackers heading to Mono Pass and the Pioneer Basin beyond, few take the time to stop at Ruby Lake, 0.25 mile off the main trail. From the trailhead, hike 0.5 mile, and bear right at the junction for Mono Pass. Grunt it out through the switchbacks as you enjoy a series of stunning vistas of the Little Lakes Valley. You'll reach the Ruby Lake spur trail at two miles out, on the left. A 0.25-mile walk brings you to cliffbound Ruby Lake, which is much larger than you'd expect and perfectly ringed by granite. The fishing is not great, but the picnicking is highly recommended. The lake's elevation is 11,121 feet.

User Groups: Hikers, dogs, and horses. No mountain bikes. No wheelchair facilities.

Permits: No permits are required. Parking and access are free.

Maps: A Mono Divide High Country map is available from Tom Harrison Maps. A John Muir Wilderness map is available from the U.S. Forest Service. For topographic maps, ask the USGS for Mount Abbot and Mount Morgan.
Directions: From U.S. 395 at the Mammoth Lakes junction, drive south 15 miles to Tom's Place and the Rock Creek Road turnoff, on the right (24 miles north of Bishop). Follow Rock Creek Road southwest for 10.5 miles to its end, at the Mosquito Flat parking area.
Contact: Inyo National Forest, White Mountain Ranger District, 798 N. Main Street, Bishop, CA 93514, 760/873-2500, www.fs.fed.us/r5/inyo.

101 WHITE MOUNTAIN PEAK TRAIL

14.4 mi / 8.0 hr 5 10

in Inyo National Forest northeast of Bishop

BEST

White Mountain Peak is the third-tallest peak in California, only 249 feet lower than the highest, Mount Whitney (Mount Williamson is second in line), yet it is little known to hikers outside of the area. In contrast to Whitney, this 14,246-foot summit is not reached by a narrow foot trail, but instead via an old Navy-built road that climbs 2,600 feet in 7.2 miles. The trail starts at a locked gate at 11,630 feet in elevation and then leads past Mount Barcroft (13,040 feet) on a long grind. The road/trail is completely above tree line, so it's exposed and often windswept. Sunscreen alone won't do it here—wear a hat to give yourself a break from the sun. If you aren't acclimated, the high altitude will make the trip very difficult. The summit constitutes an impressive granite massif with grand views. To the east, you can see 200 miles into Nevada; to the west, the Owens Valley and Volcanic Tableland, plus a wide panorama of the Sierra Nevada. Some hikers choose to pack along their headlamps and do all or part of the trip by moonlight. The road/trail is simple to navigate, so this is easily accomplished. Forget turning this into a backpack trip: The area is so exposed that you won't find a suitable place to camp. Also, if you are planning an early summer visit, call the White Mountain Ranger Station to be sure the dirt road to the trailhead is open.
User Groups: Hikers only. Dogs, horses, and mountain bikes permitted, but not advised due to extremely high altitudes. No wheelchair facilities.
Permits: No permits are required. Parking and access are free.
Maps: An Inyo National Forest map is available from the U.S. Forest Service. For a topographic map, ask the USGS for White Mountain Peak.
Directions: From U.S. 395 at Big Pine, take Highway 168 east for 13 miles to White Mountain Road. Turn left on White Mountain Road and drive north for 10.5 miles to Schulman Grove. Continue on White Mountain Road (it becomes unpaved just past the Schulman Grove turnoff) for 16 miles to the locked gate and trailhead, at the road's end.
Contact: Inyo National Forest, White Mountain Ranger Station, 798 N. Main Street, Bishop, CA 93514, 760/873-2500, www.fs.fed.us/r5/inyo.

102 METHUSELAH TRAIL

4.2 mi / 2.5 hr 2 8

in Inyo National Forest northeast of Bishop

BEST

The Methuselah Tree is the prize of the Ancient Bristlecone Pine Forest. Here for more than 4,000 years, it's the oldest documented living tree in the world. But forest rangers won't tell you which one it is, out of fear that some dimwit will cut it down. So you have to be satisfied just knowing you have walked among the ancients, rather than actually seeing the grandfather of all trees. No matter—each one of the thousands of trees here will impress you with its beautifully sculpted form. Amateur photographers have a field day along this trail. The path starts at the patio of the Schulman Grove Visitors Center (elevation 10,100 feet) and follows a meandering route through a forest of ancient and younger bristlecone pines, plus a few limber pines (the only other trees that grow up here). The first half of the loop drops 800 feet, which of course must be regained on your return, but the climb is nicely spread out. Still, if you're not acclimated, the high elevation will leave you huffing and puffing. Plan on bringing a picnic with you (you're a long way from the nearest convenience store), and make sure you spend some time at the excellent visitors center, which is open daily. If you want to hike a bit more, try the one-mile Discovery Trail loop (more bristlecone pines) or the one-mile Bristlecone Cabin Trail, which leads to an old Mexican mine site.

User Groups: Hikers and leashed dogs. No horses or mountain bikes. No wheelchair facilities.

Permits: No permits are required. There is a $2 fee per person, with a maximum of $5 per group.

Maps: Brochures and trail maps are available at the trailhead. An Inyo National Forest map is available from the U.S. Forest Service. For a topographic map, ask the USGS for Westgard Pass.

Directions: From U.S. 395 at Big Pine, take Highway 168 east for 13 miles to White Mountain Road. Turn left on White Mountain Road and drive north for 10.5 miles to Schulman Grove, on the right.

Contact: Inyo National Forest, White Mountain Ranger Station, 798 N. Main Street, Bishop, CA 93514, 760/873-2500, www.fs.fed.us/r5/inyo.

Index

Camping

A–C

Agnew Meadows and Equestrian Camp: 44
Aspen Group Camp: 58
Aspen: 39
Big Bend: 38
Big Meadow: 58
Big Sandy: 29
Big Springs: 49
Bridalveil Creek and Equestrian and Group Camp: 24
Brown's Owens River Campground: 50
Buckeye: 32
Camp 4: 22
Cattleguard Camp: 38
Cherry Valley and Boat-In: 16
Clover Meadow: 28
Coldwater: 54
Convict Lake: 54
Crags Campground: 34
Crane Flat: 24
Crowley Lake: 56

D–H

Deadman: 50
Devils Postpile National Monument: 47
Dimond "O": 19
East Fork: 59
Ellery Lake: 40
French Camp: 57
Fresno Dome: 30
Glass Creek: 49
Granite Creek and Equestrian Camp: 29
Green Creek: 35
Grey's Mountain: 32
Gull Lake: 42
Hartley Springs: 44
Herring Reservoir: 15
Highlands RV Park: 61
Hodgdon Meadow: 21
Holiday Group Camp: 57
Honeymoon Flat: 33

I–M

Iris Meadow: 58
Jerseydale: 26
Junction: 39
June Lake: 43
Kelty Meadow and Equestrian Camp: 30
Lake George: 48
Lake Mary: 53
Lower Lee Vining Camp: 37
Lower Pines: 22
Lower Twin Lake: 35
Lundy Canyon Campground: 36
Mammoth Mountain RV Park: 52
McGee Creek: 56
McGee Creek RV Park: 55
Meadowview: 16
Merced Recreation Area: 25
Minaret Falls: 46
Moore Creek Group Camp: 20
Moraine Camp: 38

N–Q

Nelder Grove: 30
New Shady Rest: 51
North Pines: 23
Oh! Ridge: 41
Old Shady Rest: 51
Paha: 33
Palisade: 59
Pine City: 54
Pine Cliff Resort: 42
Pine Glen: 50
Pine Grove Upper and Lower: 60
Pinecrest: 15
Pioneer Trail Group Camp: 15
Pleasant Valley Pit Campground: 61
Pleasant Valley: 61
Porcupine Flat: 19
Pumice Flat Group Camp: 46
Pumice Flat: 45

R–T

Red's Meadow: 48
Reversed Creek: 43
Robinson Creek: 34
Rock Creek Lake: 60
Saddlebag Lake: 37
Sherwin Creek: 53
Silver Lake: 41
Soquel: 31
Summerdale: 27
Summit Camp: 27
Sweetwater: 18
Tamarack Flat: 21
Texas Flat Group Camp: 31
Tioga Lake: 40
Trumbull Lake: 36
Tuff: 56
Tuolumne Meadows: 17
Twin Lakes: 52

U–Z

Upper Chiquito: 28
Upper Pines: 23
Upper Soda Springs: 45
Wawona: 26
White Wolf: 17
Willow Springs RV Park: 33
Yosemite Creek: 19
Yosemite Lakes: 20
Yosemite-Mariposa KOA: 25

Hiking

A–C

Agnew Meadows to Tuolumne Meadows (JMT/PCT): 114
Alder Creek Falls: 127
Barney Lake Trail: 71
Barrett and TJ Lakes: 106
Bennettville: 99
Bloody Canyon Trail: 103
Bridalveil Creek: 123
Bridalveil Fall: 121
Buckeye Creek Trail: 71
Burst Rock/Powell Lake: 70
Camp and Bear Lakes: 69
Carlon Falls: 80
Cathedral Lakes: 87
Chilnualna Fall: 129
Clouds Rest: 85
Convict Canyon to Lake Dorothy: 133
Crystal Lake: 107

D–G

Devils Postpile and Rainbow Falls: 110
Dog Lake: 93
Duck Lake: 108
Eagle Peak: 116
Elizabeth Lake: 89
Emerald Lake and Sky Meadows: 107
Fern Lake Loop: 112
Four-Mile Trail: 122
Fresno Dome: 131
Gardisky Lake: 100
Gibbs Lake: 102
Glen Aulin and Tuolumne Falls: 92
Green, East, and West Lakes: 72

H–K

Half Dome: 120
Harden Lake: 82
Hite Cove Trail: 114
Illilouette Fall: 127
Inspiration and Stanford Points: 121
Inyo Craters: 106
Jackass Lakes: 132
Kibbie Lake: 70

L–M

Lake Canyon and May Lundy Mine: 74
Lake Eleanor: 76
Laurel Lake: 78
Lembert Dome: 93
Lewis Creek Trail: 130
Little Lakes Valley: 135
Lookout Point: 79
Lower Gaylor Lake: 89
Lower Yosemite Fall: 117
Lukens Lake: 82
Lundy Canyon Trail: 74
Lyell Canyon: 90
Mariposa Grove: 129
May Lake and Mount Hoffman: 85
McGee Creek to Steelhead Lake: 133
McGurk Meadow and Dewey Point: 122
Merced Grove: 81
Methuselah Trail: 137
Middle and Upper Gaylor Lakes: 97
Minaret Lake: 111
Mirror Lake Loop: 119
Mist and John Muir Loop to Nevada Fall: 118
Mist Trail to Top of Vernal Fall: 117
Mono Lake South Tufa Trail: 102
Mono Pass: 134
Mono Pass: 96
Mount Dana: 98

N–Q

North Dome: 84
Ostrander Lake: 124
Panorama Trail: 126
Parker Lake Trail: 104
Pinecrest Lake National Recreation Trail: 69
Pohono Trail: 125
Preston Flat Trail: 75

R–T

Rancheria Falls: 77
Red Cones Loop: 109
Ruby Lake: 136
Rush Creek Trail: 104
Saddlebag Lake Loop: 101
Sentinel Dome: 124
Shadow Lake: 113
Shadow of the Giants: 131
Slate Creek Trail to Green Treble Lake: 100
Smith Peak: 79
Spillway & Helen Lakes: 97
Sunrise Lakes: 86
Taft Point and the Fissures: 125
Tamarack Lakes: 135
Ten Lakes / Grant Lakes: 83
Tenaya Lake: 87
The Niche and Cora Lakes: 132
Tuolumne Grove: 81
Tuolumne Meadows to Sonora Pass (PCT): 94
Tuolumne Meadows to Yosemite Valley (JMT): 95

U–Z

Upper Yosemite Fall: 115
Valentine Lake Trail: 109
Virginia Lakes Trail: 73
Vogelsang Loop: 88
Wapama Fall: 76
Waterwheel Falls: 91
Wawona Meadow Loop: 128
White Mountain Peak Trail: 137
Yost Lake: 105
Young Lakes Loop: 90

MOON YOSEMITE & MAMMOTH LAKES CAMPING & HIKING

Avalon Travel
a member of the Perseus Books Group
1700 Fourth Street
Berkeley, CA 94710, USA
www.moon.com

Editor and Series Manager: Sabrina Young
Copy Editor: Michelle Peters
Graphics Coordinator: Kathryn Osgood
Production Coordinator: Elizabeth Jang
Cover Designer: Kathryn Osgood
Interior Designer: Darren Alessi
Map Editor: Kevin Anglin
Cartographers: Kat Bennett, Suzanne Service
Proofreader: Erika Howsare

ISBN: 978-1-59880-277-1

Front cover photo: Mirror Lake, Yosemite, © Timothy Stirling/123rf.com.
Title page photo: Young hiker checking his map in front of Yosemite lake, © Christophe Testi/dreamstime.com

Printed in the United States of America

ABOUT THE AUTHORS

© SHELLY LEWIS

Tom Stienstra

For 30 years, Tom Stienstra's full-time job has been to capture and communicate the outdoor experience. This has led him across California – hiking, boating, fishing, camping, biking, and flying – searching for the best of the outdoors and then writing about it.

Tom is the nation's top-selling author of outdoors guidebooks. He has been inducted into the California Outdoor Hall of Fame and has twice been awarded National Outdoor Writer of the Year, newspaper division, by the Outdoor Writers Association of America. He has also been named California Outdoor Writer of the Year five times, most recently in 2007. Tom is the outdoors columnist for the *San Francisco Chronicle;* his articles also appear on www.SFGate.com and in newspapers around the country. He broadcasts a weekly radio show on KCBS-San Francisco and hosts an outdoor television show on CBS/CW San Francisco.

Tom lives with his wife and sons in Northern California. You can contact him directly via the website www.tomstienstra.com. His recent guidebooks include:

Moon California Camping
Moon California Fishing
Moon California Recreational Lakes and Rivers
Moon Northern California Cabins & Cottages
Moon Northern California Camping
Moon Oregon Camping
Moon Pacific Northwest Camping
Moon Washington Camping
Moon West Coast RV Camping

© BILL RHOADES

Ann Marie Brown

The author of 13 outdoor guidebooks, Ann Marie Brown is a dedicated California outdoorswoman. She hikes, bikes, and camps more than 150 days each year in a dedicated effort to avoid routine, complacency, and getting a real job.

Ann Marie's work has appeared in *Sunset, VIA, Backpacker,* and *California* magazines. As a way of giving back a little of what she gets from her experiences in nature, she writes and edits for several environmental groups, including the Sierra Club and the Natural Resources Defense Council. When not traipsing along a California trail, Ann Marie can be found at her home near South Lake Tahoe.

Ann Marie's recent guidebooks include:

Moon 101 Great Hikes of the San Francisco Bay Area
Moon Bay Area Biking
Moon Northern California Biking
Moon Tahoe
Moon Take a Hike Los Angeles
Moon Yosemite

For more information on these titles, visit Ann Marie's website, www.annmariebrown.com.